Philosophy of Religion

for A Level

ANNE JORDAN

NEIL LOCKYER

EDWIN TATE

First published in 1999 by:
Stanley Thornes (Publishers) Ltd
Second edition published in 2002 by:
Nelson Thornes Ltd
Delta Place
27 Bath Road
Cheltenham GL53 7TH
United Kingdom

03 04 05 06 / 10 9 8 7 6 5 4 3

A catalogue record for this book is available from the British Library.

ISBN 0–7487–6760–6

First edition typeset by Wyvern 21 Ltd, Bristol
Second edition typeset by Tech-Set Ltd
First edition edited by Geoffrey D. Palmer
Second edition edited by Sue Whimster
Illustrated by Linda Jeffrey and Oxford Designers and Illustrators

Printed and bound in Spain by GraphyCems

Acknowledgements
With thanks to the following for permission to reproduce copyright photographs in this book:
Bridgeman Art Library, London, pages 150 (Vatican Museums and Galleries, Rome), 193 (Museo Nacional Centro de Arte Reina Sofia, Madrid)
Ronald Grant Archive, page 87
Hulton Getty, pages 59, 102, 164
Mary Evans Picture Library, pages 43, 111 (Sigmund Freud Copyrights), 134

Every effort has been made to contact copyright holders. The publishers apologise to anyone whose rights have been inadvertently overlooked, and will be happy to rectify any errors or omissions.

Contents

Introduction

What is the 'Philosophy of Religion'?

Any definition of the philosophy of religion will be controversial. This is because it is traditionally used and interpreted in very different contexts. In modern times, particularly in Europe and America, the philosophy of religion has meant an analysis of certain elements and concepts of (particularly Western) religions. In the main, this has meant a critical study of Christianity and, to some extent, Judaism.

The questions raised by this study are far too numerous to be listed here, but they include the following:

- Does God exist?
- How can we talk about God?
- Can God be experienced?
- How can God be all-powerful and loving if evil and suffering exist?
- Do miracles occur?
- Is there life after death?

All of these questions and more will be discussed in this book.

Why study the Philosophy of Religion?

Socrates (470–399 BC) is regarded by many as the 'Father of Philosophy'. However, he was tried, condemned and executed for his teachings. This was because many of his contemporaries (such as Aristophanes) argued that his method of inquiry was irreligious, as it attempted to understand 'the Divine'.

Despite the physical demise of Socrates, his impact upon logical investigation and what would become the philosophy of religion was profound. Indeed, it is because of the method of critical inquiry that Socrates, and others, developed that this academic area is of such interest today.

Many people have suggested that science was the 'new religion' of the nineteenth century. If this is the case, then surely philosophy is the 'new religion' of the twenty-first, for exactly the same reasons; that is, it enables an individual to question what he or she is told, and to reach *his or her own conclusions*.

As such, the study of the philosophy of religion develops an inquiring mind, the ability to analyse a point of view, the ability to develop and reason through an argument, and the ability to reach a logical and justified conclusion.

What is Involved?

The simple answer to this is *reading* – and lots of it! You will find some primary source material in this book, but mainly summary, comment and evaluation. Therefore, background reading to back up the material here is essential for a full understanding.

In each chapter you will find panels entitled 'You need to know' and 'Something to think about'. The 'You need to know' sections contain points to supplement your knowledge and understanding of a particular point or topic. The 'Something to think about' sections usually contain short tasks or points for discussion within small groups or your class.

At the end of each chapter you will find 'Essay Questions'. These questions are typical of questions for both the AS and A2 papers. Students need to be certain whether the topic covered by the chapter is from the AS or A2 specification so check the specification of the examination board you are following carefully. The questions at A2 level will expect students to be able to answer in greater depth than those at AS.

Chapter 1

Some Influential Philosophers

There are many important commentators who have contributed to the historical development of the philosophy of religion: not only is it impossible to mention them all here, but it is also impossible to go into any great depth in discussing their work. However, in this chapter we will attempt to encompass nearly two and a half thousand years of historical development by mentioning the *key* points of the *key* contributors. We will begin with the ancient Greeks.

To a Philosopher no circumstance, however trifling, is too minute.
Oliver Goldsmith (1728–1774)

Socrates (470–399 BC)

As mentioned in the Introduction, Socrates was a very important figure in terms of the development of philosophy. His teachings were largely revealed by his student Plato (see below). The fact that Socrates wrote very little himself makes any form of reconstruction of his ideas quite difficult. Accessing his thought through the work of Plato also presents us with problems, as it is often very difficult to distinguish between the two of them.

Socrates' most famous claim was that he knew nothing at all! This may sound strange coming from the alleged 'Father of Philosophy', but it was actually the recognition of the fact that we must be incredibly careful before asserting that we *know* anything. As suggested in the Introduction, it was not Socrates' knowledge that made him such an important figure, but the *method* that he developed of inquiring into knowledge. This method was based on critical scrutiny, and was demonstrated in his interest in the definition of things and his use of inductive arguments (see 'David Hume' below).

Socrates' contribution to moral philosophy was also profound. He saw knowledge as the greatest virtue, claiming that it was through knowledge and understanding of the human condition that people could live properly. This idea clearly inspired his student, Plato.

Plato (c. 428–347 BC)

In 399 BC, Plato left Athens, disgusted with the condemnation and execution of his teacher Socrates. Indeed, much of Plato's early philosophical work recorded and developed Socrates' teachings, and included investigations into ethical questions, the immortality of the soul and political philosophy.

While his work is both profound and fairly lengthy, one of the most important areas – as far as we are concerned – was Plato's development of Socrates' notion that we cannot say anything about X before we establish what X is. This idea underpinned Socrates' ethical thinking, and was clearly important to Plato.

Aristotle (384–322 BC)

Aristotle studied under Plato in Athens from the age of 17. His philosophical output was considerable, but there are two specific areas that are of interest here, his work on **logic** and **ethics**.

In studying logic, Aristotle developed the concept of the **syllogism** (see Chapter 4, page 61) and the use of deductive arguments (see 'David Hume' below). His classic syllogism was as follows:

*All **as** are **bs***
*All **bs** are **cs***
*Therefore, all **as** are **cs***

Something to think about

Consider the following two statements:

It is good to help people

Pete Sampras is a good tennis player

What is the difference in the use of the word *good*? Is it acceptable to use the word *good* in both of these situations? How can we know?

He also applied this type of deductive thinking to ethics, producing what has become known as the **Aristotelian Circle**. This aimed to provide a thorough understanding of what Aristotle terms 'the Good Life'. It suggests that 'practical wisdom' can lead directly to 'well-being'. Individuals who experience a general 'well-being' are individuals with 'virtue'. Aristotle considered 'virtues' to be moral and intellectual characteristics, which he thought we must possess in order to achieve 'the good life'. Virtue is the root of 'practical wisdom'. Aristotle defined *good* in terms of emotion, intention, desire and imagination.

Something to think about

How can *good* be defined in these terms?

St Augustine (AD 354–430)

Augustine was a Christian, the bishop of Hippo Regius (now in Algeria). He was primarily concerned with the pursuit of truth. His most famous works touch on areas such as:

- the immortality of the soul
- the problem of evil (see Chapter 8)
- language and learning

Augustine agreed with Plato that there were three 'natures':

1 bodies, which are limited in space and time
2 souls, which are limited in time, but not in space
3 God, who is not limited by space or time

You need to know

Epistemology is the study of the nature, structure and interaction of *knowledge*.

Augustine saw God not just as the cause of absolutely everything, but also as the cause of our knowing things. This was evidence of the philosophical development of **epistemology**.

Something to think about

Why do you think Augustine made this assertion?

'Free will' was a major aspect of Augustine's work. Without it, he believed that God could not punish the wrongdoer or reward the righteous person.

St Thomas Aquinas (1224–1274)

Aquinas produced an enormous amount of written work, estimated by some at being over 8 million words. His chief work was *Summa Theologiae* ('Summation of Theology'), which was left unfinished when he died. Four months before his death, Aquinas underwent some sort of religious experience (see Chapter 3) while saying Mass. He never wrote again, saying 'All that I have written seems to me like straw compared to what has now been revealed to me.'

Aquinas felt that Aristotle's system of logic and ethics was compatible with Christianity. He distinguished between the two different routes that an individual could take to God. The first was through divine revelation, and the second was through human reasoning. Although Aquinas acknowledged the superiority of revelation in 'finding' God, he suggested that the same knowledge could eventually be found through reason.

Aquinas did not accept that the statement 'God exists' is self-evident. He states that it is a proposition that requires demonstration. His demonstration, from *Summa Theologiae*, can be found in Chapters 5 and 6.

You need to know

A **concept** is the way in which a term is perceived, or understood.

A **proposition** is a statement of what a person believes to be the case, which is put forward for consideration. For example, *the truth is out there* is a proposition.

You need to know

Empiricism is the view that concepts or knowledge of the external world are based on sense experience. It is through touch, sight, smell and hearing that something is proved true or false. An empiricist believes that knowledge is gained through experience and/or experiment.

Rationalism is the view that true knowledge of the external world does not come through experience. It is through reason alone, without reference to the external world, that the truth is known.

Something to think about

In groups, make lists of propositions that we know to be true and propositions that we know to be false.

Look at your lists and think about how you decided whether a proposition was true or false.

Discuss your findings with the rest of the class.

You may have decided that a proposition was true by using past experience, or you may have reasoned that a proposition was true on the basis of knowledge. Philosophers decide the truth of a proposition through the application of experience, logic or a combination of the two.

René Descartes (1596–1650)

Descartes sought a 'firm principle of philosophy' that could not be doubted. He began by doubting everything, including truths that he had previously accepted. He would not accept empirical evidence to prove something true. He believed that our senses could deceive us. What we think we are experiencing could be hallucinations, dreams, or false experiences caused by a 'malicious demon'. Descartes' doubt of everything included doubt of his own existence. He decided that the only certainty was doubt itself.

Descartes realised that the only thing he could not doubt was his thoughts. Even if he was dreaming or hallucinating, he was still thinking. Even if he did not have a body, he was still thinking. He had found a solution to proving his existence: 'I think, therefore I am' (in Latin, *cogito ergo sum*). Descartes said that he

> ... noticed that while I was thinking in this way, regarding everything as false, it was nonetheless absolutely necessary that I, who was doing this thinking, was still something. And observing that this truth 'I think, therefore I am' was so sure and certain that no ground for doubt, be it ever so extravagantly sceptical, was capable of shaking it, I therefore decided that I could accept it without scruple as the first principle of the philosopher I was seeking to create.

> *René Descartes, Discourses on the Method of Right Reason, 1637*

Descartes had proved his own existence, but he had not proved the existence of the outside world. In order to do so, he concluded that he needed to prove the existence of God. This was because he believed that God was perfect and would not allow deception. If God existed and had created the world, then Descartes was satisfied that we could accept the reality of the external world's existence.

John Locke (1632–1704)

Locke was an empiricist. He argued that knowledge comes from experience, and that these experiences prove the existence of the external world. He believed that our mind at birth is a *tabula rasa* ('blank tablet'), on to which life's experiences write the general principles and the details of our knowledge. It is through our senses that we know what the world is like. We experience simple ideas, such as blue, hot and sour, and reflect on these sensations. Through reflection, we combine simple ideas together to make complex ones. For example, the simple ideas of a horse and a horn could be combined together to form the complex idea of a unicorn.

Locke agreed with Descartes that our experience of the world is indirect. There *is* an external world, but our senses are unable to give us direct knowledge of that world. Locke argued that everything possesses primary and secondary qualities. A **primary quality** is a quality that any object has regardless of the situation. For example, the primary qualities of a brick are its hardness, size and shape. Whether or not we can see a brick, it will always have these qualities. Our senses add **secondary qualities** to an object, such as colour, smell and taste. These are not properties of the object, and change according to each individual's sense experience of the object. For example, the

Something to think about

Descartes believed that knowledge is acquired through reason. Things are only proved true by logical thought alone:

1 Do you think that Descartes was a rationalist or an empiricist?

2 What reasons would you give for the answer that you have chosen?

You need to know

Descartes used the **ontological argument** to prove God's existence. Read Descartes' version of the argument in Chapter 4 to find out how he did this.

colour of the brick that I observe is the result of the way in which I see the brick, and therefore the appearance of an object does not exist independently of the observer:

> Let us suppose that the mind be, as we say, white paper void of all characters, without any ideas. How comes it to be furnished? Whence comes it by the vast store which the busy and boundless fancy of man has painted in it with almost endless variety? Whence has it all the materials of reason and knowledge? To this I answer, in one word, from experience, in that all our knowledge is founded, and from that it ultimately derives itself.
>
> John Locke, 'An essay concerning human understanding', 1690

Something to think about

1 Explain how Locke argues that knowledge of the external world is acquired.

2 Explain how Locke's understanding of how we know that things exist in the external world differs from the philosophy of Descartes.

You need to know

An **a priori** argument is one in which the truth of a proposition does not depend on experience, but on knowledge acquired independent of experience. Some philosophers believe that we are born with this knowledge – that it is *innate*. For example, many religious believers would argue that they have innate knowledge of God.

An **a posteriori** argument is one in which the truth of a proposition may only be known to be true after empirical evidence has been used to prove the proposition true or false. For example, the statement *0°C is the temperature at which water becomes ice* can be proved true or false by freezing water at that temperature to see what happens.

David Hume (1711–1776)

Hume believed that all knowledge comes from our sense experience; that any idea, however complex, can be reduced to some experience that our senses have provided. Hume's examination of people's modes of thinking led him to conclude that humans think that they know a great deal more about the external world than is warranted. Hume argued that the mistake humans make is to allow imagination to make a connection between cause and effect. We have seen something happen in the same way several times in the past, and we imagine that the same cause will result in the same effect in the future. For example, events such as the Sun rising each day may lead to the conclusion that it is a certainty that the Sun will rise each day. Hume believed that this would be an unreliable statement. However likely it may appear that the Sun will rise every day, *it is not a certainty*. It would be just as valid to say *one day the Sun may not rise*, because that is a possibility. Hume says that we cannot assume that the laws of nature are uniform. We cannot assume a connection between cause and effect. We observe a conjunction of events – *the Sun rising* and *the beginning of the day* – but they are in fact two separate events, occurring at separate times. It is just the habit of the mind that has made the connection between the two events. It is **induction**.

You need to know

Deduction is a method of reasoning by logical stages to reach a conclusion.

Induction is a method of reasoning where a conclusion is reached by linking observations of cause(s) and effect(s) to draw a conclusion.

Arbitrary means in accordance with impulse and whim, rather than reasoned judgement. The result is not fixed or certain.

Scepticism is an attitude of mind in which the individual is inclined to doubt the truth of something in the absence of absolute proof.

To prove his point that we cannot link cause and effect with certainty, Hume used the example of a game of billiards. He pointed out that when you hit a white billiard ball, you cannot be certain that it will in turn hit a red one and cause it to move. Even if the red ball moves, we cannot be certain that it was the white ball that caused this to happen. When we see the white ball moving towards the red ball, we reason that the red ball will move if the white ball hits it. We are reaching a conclusion based on previous observation of cause and effect. We are using past experience to make an assumption about what is going to happen; but, in fact, there is no certainty that the red ball will move on this occasion. Hume argued that until the two balls come into contact there can be no certainty of the reason for the outcome. Hume does not accept induction as a reliable method of argument:

Something to think about

1 Why did Hume believe that an *a priori* proposition 'must be entirely arbitrary'?

2 Hume rejected induction. Why did he feel that this was an unreliable method of reasoning?

3 Hume is considered a sceptic. Why do you think that he is often classed as a sceptic rather than as an empiricist?

> In a word, then, every effect is a distinct event from its cause. It could not, therefore, be discovered in the cause, and the first invention or conception of it, a priori must be entirely arbitrary. And even after it is suggested, the conjunction of it with the cause must appear equally arbitrary; since there are always many other effects which, to reason, must seem fully as consistent and natural. In vain, therefore, should we pretend to determine any single event or infer any cause or effect, without the assistance of observation and experience.

David Hume, 'An enquiry concerning human understanding', 1748

Analytical propositions are propositions that show a relationship between ideas. Analytical propositions are known to be true before experience, because their denial would involve a contradiction. Analytical propositions are judged true because of the meaning assigned to the words. For example, *a bachelor is an unmarried man* or *a horse is a quadruped* are analytical propositions. The propositions are true by definition. Some philosophers have maintained that the truths of mathematics are analytical propositions. For example, it is accepted as true that *2 + 2 = 4*. Analytical propositions are *a priori* propositions. Many philosophers have thought that the truths of logic and mathematics are *a priori*, although there are philosophers who disagree.

Synthetic propositions are propositions that have to be judged true or false on the basis of experience of the world. Synthetic propositions are *a posteriori* propositions. For example, *there are four people in the next room* or *aliens have landed in London* are synthetic propositions. It is possible to go and see if the proposition is true or false. Many philosophers have thought that the truths of the empirical and non-mathematical sciences are entirely *a posteriori*, although many rationalists would deny this.

Hume's Fork

Hume argued that there are two questions to ask of any statement to decide whether it is possible to prove the proposition true or false:

- Does it contain matters of fact? If so, can you relate them to your experience to prove that they are true?
- Does it give the relationship between two abstract ideas, or reasoning of the sort found in mathematics or geometry?

If the answer to both of these questions is *no*, then Hume says that we should reject the statement as meaningless, because it will not give any reliable knowledge about the external world.

Immanuel Kant (1724–1804)

Kant was worried that rationalism and empiricism alone did not seem to be a solid basis for knowledge of the external world. He set out, in his *Critique of Pure Reason* (1781), to discover how we acquire knowledge. He concluded that knowledge is acquired from both experience and ideas. He used the terms **synthetic** and **analytic** to distinguish between these two sources of knowledge. He believed that our senses make us aware of the external world. Our minds turns these experiences into ideas by imposing time, space and causality on to them, to organise them into logical thought so that we understand the world.

Kant distinguished between those things about the external world that are knowable through the senses (**phenomena**, singular **phenomenon**) and the reality behind them (**noumena**, singular **noumenon**). The noumenon is beyond our understanding, and the reality cannot be known, because it lies behind the mind-imposed forms of time, space and causation. It is not accessible to us. For example, the appearance of the billiard balls is the phenomenon. The reality of the balls (the noumenon) that lies behind their appearance is unknowable, because it is beyond human experience and understanding.

Kant had brought the empiricist and rationalist strains together. He had developed a form of **Idealism**, which is generally the view that our understanding of the reality of the world depends on the way in which the mind has organised experience. The way in which we see the world may not be the way it really is, but only the way we think it is. The reality is independent of our observations.

Something to think about

Does this mean that if we stop looking at something it ceases to exist? What answer do you think Kant might give to such a suggestion?

Something to think about

Before reading on, list as many different uses for the word *is* as you can think of.

Examples of the use of this word might include:

*John **is** happy* (here it is used to characterise John as being happy)

*a carrot **is** a vegetable* (here it is used to mean *equals*)

*Jane **is** human* (here it is used to make a prediction; we might not know that Jane is human, but we assume that she is!)

Bertrand Russell (1872–1970)

In 1914, Bertrand Russell introduced the expression **philosophical logic**. This referred to a process, in which key philosophical questions were re-worded in mathematical terms. This resulted in Russell's work being presented as such; an example can be found in the syllogism given in Chapter 4. The reason why Russell felt this to be necessary was because of the fact that normal (that is, 'everyday') language can be extremely misleading. Fundamentally, his argument was that every word stands for something. He believed that words were often used without the user knowing what they stood for – or, in some cases, without standing for anything! As an example, he cited the uses of the word *is*.

Further examples of the confusion that Russell is referring to can be found in Chapter 4.

William Ockham (1285–1347)

Before moving on to to a detailed discussion of religious language in Chapter 2, it is perhaps poignant to conclude this chapter by referring to William Ockham. Although, in some respects, he might have agreed with Russell's commitment to precise and meaningful language, he would have rejected Russell's idea that all words stand for something specific. In fact, he referred to the idea that objects are real things, and are more than simply names or concepts, as 'the worst error of philosophy'!

In a theory popularly known as **Ockham's razor**, he concluded that the most productive and most efficient form of philosophical inquiry was the simplest. It is possibly worth bearing that in mind as you read on!

Chapter 2   Religious Language

Some philosophers have looked at the language in which philosophical ideas are expressed to see if truths are conveyed.

The Verification Principle

Logical Positivism developed from the work of a group of philosophers known as the Vienna Circle. These philosophers, working in Vienna in the 1920s, included Moritz Schlick and Rudolf Carnap. The philosophical group did not want to understand how we gain knowledge about the external world, but how we use language as the means of conveying knowledge. The fundamental principle of Logical Positivism was that only those propositions *that can be verified empirically* have meaning. As the leader of the Vienna Circle, Moritz Schlick (1882–1936) put it, 'The meaning of a proposition is the method of verification.'

The logical positivists only accepted two forms of verifiable language:

- analytic propositions (*a priori*) by which knowledge is gained though logical reasoning – to deny the propositions within the statements would be a contradiction
- synthetic propositions (*a posteriori*) by which knowledge could be proved true or false (**verified**) by some form of sense experience or experiment

This became known as the **Verification Principle**. The meaning of a statement is its method of verification. The principle says that *we know the meaning of a statement if we know the conditions under which the statement is true or false*. If it is not possible to know how to prove the statement true or false, then the logical positivists regard it as meaningless, because it is not logical to make such a statement.

The logical positivists argued that it was pointless to talk about God, ethics, art and metaphysics, as such propositions could not be verified using the senses. It was not possible to know the conditions under which such propositions could be proved true or false, and therefore such talk must be meaningless.

This opened a debate on the function of religious language. Some philosophers claimed that religious language served a different function from normal everyday speech, and that – in this context, of the realm of the infinite – the language *is* meaningful. Other philosophers, including the logical positivists, claimed that religious language has no meaning at all, because it talks about things that cannot be proved using empirical evidence.

You need to know

Language is communication between people. It is used **univocally** or **equivocally**.

Univocal language is straightforward and clear. The statement *Paris and Rome are cities* is univocal. There is no doubting the statement, because the concept of a *city* is unambiguous.

Equivocal language is unclear and ambiguous. There can be confusion over the use of a word or phrase, because that word or phrase can have more than one meaning. The statement *John is on the right* is equivocal. The meaning is unclear because *right* could refer to John's political views or the position in which he is standing.

Is Religious Language Meaningful?

Religious language is the communication of ideas about God, faith, belief and practice. The problem with the communication of these ideas is that behind the words used are concepts. Individuals have different understandings of the concepts and this might result in differences of interpretation. Some philosophers argue that religious language is used in different ways from everyday language. It could be used to show one's commitment to a particular faith tradition or to make a claim on behalf of that tradition.

Religious language is used to consider things beyond human experience and this leads to problems in understanding the meaning of any assertions made. The problems arise because:

*   any discussion related to God and belief cannot be based on common ground
*   religious language is not univocal and therefore the meaning of an assertion may be unclear
*   religious language is equivocal language, because it is talking about the realm of infinite existence – the result is different interpretations and understandings of the words used

A. J. Ayer (CE 1910–1989)

Ayer was a logical positivist. He believed that empirical methods have to be used to assess whether a proposition is *in principle* verifiable, and therefore meaningful. It is the steps taken to verify a proposition that make it meaningful. A proposition needs to be analysed to find out what is meaningful and what is not. A physicist makes propositions about the universe that might be challenged or proved untrue

Something to think about

1 Write down how an atheist's concept of God would be different from that of a believer.
2 What problems do you think could arise when an atheist and believer try to discuss their respective concept(s) of God?

Something to think about

The criterion, which we use to test the genuineness of apparent propositions of fact, is the criterion of verifiability. We say that a sentence is factually significant to any given person, if, and only if, he knows how to verify the proposition which it purports to express – that is, if he knows what observations would lead him, under certain conditions, to accept the proposition as being true, or reject it as being false.

A. J. Ayer, Language, Truth and Logic, Victor Gollancz, 1936

On the basis of this statement from A. J. Ayer, why do you think he would reject propositions such as *God is good* or *God loves me*? Support your answer with direct quotes from Ayer.

at some future date. Ayer considered such propositions meaningful, because the physicist bases his findings on experiments. A scientific theory may not be verifiable 'in practice', but because scientists know how to verify a theory it is verifiable 'in principle'. Ayer decided that a proposition is meaningful if it is known how to prove it true or false. If such verification cannot take place, then a proposition is meaningless. *Therefore, according to the logical positivists, as religious propositions cannot be analysed using empirical methods, they are meaningless.*

Later, Ayer realised that we accept some scientific and historical propositions which have not been verified with certainty. He introduced two forms of the Verification Principle, 'strong' and 'weak' verification, to deal with this problem.

'Strong' verification occurs when there is no doubt that a statement is true, as one verifies it using sense experience, observation. An example of the strong form would be the statement *Mary has red hair*, which could be proved true or false by visiting Mary.

'Weak' verification is a statement that there are some observations that are relevant to proving a proposition true or false. For example, *Columbus discovered America* is accepted as true because people affirmed the event at the time. Similarly, statements that could be affirmed in the future are meaningful: 'A proposition is . . . verifiable in the strong sense of the term, if, and only if, its truth could be conclusively established. . .But it is verifiable in the weak sense if it is possible for experience to render it probable.'

Ayer considered that empiricism cannot 'account for our knowledge of necessary truths'. He accepted analytic propositions because to reject such statements would be illogical. He accepted *a priori* truth in both mathematical and linguistic statements because they 'add nothing to our knowledge'. He accepted them because:

> . . . the power of logic and mathematics to surprise us depends, like their usefulness, on the limitations of our reason. A being whose intellect was infinitely powerful would take no interest in logic and mathematics. For he would be able to see at a glance everything that his definitions implied, and accordingly could never learn anything from logical inference which he was not fully conscious of already.

A. J. Ayer, Language, Truth and Logic, Victor Gollancz, 1936

Something to think about

Which of the following statements would Ayer consider meaningful and which would he reject as meaningless? Give reasons for your choice:

When water reaches boiling point, it turns to steam

Unicorns exist

There is life on other planets

A spinster is an unmarried woman

God exists

3 + 3 = 6

An occultist is an eye-doctor

91 × 79 = 7189

You need to know

Eschatology is the doctrine of last things. It is the theological teaching about death and the final judgement after death.

You need to know

Falsification means to prove something false. The **Falsification Principle** accepts that a statement is verifiable if it is known what empirical evidence could count against it, or prove it wrong (false). For example, *aliens live on Saturn* is a meaningful statement because we know how to verify the statement.

A Challenge to Logical Positivism

Many philosophers have rejected the Verification Principle. The reasons for its rejection include the following:

- The principle itself is not meaningful because it cannot be verified using the Verification Principle.
- The logical positivists reject religious language because there is no way of verifying it. The philosopher **John Hick** argued that when we die the truth of God's existence will be proved true or false (verified). Hick calls this '**eschatological verification**'. He is making the point that as we do know how to verify propositions such as *God exists*, religious statements do have meaning.
- The 'weak' form of verification would support some religious statements. There is some sense experience that could count towards them. For example, the proposition *God is the Creator* could be supported by evidence of possible design in the world. There is historical evidence that counts towards propositions such as *Muhammad is the Prophet of Allah* or *Jesus rose from the dead on the first Easter Sunday*.

The Falsification Principle

In the 1950s, **Antony Flew** applied the **Falsification Principle** to religious language and concluded that religious statements are meaningless. Flew argued that this is because there is nothing that can count against religious statements. Religious statements can neither be proved true (verified) nor false, because religious believers do not accept any evidence to count against (falsify) their beliefs. For example, Flew argued that Christians hold to their belief that *God is good*, whatever evidence is offered against God's goodness. The believer gives reasons why God remains good, and Flew stated that these constant qualifications render religious statements meaningless because they die the 'death by a thousand qualifications'. He used **John Wisdom's** Parable of the Gardener to prove his point that religious statements are meaningless because a religious believer will allow nothing to count against his or her beliefs:

> Two people return to their long-neglected garden and find among the weeds a few of the old plants surprisingly vigorous. One says to the other 'It must be that a gardener has been coming and doing something about these plants.' Upon

Read John Wisdom's Parable of the Gardener.

Flew said that a believer's continual refusal to accept things which count against the existence of God made any such discussion meaningless. He described this as 'death of a thousand qualifications'. What do you think Flew meant by this statement? Support your answer with reference to the Parable of the Gardener.

inquiry, they find that no neighbour has ever seen anyone at work in their garden. The first man says to the other 'He must have worked while people slept.' The other says, 'No, someone would have heard him and besides, anybody who cared about the plants would have kept down these weeds.' The first man says, 'Look at the way these are arranged. There is purpose and a feeling for beauty here. I believe that someone comes, someone invisible to mortal eyes. I believe that the more carefully we look the more we shall find confirmation of this.' They examine the garden ever so carefully and sometimes they come on new things suggesting that a gardener comes and sometimes they come on new things suggesting the contrary and even that a malicious person has been at work. Besides examining the garden carefully, they also study what happens to gardens left without attention. Each learns all the other learns about this and about the garden. Consequently, when after all this, one says 'I still believe a gardener comes' while the other says 'I don't' their different words now reflect no difference as to what they have found in the garden, no difference as to what they would find in the garden if they looked further and no difference about how fast untended gardens fall into disorder. At this stage, in this context, the gardener hypothesis has ceased to be experimental, the difference between one who accepts and one who rejects it is not now a matter of the one expecting something the other does not expect. What is the difference between them? The one says, 'A gardener comes unseen and unheard. He is manifested only in his works with which we are all familiar,' the other says 'There is no gardener' and with this difference in what they say about the gardener goes a difference in how they feel towards the garden, in spite of the fact that neither expects anything of it which the other does not expect.

John Wisdom

The Falsification theory differs from Logical Positivism in two ways:

- It depends on falsification rather than verification to decide whether or not a statement is meaningful.
- The challenge of falsification is based not on the language used but on the basic insight that to assert something is to deny something else. Flew is asking that the proof of the existence of God must be based on what the believer is in a position to *know*, and not just to *believe*.

Cognitive refers to propositions based on knowledge. Facts are known to be true or false through this knowledge.

Non-cognitive refers to propositions that cannot be proved true or false through knowledge. Non-cognitive propositions include ethical or moral propositions, or an expression of an emotion.

The Challenge to the Falsification Principle

Other philosophers wanted to prove that religious language does have meaning even if it cannot be verified or falsified. Many philosophers argued that the statements are not cognitive and that it is wrong to treat them as such. Religious statements are non-cognitive. Religious statements do not contain facts that could be proved true or false. The reasons for the rejection of the principle include the following:

- There are statements that cannot be falsified, and yet we understand the meaning behind the statement. **Richard Swinburne** used the example of toys in the toy cupboard to support this point. We can never prove that the toys do not come out of the toy cupboard and move around when we are not watching them. We might not be able to falsify whether or not the toys move, but we still understand the idea of toys moving.

Do these toys move when we are not looking?

- **Basil Mitchell** wanted to show that religious statements are meaningful even if they are not straightforwardly verifiable or falsifiable. Mitchell argued that Flew was wrong in supposing that believers never allow anything to count against their beliefs. Mitchell claimed that Flew missed the point that believers have a prior commitment to trust in God based on faith, and for this reason do not allow evidence to undermine their faith. Believers have to look for qualifications that can explain why there is, for example, evil in the world and still accept a 'God who loves us'.

Something to think about

1 In small groups, make lists of examples of cognitive propositions and non-cognitive propositions.

2 Explain to the other groups your choice of propositions and the reason for your classification of them.

- **R. M. Hare** agreed that falsification could be used to decide the meaningfulness of cognitive statements, but said that religious statements are non-cognitive. Religious language cannot make factual claims but it still has meaning – not because it imparts knowledge, but because it influences the way in which people look at the world. Hare illustrated this point with the example of a university student who was convinced the dons were plotting to kill him. He would not accept any evidence that he was shown to the contrary. The student would not accept evidence that would falsify his belief, but the belief was meaningful for the student even if it was not true, as it influenced the way he saw the university. The student's way of looking at the university was significant for him. Hare called this way of looking at the world a '**blik**'. Religious beliefs are 'bliks' because of the impact they have on the way in which people look at the world and live their lives.

The Purpose of Religious Language

Other philosophers wanted to prove that religious language has a purpose because it has the function of conveying ideas, and this in itself makes it meaningful.

R. B. Braithwaite pointed out that the error of the Verification and Falsification Principles had been to treat religious language as cognitive language when in fact it is non-cognitive.

Religious Language is Moral Discourse

Religious language is about the way in which people should behave towards each other. Braithwaite argued that 'Theological propositions are not explanations of facts in the world of nature in the way in which established scientific hypotheses are.' He asserted that religious claims are meaningful because:

- a religious claim is primarily a moral claim expressing an attitude – it expresses an intention to follow a specified code of behaviour
- it is different from a moral claim, as a religious one will refer to a story as well as to an intention
- it is not necessary for the religious person to believe in the truth of the story referred to in order to resolve to adopt a certain way of life

Read the relevant section in Chapter 3, to understand what is involved in a **mystical experience**.

An **analogy** is a comparison between two things; when a similarity between two things is suggested by the use of the same word. In the phrases *a good book* and *a good dog*, the word *good* is not used in exactly the same way, but there is a similarity between the ways in which it is used, and so there is understanding of the meaning behind the word.

Look at the section about **St Thomas Aquinas** in Chapter 1 (pages 3–4), to help you understand his philosophy.

Religious Language is Equivocal

Religious language is the way in which human language is able to refer to things beyond their understanding, the infinite. Many mystics, such as **St John of the Cross**, believe that it is possible to talk about God not by saying what He is but by saying what He is not – the *via negativa*. A mystical experience is ineffable: mystics resort to saying what God is not; for example, by saying that God is 'not evil' and 'not human'. By joining phrases together, people learn about God. Although other philosophers agree that negative propositions take people nearer to understanding God, they do not think that they help people to understand what God is, or say anything about God that is definitely true.

Religious Language is Analogical

It is possible to apply words that describe human qualities and characteristics to help the understanding of God. People need to realise that there is a difference between the way in which a word is used to describe human characteristics and the way in which the same word is applied to God.

St Thomas Aquinas

Aquinas argued that we only have our day-to-day language with which to talk about God. We understand that a word, when applied to God, has a different meaning from its everyday use because we understand that God is perfect. We are therefore using analogies.

Some philosophers have rejected the use of analogies. They argue that an analogy has to have some shared understanding, some basis for comparison. This is not possible when speaking about God, because God is beyond human understanding. They believe that the use of analogies within religious language is meaningless. Aquinas disagreed. He argued that there is a relationship between the world and God. God created the world, and sustains it, so there is a point of comparison. Aquinas developed two forms of analogy to talk about God.

Analogy of proportion occurs when a word is employed to refer to a quality that a thing possesses in proportion to the kind of reality it possesses. For example, a dog is loyal in the way in which dogs are loyal, and humans are loyal in proportion to the loyalty of being a human. Similarly, one can understand God as all-powerful, as we have the human idea of power. God is proportionally more powerful than humans, so although we cannot completely understand the idea of God's omnipotence, we can have an insight into God's power because of our human experience of power.

Analogy of attribution applies when a term, originally used with reference to one thing, is applied to a second thing because the one causes the other. For example, we may speak of someone having a 'sickly' look because his or her appearance is the result of sickness. Aquinas saw human wisdom as a reflection of God's wisdom. God is the source of love and life, and therefore it is possible to speak of 'the Living God' or say 'God loves us'.

Ian Ramsey developed the theory of analogy in the twentieth century. Ramsey refers to 'models' and 'qualifiers'. A model is an analogy to help us express something about God. For example, if we say *God is good*, the model is the word *good*. We have human understanding of *good*, and when applied to God, it is a model for understanding God's goodness. Ramsey states that if we want to understand God's goodness we need to adapt the model, to **qualify** it, so that we realise that it is not literally what God is like. To the statement *God is good*, we need to add the qualifier that God is *infinitely good*. This will make us think of God's goodness in greater and greater depth, until eventually we have an insight into God's goodness, and we will then respond to this insight with awe and wonder.

Something to think about

Analogy lacks a clear, precise understanding about God. Do you think analogies do allow a discussion of God and His characteristics? Give reasons for your answer, showing that you have thought about more than one point of view.

You need to know

A **symbol** is something that stands, or is used, in place of some other thing.

A **metaphor** is a figure of speech. A word or phrase is used to denote or describe something entirely different from the object or idea with which it is usually associated. The result is that a resemblance or analogy is suggested.

Religious Language is Metaphorical and Symbolic

It is through metaphors and symbols that we are helped towards an understanding of God. **Paul Tillich** (1886–1965) believed that it is through symbols that religious language communicates religious experiences. Religious language tries to interpret that experience and it is therefore:

- closer to poetry than to prose
- mythical, heroic and imaginable
- evocative of the experience that it seeks to describe

Tillich believed that religious language is symbolic because it 'opens up' new levels of reality. Tillich argued that symbols go beyond the external world to what he described as their 'internal reality'. Religious symbols 'open up levels of reality which otherwise were closed to us'. When the Bible speaks of the *kingdom of God*, the symbol of a *kingdom* is concerned with the reality of God's power and rule. We understand a kingdom on Earth, and by thinking about an earthly kingdom we can go beyond to understand the ultimate reality of the power in the universe that is God. Tillich believed that a symbol 'unlocks dimensions and elements of our soul'. Religious symbols take us to 'being itself'. Tillich suggested that the power of symbols to direct ways of thinking changes through time. This is because the impact and meaning of words change, and the symbol is no longer able to direct us towards what 'concerns us ultimately' as it did in the past.

Opposition to Religious Language as Symbolic

The arguments of those opposed to religious language as symbolic include the following:

- **Paul Edwards** did not believe that symbols convey any factual knowledge, and asserted that they were meaningless. Tillich argued that symbols were intended to convey facts, and therefore that they cannot be verified or falsified using empirical evidence.
- The symbols used are neither adequate nor appropriate. A symbol is intended to point the way to understanding something. It is not possible for religious symbols successfully to represent that which is beyond human experience. There is no way of knowing if the symbols gives the wrong insights about the ultimate reality. Therefore, there is no way of knowing if the symbols are appropriate.
- Symbols are about the real world. Tillich does not apply symbols to an objective reality, and therefore this might lead to misunderstandings of the way in which religious symbols are understood.

Language Games

Ludwig Wittgenstein (1889–1951) had supported the logical positivists, but he came to reject the Verification Principle. He decided that the meaning of words is in their use; the function they perform as agreed by the particular group or society using them. Each activity has its own language, and Wittgenstein regarded this rather like a game with its own set of rules. **Language games** exist within all forms of human activity and life. People not in the game will be unable to understand the use of the language. If people do not understand the language, then it will seem to be meaningless. Religious belief has its own language. A non-believer will find religious language meaningless because he or she is not in the religious 'game'. But an outsider cannot claim that the language used in a particular 'game' is meaningless just because it does not make sense to them.

René Descartes believed that he had proved his existence because of his private thoughts. Wittgenstein argued that individuals could not create a private language: How would individuals know that they were using words correctly? Language is a social product and therefore any thoughts are not in private but in public language, with socially agreed rules on how they are to be used and understood. Wittgenstein denied the first-person certainty that had underlined both rationalist and empiricist approaches to philosophy.

You need to know

Look back at the section on **René Descartes** in Chapter 1 (pages 4–5) to help you to understand his philosophy.

Criticisms of Wittgenstein

The criticisms of Wittgenstein's view of religious language have included the following:

- If people in different faiths are playing their own language game, how is it possible for discussion to take place between the different faith traditions about God's existence?
- Religious believers are involved in other language games because they are involved in other aspects of life. This means that religious language is not totally isolated. This means that there will be common ground between religious language and other 'language games'. This common ground means that non-believers are able to understand religious language and decide whether it has meaning for them.
- Non-believers might be able to understand religious language better than believers. This is because non-believers have an objective view of the use of religious language.

Conclusion

Believers would agree that it is difficult to talk about God. The meaning of the word *god* applies to a being beyond human understanding. Believers recognise that any discussion of God is limited, but they would argue that religious language does have meaning and/or purpose.

Essay questions

AS

(a) Explain the reasons why the Logical Positivists argued that to state 'God exists' was a meaningless statement.

(b) With reference to philosophers you have studied, how far is it true to say that all religious statements are meaningless?

A2

(a) " 'God is life' and 'God is love' are meaningless statements." Examine the reasons why some philosophers might agree with this statement.

(b) Explain and assess the claim that such statements as 'God is life' and 'God is love' have meaning for a believer.

Chapter 3   Religious Experience and Authority

The term **religious experience** can conjure up a wide and diverse series of images. We might assume that it can mean anything from saying a prayer, to attending a service at a place of worship, to 'hearing the voice of God'. Indeed, our understanding of the term is important in investigating the concept.

If your definition incorporates the idea of personal involvement in any form of prayer, reflection, worship or meditation, then you are focusing in the right direction. However, for our purposes it is important to have a definitive answer, to enable thorough analysis.

Something to think about

Write a sentence to express how you would interpret the term **religious experience**.

Something to think about

Remind yourself of the meaning of **empiricism**. Find out what the term **non-empirical** means.

What is Religious Experience?

- A religious experience is a non-empirical occurrence, and may even be perceived as supernatural.
- It can be described as a 'mental event' which is undergone by an individual, and of which that person is aware.
- Such an experience can be spontaneous, or it may be brought about as a result of intensive training and self-discipline.

You need to know

For an example of a 'spontaneous' religious experience, look up the story of the conversion of St Paul in a Bible (Acts of the Apostles, Chapter 9).

For an example of religious experiences brought about by training and meditation, find out about the practices of the **Sufi** orders of Islam.

- Recipients of religious experiences usually say that what has happened to them has 'drawn them into' a deeper knowledge or awareness of God.
- It is very important to remember that the experience itself is not a *substitute* for the Divine, but a vehicle that is used to bring people closer to the Divine.

- The experience that each individual has is absolutely unique and cannot be shared with anyone.
- Finally, *genuine* religious experiences seem to be encouraging; they do not condemn the individual, but help them to live a better life or, for example, to help others.

Different Forms of Religious Experience

As mentioned above, there is an infinite number of different religious experiences, as each one is unique, but there have been attempts to classify them, based largely upon the results of the experience.

- Most religious experiences are said to be **mystical**. This means that the recipient feels a sense of 'union' with the Divine.
- Many religious experiences are classified as 'prayer' experiences. This usually refers to experiences that have been brought about by meditation and reflection.
- The effects of religious experience can sometimes be permanent and life-changing. Such experiences are often classified as 'conversion' experiences.

Numinosity

Many testimonies from those claiming to have had a religious experience refer to a sense of being in the presence of an awesome power, and yet feeling distinctly separate from it. The word given to describe this feeling is **numinous**. While many regard numinosity as a feature of religious experience some, such as C. S. Evans, classify it as a 'type' in its own right and contrast it with mystical experience.

Something to think about

Imagine being in the presence of your idol or hero/heroine. How would you feel? What would you do or say? If this reaction could be multiplied infinitely, we might have an example of numinosity.

Rudolph Otto

In *The Idea of the Holy* (1936), Otto used the term 'numinous' to refer to a being that had an awesome power. He suggested that religion *must* derive from a being that is totally separate from this world. It is in the presence of such a being that numinosity is experienced. Some commentators are unhappy with this idea. They feel that this 'otherness' of God makes religion impersonal.

You need to know

Find out about the **Deist** movement (Chapter 10, page 138) that began in the eighteenth century. There is a similarity between the views of this movement and Otto's point here.

Indeed, for many people the notion of God as being entirely separate from mankind is extremely problematic. For example, it is an apparent contradiction of the Christian belief that God is a personal being.

Martin Buber (1878–1965)

Buber stressed the existence of personal relationships that can exist regardless of the concept of the numinous. He suggested that relationships can be formed at two levels:

- I–It: viewing people and things simply as phenomena (that is, simply classifying things)
- I–Thou: taking a relationship further by 'probing deeper'. This, stresses Buber, is a truly *personal* relationship

Buber stated that God is the 'Eternal Thou' and, as such, God can reveal Himself to man on a personal level, which leads the human to a special religious experience of life and the world. This understanding of God can be interpreted as contact with God *through other people and nature*. As Buber put it, '. . . in each Thou we address the Eternal Thou'.

Søren Kierkegaard (1813–1855)

Kierkegaard's work supported the position taken by Buber. Kierkegaard saw faith as a miracle, and he stated that the only way in which God could be 'known' by an individual was through a 'leap of faith'. Faith arose through human experience which could include, in some cases, religious experience.

Buber and Kierkegaard are basically saying that 'knowledge' of God could be different for each individual. Any such knowledge will depend upon:

- the personal level of faith – for example, someone with a certain amount of theological understanding or someone led by 'blind faith'
- the personal denomination of faith – for example, a Muslim or a Jew
- the 'type' of faith – for example, a devout Catholic, or a nominal Catholic who attends only weddings and funerals

Something to think about

On the basis of what Buber and Kierkegaard said, what problems do you think might arise in relation to each of these categories of personal belief?

Something to think about

One of the most well-known forms of religious experience is **stigmata**. Try to find out about this phenomenon.

Why might it be that a considerable majority of the people claiming to have undergone this experience are Roman Catholics?

Mystical Experience

Most forms of religious experience are referred to as 'mystical'. The term is extremely versatile, and has been used to cover everything from the experiences of the Great Mystics of each religious tradition, to mildly ecstatic, mysterious or occult experiences.

As far as we are concerned in our investigation of religious experience, mysticism involves the *spiritual recognition of truths beyond normal understanding*.

It has been suggested that there are several features that accompany the experiences and enable their recognition:

- the gaining of knowledge of the 'Ultimate Reality' – this is knowledge that is normally hidden from the human intellect
- a sense of freedom from the limitations of time, space and the human ego
- a sense of 'oneness' or unity with the Divine
- a sense of bliss or serenity

Mysticism is seen as the closest that a human being can ever come to actually meeting the Divine.

William James (1842–1910)

The most famous commentator on religious experience is William James. He recognised that the term **mystical** is used in a wide variety of contexts, but suggested that using it to refer to 'any person who believes in thought-transference or spirit-return' is far too ambiguous. Therefore, in his *The Varieties of Religious Experience* (1902), he offers four characteristics which, he claims, will enable us to identify mystical experiences: ineffability, noetic quality, transciency and passivity. These characteristics require detailed consideration.

Ineffability

James suggested that ineffability is the most easily recognisable characteristic of mystical experience. This is despite the fact that it is inherently negative. As mentioned earlier, religious experiences are *private* events; the recipient goes through certain sensations that are beyond verbal description – unutterable.

There is an awareness that there is something to be described, but no way of doing so. St Teresa of Avila stated 'I wish I could give a description of at least the smallest part of what I learned, but, when I try to discover a way of doing so, I find it impossible . . .'.

Sometimes descriptions are offered, but these tend to be meaningless to the listener who has no *experience* of such occurrences. For example:

the dissolution of the personal ego

or

a sense of peace and sacredness

You need to know

The term **Divine** is used here to mean a perfect being that is all-powerful and is not comparable to anything human. Such a being is usually referred to as 'God'.

Something to think about

Try writing down a description or definition of one of the following, as though you were explaining it to someone who had never experienced it:

- being in love
- the taste of an onion

Is this an easy task? Why, or why not?

According to R. A. Gilbert, in *The Elements of Mysticism*, such phrases 'serve to illustrate the extreme difficulty of discussing non-empirical concepts solely in terms of the intellect'.

Something to think about

What we are thinking about can be compared to any unique experience. Only Neil Armstrong *knows* what it felt like to be the first man on the Moon – no one else has or will ever experience this, and therefore no one else can truly relate to it.

A unique experience that cannot be shared

Something to think about

Such an idea is familiar to many religious groups. For example, Christians read in the Bible (John 14:26) that '. . . the Holy Spirit, whom the Father will send in my name, he will teach you all things'. This is not a reference to knowledge gained in the 'normal' way, through the senses.

How do you think, therefore, that this knowledge is gained?

As **Alfred Tennyson** (1809–1892) wrote in a letter about religious experience, 'I am ashamed of my feeble description. Have I not said that the state is utterly beyond words?' In conclusion, one might suggest that one cannot truly understand what is beyond one's own experience.

Noetic Quality

Despite mystical experiences being classed as 'ineffable', recipients are quick to point out that they do provide insights into *unobtainable truths* – although not through the intellect.

Something to think about

An example of noetic quality can be found in experiences in which an individual may see 'God's handiwork' in nature. Consider a beautiful scenic view or the sky at night. Such scenes can convey information of sorts, albeit very different information to the types we are more familiar with.

Rather, knowledge is grasped through *intuition* and *perception* – it is a revelation.

The noetic quality of a religious experience, therefore, is the 'knowledge' or information that is gained, although not in the conventional manner.

Transciency

It would appear that most religious experiences last between a few minutes and about two hours. However, the *significance* and *effects* of the experience are out of proportion to its physical duration.

This can be easily considered if one thinks about dreaming. It is perfectly possible to spend five minutes dreaming about a scenario that *appears* to take hours or even days, or vice versa.

However, unlike many dreams, those who have undergone such experiences claim that the experience is well remembered.

Passivity

This final aspect as outlined by William James in *The Varieties of Religious Experience* suggests that while undergoing the experience one 'loses control' to a more powerful being, namely God, and is overwhelmed. The effects of this loss of control include individuals assuming entirely different personalities, writing or drawing certain prophetic visions or messages with the opposite hand to normal, or speaking in a completely different voice or language. This leads one to the conclusion that although many people try to control the experiences, they are in fact beyond human control.

Induced Experiences

Obviously, many of the types of experiences we have considered so far could be confused with the effects of consuming alcohol and/or drugs. James recognised this fact:

> The drunken consciousness is one bit of the mystic consciousness, and our total opinion of it must find its place in our opinion of that larger whole.

> *William James, The Varieties of Religious Experience, Longmans, Green and Co., 1902*

In conclusion, it seems apparent that mystical experiences are states of consciousness, which are either spontaneous or induced. While 'under the influence', mystics feel a greater depth of understanding. Although this understanding may be lost as the influence fades, a sense of profound feeling is retained. No matter what ties may connect different people who have these experiences – social, cultural or religious – *their experiences are unique*.

F. C. Happold (1893–1971)

F. C. Happold sought not to establish a set of criteria to identify mystical experiences, as William James had done, but to provide some sort of context in which to think about and discuss them. In *Mysticism – A Study and an Anthology* (1963), he suggests that we can divide mysticism, 'for convenience', into two types:

- The Mysticism of Love and Union
- The Mysticism of Knowledge and Understanding

The Mysticism of Love and Union

This, Happold suggests, is the longing to escape from loneliness and the feeling of being 'separate'. To look at it from the opposite perspective, it requires some sort of union (or, depending on your theological perspective, *re*-union) with God. In the words of Saint Augustine:

> Thou hast made us for thyself, O God, and our hearts are restless till they rest in Thee.

Happold believes that the two urges that govern all of us are the desire for separation (that is, the need to be an individual), and the desire to be part of something bigger than ourselves (that is, the need to be accepted in some way). Obviously these two urges are constantly in conflict with one another. Happold believes that these urges have their origin in the fact that we are in some way sharers in what we could call 'the Divine Life'. This suggests that, despite our need to be individuals, we are always trying to get back to God – hence the desire to be part of something bigger than ourselves. In the words of Happold:

> He [mankind] feels himself to be a pilgrim of eternity, a creature in time but a citizen of a timeless world.

The Mysticism of Knowledge and Understanding

Happold says that people have another 'urge', which is inherent in all of us. We need to try to find out the 'secret of the universe' ('the meaning of life', in other words).

Something to think about

What do you think Happold means by the phrases 'a pilgrim of eternity' and 'a citizen of a timeless world'?

You need to know

Look at Chapter 11, which focuses on questions regarding the meaning of life. Try to find as many different approaches as you can that suggest how we can find fulfilment.

Something to think about

The phrase 'I was led in the learning that is ignorance to grasp the incomprehensible' appears to be a complete contradiction in terms. Using William James's idea of noetic quality, can you explain what Nicholas of Cusa meant?

Something to think about

Try to find out about the Hindu concept of Brahman. How does this idea relate to Happold's explanation of *soul-mysticism*?

You need to know

Remind yourself of the concepts of immanence and transcendence in the section on 'The Attributes of God' in Chapter 4.

Importantly, he says that we do not seek this in sections, but want to know 'the whole story', as it were.

The way that we can look for answers to such an ultimate question is through experiential knowledge of God.

What form would such knowledge take?

Happold points out that philosophers often play games of 'conceptual counters'. By this he is referring to deductive arguments and logic, such as the Aristotelian Circle, referred to in Chapter 1.

The point about experiential knowledge of God is that it is intuitive. In James's terms, this suggests noetic quality. As Nicholas of Cusa wrote in *De Docta ignorantia* ('Of Learned Ignorance'):

> I was led in the learning that is ignorance to grasp the incomprehensible; and this I was able to achieve not by way of comprehension but by transcending those perennial truths that can be reached by reason.

Further to his separation of mystical experience into two types, Happold says that there are three aspects of mystical experience:

- *Soul-mysticism*
- *Nature-mysticism*
- *God-mysticism*

Soul-mysticism is the concept of *the soul* as something that is numinous or hidden. It does not deal with the concept of union with *God*, as such (in fact the existence of God is not actually considered). Rather, it sees the soul as something that is hidden or, to use Otto's terminology, *numinous*. Mystical experience in this context, therefore, is the idea of *finding* the soul and, therefore, complete self-fulfilment. As Happold says:

> The chief object of man is the quest for his own self and of right knowledge about it.

Obviously, this form of mysticism *does not deal* with the 'God of Classical Theism', although it does relate to certain Buddhist and Hindu philosophies (the concept of Brahman, for example).

Nature-mysticism is found in the belief that God is immanent. He is everywhere, and can therefore be 'united with' in many aspects of nature. Happold suggests that the poet William Wordsworth expressed this idea well:

A motion and a spirit,
that impels all thinking things,
all objects of all thought,
and rolls through all things.

and

That Light whose smile kindles the Universe,
that Beauty in which all things work and move.

God-mysticism is the contention that the souls of humankind desire to return to their 'immortal and infinite Ground, which is God'. There are suggestions that mystical union with God requires the human soul to be 'deified' – it almost *becomes* God whilst retaining its own identity. This is something that Sufi Muslims seek through their various forms of worship.

Prayer

Some people refer to mystics as those who experience a particular type of **mental prayer**.

In simple terms, prayer is a method of communication between man and God. In particular, this should be focused upon for the purpose of religious experience, as opposed to 'set formulas' of prayer.

Auguste Sabatier (1839–1901)

Sabatier attempted to place prayer in its authentic religious context by stating the following:

> Religion is an intercourse, a conscious and voluntary relation entered into by a soul in distress with the mysterious power upon which it feels itself to depend . . . Prayer is religion in act . . . Wherever prayer rises and stirs the soul, even in the absence of forms or of doctrines, we have living religion.
>
> *Auguste Sabatier, Outlines of a Philosophy of Religion Based on Psychology and History, Hodder and Stoughton, 1897*

Petitionary prayers are prayers that ask for something, and they form an important part of prayer activity. However, there is a problem inherent within such a notion:

How can human petition affect divine will?

Instead of petition, therefore, the prayer may involve recognition of the power and goodness of God, and a **resignation** to His will. Islam is a prime example of such resignation and/or submission. Some would object to this, maintaining that a petitionary prayer is a natural reaction to a *personal* God. To conclude this point in a logical fashion, therefore, one might suggest that the 'reward' sought after by the person praying is not a detailed fulfilment of his or her 'wish', but relaxation from his or her state of tension. How can this be gained? – by the recognition of the fact that the matter is now in the hands of God.

Frederic W. H. Myers

Writing in 1898, Myers saw prayer as a vital component of the psychological well-being of many individuals. He defined prayer as the general name for an 'attitude of open expectancy'. Indeed, he suggested that it really does not matter *who* one prays to! This is because prayer is so completely subjective that 'it would be rash to say that Christ himself hears us'. Myers' points rest on the recognition that we have absolutely no idea as to how prayer operates.

Mystical States of Prayer

There have been many attempts to define prayer into various classifications – one being that of St Teresa of Avila (1515–1582). St Teresa was a passionate mystic but also a very methodical and practical woman. It is these qualities that provide us with a classification that is particularly useful, as it moves from clearly distinguishable psychological points. Following R. A. Gilbert, it can be illustrated as follows:

1 The prayer of quiet
   ↓
2 The prayer of union
   ↓
3 Ecstasy
   ↓
4 Spiritual marriage

The Prayer of Quiet

This is brought about by consistent meditation and/or contemplation. The state does not interfere with other mental functions as later ones do. To begin with, the state can only be maintained for a few seconds, but as the individual becomes more experienced it can be maintained for many hours – even continuing during physical activities. The contemplation itself is accompanied by 'distractions', which are best described as 'images' or 'thoughts'. The power to make voluntary body movements is not lost, although movement can result in a loss of the state.

The Prayer of Union

This is the intermediate stage between 'quiet' and 'ecstasy'. It would appear to be a more intense and emotional experience than the prayer of quiet, and the 'distractions' are not reported to occur. Again, the powers of voluntary movement and sensory perception are not lost.

Ecstasy and Spiritual Marriage

This stage of the classification always attracts the most interest out of the four stages – mainly because of the striking bodily movements. This can often appear like fairly erratic dancing, and can be accompanied by phenomena such as 'speaking in tongues'. The state of ecstasy is accompanied by a *complete loss* of sensory perception and of the power to make voluntary movements. However, it would appear that commands from the 'spiritual superior' are obeyed. The power held by the spiritual superior has been likened to that of the hypnotist over his subject. *But 'ecstasy' is not a hypnotic trance.* It is often a state entered into by a person when in a less intense state of contemplation. It is in this state that visions and revelations can occur. Furthermore, it is in this state that the individual can access the 'ultimate' state of contemplative prayer – 'spiritual marriage' – so-called because the person feels that they are in a condition of 'complete wedded bliss' with God. St Teresa of Avila described this feeling as:

> . . .a sweetness impossible to describe, for which reason it is better to say no more about it.

Conversion

What is Conversion?

The term **conversion**, in the sense of religious experience, refers explicitly to a 'regeneration', an assurance of the 'truth of the Divine'. On a personal level, the result of a conversion is usually a greater understanding of faith. 'Religious conversion' is the process that leads to the adoption of a religious attitude or way of life.

The Psychological Background to Conversion

In the mind of every individual, there are a whole series of diverse aims, each one consisting of a group of ideas ranked in order of importance. At certain times, different aims will be

of paramount importance to the individual to such an extent that the other aims – or at least some of them – will be of very little consequence indeed.

If certain circumstances should arise that establish one aim as having *permanent* priority in one's mind – to the complete *exclusion* of others – we refer to this as a **transformation** (for example, winning the lottery).

Obviously, as an individual passes through life, certain priorities shift from peripheral to central areas of conscious thought. Often, what brings about such changes is *emotional excitement* – that is, what excites us or upsets us one day might not do so in a week's time.

If a person is prone to sudden and dramatic changes in emotional excitement, he or she can be weakened, as his or her aims will be divided and it will be very difficult on any one particular objective. But how does this relate to religion?

If, as mentioned above, a permanent shift in the focus of a person's aim can be observed, we are probably dealing with *some sort* of conversion. If the emotional excitement that inspired the shift is *religious*, then it could well be a religious conversion. In such a case, religious ideas that were previously insignificant in the consciousness of the individual will now take a central place; that is, religious aims will now form the 'habitual centre' of that person's energy; the area of the conscious mind devoted to mankind's ideas. It is interesting to note that neither the outside observer nor the subject him- or herself is in any way able to explain *how* the experience undergone has been able to change that person's life so dramatically, by changing his or her aims as discussed.

One thing that can put the process of conversion into its rightful perspective is to consider how *violent* explosions of emotion can affect people. Love, jealousy, guilt, fear, hatred, anger, joy or compassion rarely leave the individual unchanged by their involvement in their life.

Edwin D. Starbuck

Professor Starbuck demonstrated that the *ordinary* – that is, 'non-religious' – 'conversion' of young people (14–17 years old) brought up in evangelical circles into a spiritual life is very similar to the conversions experienced by most adolescents. The symptoms would appear to be the same – a sense of incompleteness and imperfection, brooding, depression, introspection, anxiety about the future and distress over doubts. The result of the conversion is universally similar, whether religious or not – a 'happy relief' and objectivity. Starbuck's conclusion is as follows:

> Conversion is, in its essence, a normal adolescent phenomenon, incidental to the passage from the child's small universe to the wider intellectual and spiritual life of maturity.

It is interesting to note, however, that while Starbuck points out the similarities between religious and non-religious conversion, he does note that theology shortens the period of storm and stress. His definition of conversion is:

> . . . a process of struggling away from sin rather than striving towards righteousness.

> *E. D. Starbuck, The Psychology of Religion,*
> *Walter Scott, 1899*

William James maintains that there are some people who could never be converted, as religious ideas could never become the centre of their spiritual energy. There are a variety of reasons for this: for example, they may be exceptionally cynical, or any chance of religious belief may be hindered because of natural, pessimistic beliefs about the world. Inhibitions such as these are rarely overcome, according to James. There are other people who have 'temporary inhibitions'; that is, they 'refuse to believe', but may change their minds, even late in life.

With more than one group of people to consider in the area of religious conversion, there are obviously different types.

Types of Conversion

There are basically *two* forms of mental occurrence which lead to a difference in the conversion process:

- a conscious and voluntary experience – the **volitional** type
- an involuntary and unconscious experience – the **self-surrender** type

The **volitional** type features a gradual change and consists of the slow development of new moral and spiritual habits. It may be the case that the person suddenly 'becomes aware' of the change one day. The subconscious effects are more evident, however, in the **self-surrender** type. For William James, the concept of conversion by self-surrender can be illustrated by the expression 'man's extremity is God's opportunity'. What is also evident is that even in the most voluntary forms of conversion, there *has* to be some element of self-surrender. It would appear that one can only go so far in *bringing about* conversion; after a certain stage it must be left to 'other forces'. Starbuck maintains that quite often a person must stop 'trying' to change; only then will conversion occur naturally.

As a rule, there are two things in the mind of the candidate for conversion:

- the present 'wrongness' in their life – their sins, perhaps – that they want to change
- the positive changes that they wish to make

Recently, there has been much interest in the concept of sudden conversion experiences, leading to the assertion that *all* religious believers probably had undergone such an occurrence. While the majority of conversions are clearly *gradual*, the *sudden* experience would appear to be the most significant and profound, as far as its effects are concerned. It often affects people who had no religious faith whatsoever before the experience. In turn, what is most significant about the gradual conversion is the process involved. It would appear that, to begin with, a person rejects any notion of religious faith, for whatever reason. He or she then reaches a position in which *some* elements seem acceptable. This continues until such time as there is a 'climax', at which point complete conversion occurs. This process is a vehicle with which the most complicated series of objections to the faith can be resolved. The process can often result in some of the most passionate and fundamentalist advocates of a given religious group.

How Permanent is Conversion?

In many cases, those who experience sudden conversion may know very little about what they have come to believe and testify in! Their knowledge may amount to little more than what they have read in a series of leaflets, or what they have heard from a local preacher. As such, there is far more chance of their deciding at some future point that there are inherent problems in what the preacher has told them, or that there are flaws in the literature upon which they have based their 'new outlook'.

As illustrated, such problems of 'fall-off' rate are far less likely in the case of gradual conversion.

Something to think about

Gradual conversion is always more likely to be permanent than sudden conversion. This is probably because a slower procedure is more likely to be thorough. For example, a *well-planned* essay will always be more thorough than a quickly scribbled effort!

Examples of Conversions

Religious conversion is likely to include a change in belief on religious topics, which in turn leads to changes in the motivation for one's behaviour within the social environment. As a result, it is appropriate to speak of **intellectual**, **moral** or **social** conversions.

Intellectual conversions involve conflicts between two systems of thought. The result of the conflict is often that the new one is 'true' and the old one is 'false'. It can either be to or from a religious system of thought, or from one religion to another.

James H. Leuba (1868–1946)

Professor Leuba clearly views religious life as almost purely **moral**. He defines the religious sense as:

> The feeling of unwholeness, of moral imperfection of sin, to use the technical word, accompanied by the yearning after the peace of unity. . .The word religion is getting more and more to signify the conglomerate of desires and emotions springing from the sense of sin and its release.

> *J. H. Leuba, 'Studies in the psychology of religious phenomena',*
> *The American Journal of Psychology, vol. vii, 1896*

Indeed, Leuba gives a series of examples in which sin ranges from drunkenness to spiritual pride.

An example of **moral conversion** can be found in the story of 'Swearing Tom', as told by **Robert H. Thouless**. Tom's story illustrates a moral conversion – it does not revolve around a system of thought, as the intellectual one does, but around one's lifestyle.

Swearing Tom

For 17 years, 'Tom' lived a most profane and godless life, until one day he entered a church and heard a preacher say that even the most wicked of men could undergo a change of heart, if they prayed to God. Tom left the church and went home, ignoring the public house for a change, and prayed using the words the preacher had used.

Sure enough, a change took place and soon his name was changed from 'Swearing Tom' to 'Praying Tom' – a name he went by until his death.

You need to know

Look back to the notes you took earlier in the chapter, to remind yourself of the details of St Paul's conversion.

An example of a sudden, **social** conversion is that of St Paul on the road to Damascus. Indeed, it is this idea of a conversion taking place slowly *in the subconscious*, followed by a rapid and sudden conscious experience, that William James calls 'subconscious incubation'.

William James' conclusions about religious conversion are as follows:

1 Sudden conversion is very real to those who have had the experience. They feel that the process has been 'performed' upon them. God causes the conversion.
2 For Methodists, salvation is not truly received unless they have been through a crisis of the sort which is involved in conversion.
3 Those having a sudden conversion feel it to be a miracle rather than a natural process.
4 Even when James saw conversion as being a natural process, he maintained that it was inspired by the Divine.

The Value of Religious Experience as a Basis for Belief

As we have seen, religious experiences can take many different forms, and those who experience them are affected in particularly diverse ways. However, could one go as far as to suggest that the 'existence' of religious experiences is proof for the existence of God?

Something to think about

Consider the problems in suggesting that one can accept the existence of God from the testimony of those who claim to have undergone religious experiences.

Also, suggest any ways in which these testimonies could affect an existing believer's faith.

Religious Experience as an Argument for the Existence of God

An individual who believed in the existence of God would probably suggest that His involvement in human affairs is perfectly understandable, acceptable and even to be expected. This is why many religious believers refer to God as a *personal* being.

However, few would suggest that God could reveal Himself too frequently in our affairs, as this would seriously jeopardise our free will. This problem is highlighted in more detail in Chapter 8.

Consequently, it would appear that the argument for the existence of God based on religious experience is based upon the idea that God manifests Himself occasionally and privately in some people's lives. The only way we can 'know' this is by the testimony of the recipients of these experiences. They assure us that God has been experienced through:

- creation
- redemption
- the fellowship, or community, of believers
- prayer, worship and meditation
- His love (as displayed by others)

Obviously, areas of life such as these are not open to any form of empirical scrutiny or rational justification, but demand *spiritual recognition*. The problem with such a notion is, arguably, that such areas are accessed far more easily by the believer than the non-believer.

A common criticism of religious experience as evidence for the existence of God is that many reported experiences do not seem to involve God. Rather, we are told of 'mystical union' with angels, saints or 'messengers'. While, superficially, this apparent inconsistency indicates a flaw within the argument, it is not necessarily so. The existence of angels, saints and God's 'messengers' must surely affirm the existence of God – otherwise, where are they from and what purpose do they serve?

This argument is further strengthened by what many philosophers call the **Principle of Credulity**. This asserts that we must accept what appears to be the case unless we have evidence which suggests that we are wrong to do so. This can be thought about in terms of the legal concept 'innocent until proven guilty'. A person could commit the most atrocious crime but be regarded as innocent of that crime until those sitting in judgement have 'experienced' – usually through observation in court – sufficient evidence to be sure of the person's guilt.

The implications of this principle for religious experience are clear. Unless there are sufficient grounds for asserting that the experiences are *not* authentic, we should take them as they are described – encounters with the Divine. You will probably have concluded that many of the experiences that we are considering might be brought about by natural causes, and have nothing to do with God. This is quite true, yet the fact remains that there will always be a greater chance of such experiences taking place if God *does* exist.

Problems of Verification of the Experience

What are the difficulties that confront us when we try to assess the authenticity of these experiences?

- As we have seen, individuals rather than groups undergo these experiences. As a result, we only have one person's testimony as to what has happened. For example, St Bernadette testified that the Virgin Mary had spoken to her; others who witnessed the 'experience' only saw her talking to an unseen 'someone'.
- Religious experience is very like emotion – it is a personal response, which means that any form of empirical testing is useless.
- It would appear that those who encounter these experiences portray the 'being' revealed to them quite differently. In some cases it is clearly the God of their respective faith. For example, stigmata is linked with Jesus, whereas Muhammad experienced the message of Allah. In other cases it would appear to be a deity quite distinct from the God of formal or organised religion. For some, it is simply the force of nature.
- In many cases, drugs or alcohol can produce very similar effects to a religious experience. In *The Varieties of Religious Experience* (1902), James refers to experiments using nitrous oxide and anaesthetics. He suggests that, when mixed sufficiently with air, these substances 'stimulate the mystical consciousness in an extraordinary degree'.

The Objective/Subjective Distinction

Consider the following two statements about the same person:

Kierkegaard was a philosopher
Kierkegaard was a great philosopher

The key difference between these two statements illustrates the objective/subjective distinction.

The first statement is clearly **objective** – that is, it is open to testing. It can be empirically verified or falsified and shared.

The second statement is clearly **subjective** – that Kierkegaard was a great philosopher is a private decision. It may be the case that there is something in his work that *I* find inspiring

Something to think about

Try to construct your own examples of objective and subjective statements about the same issue.

Is there any overlap? Why, or why not, might this be?

and brilliant, but it is a decision based on a *personal* conviction. The fact that *you* or anybody else might agree is irrelevant to the conviction.

As has been demonstrated throughout this chapter, religious experiences are regarded as subjective because no objective criteria can be applied to them in order to judge their merit, authenticity or anything else.

This presents us with three areas worthy of consideration:

- A subjective experience cannot be offered as 'scientific'; that is, as empirical or intellectual proof. This is basically because experiences happen to people, and will always be open to interpretation. However, the apparent lack of uniformity between different reports of religious experience does not render them all 'incorrect' or 'inauthentic'. The consequence of all the experiences being different and none being necessarily inauthentic is that Kierkegaard was right – there is no 'objective' way of reaching God.

You need to know

Look at the way in which God is physically represented in the following 'appearances':

- to Adam (Genesis 3)
- to Abraham (Genesis 17)
- to Moses (Exodus 3)

What problems could these appearances raise in relation to the claim 'I have seen God'?

- Surely anything as abstract from 'everyday life' as a religious experience can be deceptive. It may be the case that whatever experience takes place is *perceived* as religious by the recipient. In particular, this would apply to situations in which the recipient claims to have actually seen God. Such a conviction raises considerable theological problems, as even the Scriptures do not feature any physical appearances by God. There are two suggestions as to how such audiovisual experiences could occur:

  1 psychopathological – the recipient suffers from a medical condition
  2 the mind can 'misjudge' experiences under extreme conditions (for example, mirages in the desert)

- Many would suggest that conversion *is* a form of religious experience that can be verified fairly easily, because the results are readily observed. On the other hand, conversion could be put down to psychological causes, not divine intervention; that is, a person might undergo a conversion because it meets his or her psychological needs as an individual. This idea was supported by Freud, who suggested that conversion was a 'reaction to a hostile world', in which insecure people reach out to God as a father figure who can provide them with love and comfort. Voltaire was of a similar mind when he commented that 'If God did not exist, it would be necessary to invent him.' However, some philosophers feel that approaches such as these are simply attempts to reduce the phenomenon of conversion and/or religious experience into its most basic components, so as to dispute its authenticity.

An Evaluation of the Argument

The study of philosophy highlights the fact that there are many ways of considering what the 'truth' in a given situation might be. Indeed, the very *concept* of 'truth' can soon become extremely diverse. With this in mind, we must accept that evaluating any argument involves a search for a theory or theories of truth. In this case there are several theories that could be applied.

Something to think about

What problems might arise if we assert that things are *only* 'true' if they correspond with certain earthly facts?

You may wish to consider what the word *fact* actually means.

The **correspondence theory** asks whether or not a particular statement corresponds to something in the 'real world'. For example, if one is told that the Earth is flat, one could undertake various scientific tests that focus upon a specific hypothesis to check this out. However, it is not quite so straightforward when dealing with a statement about God. We cannot exactly contact Him, and ask Him if He *did* actually contact a certain individual last Thursday! As a result, this theory is not appropriate to prove the truth of a religious experience, and therefore the existence of God from such experience.

The **coherence theory** evaluates the truth of statements by relating them to other proven truths within a given system of thought. If an inconsistency should be discovered, it is either deemed untrue or the system is suitably modified to remove the problem. In extreme cases the entire system may have to be abandoned. For example, if we are told that Spiderman actually exists, but do not actually see him, we can apply the coherence theory. We would consider whether the concept of a human being climbing walls without assistance is consistent with what we know of humans generally. Obviously it is not consistent. Therefore, we can either dismiss the statement about 'Spidey', or suitably adjust our system of understanding human beings to *include* those who can climb walls, and so on. Of course, the problem with such a theory is that there may be a large number of 'sets' of cohering statements, each with a reasonable claim to be 'telling the truth' about the world or anything in it.

To apply the theory to religious experience, one would have to ask whether:

- whatever description of the experience is given, and
- the effects and/or consequences of the experience

were consistent with our system of understanding pertaining to God.

A genuinely religious experience should develop a deeper knowledge and awareness of God – it should not result in something or someone else as a substitute for God.

The difference between religious experiences as examples, and the example pertaining to Spiderman, is that if the experience *of God* seems inconsistent, we would not know whether to dismiss the statement or the initial system of understanding about God.

The **pragmatic theory** focuses upon the *consequences* of accepting the experience; the 'truth' of a statement is seen purely in *practical* terms. Therefore, acceptance of a religious experience would have to produce beneficial results. But how could clearly beneficial results *prove* the experience to be authentic and therefore from God? The answer lies in the notion that truth is always life-enhancing, in some way or other, whereas delusion will always be, ultimately, life-diminishing. Consequently, religious experience would have to be found to be life-enhancing to be worthy of our credence. Many of the philosophers from the so-called 'pragmatic' school of thinking would support this attempt to ascertain the truth. For William James, *true* beliefs 'lead to consistency, stability and flowing human intercourse'. **John Dewey** (1859–1952) states that all inquiries into the truth start with a 'problematic situation'. If the inquiry is successful, the result will be a 'determined and unified' situation, which will enable a person to act on this truth.

Authoritarianism

You need to know

Many people have either claimed or been given great status as the result of having (or claiming to have had) religious experiences. In this section, two examples are considered – Padre Pio and the recipients of 'The Toronto Blessing'. In addition, you should try to find out about individuals such as St Augustine of Hippo, Julian of Norwich, St Francis of Assisi, Richard Rolle of Hampole and John Wesley.

Something to think about

Consider, for example, cult leaders who demand adoration and praise befitting a deity from their followers. Find out about some of the more famous examples, such as the group led by David Koresh in Texas.

Historically, those who have undergone religious experiences have often been the focus of attention, adoration and, sometimes, even worship. An example of such a following relates to the Italian priest, **Padre Pio** (1887–1968). Both during his life and since his death, he has had a worldwide following because of his stigmata (the reproduction of the wounds of Christ on the Cross). However, although it is recognised that people who undergo religious experiences do carry 'a curious sense of authority' regarding the afterlife, according to James, no one can really claim authority on the grounds of religious experience. This is not to suggest that Pio did, as his following seems to have been the result of an accumulative religious fervour.

Padre Pio

But what about when an experience *appears* to be shared by many people? As we have already established, the experiences themselves are unique but the effects, it would seem, can be shared.

On 10 January 1994, a bizarre phenomenon is reported to have occurred at the Toronto Airport Vineyard Church. The phenomenon, which has since been referred to as the 'Toronto Blessing', is said to have been an 'outpouring of the Holy Spirit'. Whilst individual testimonies of the experience may differ, the descriptions of the effects by witnesses are strikingly similar.

The 'blessing' occurred during a sermon by Pastor Randy Clark. Another senior Pastor, John Arnott, described what he saw:

> When Randy Clark preached at the Airport Vineyard . . . almost 80 per cent of the people were on the floor . . . It was like an explosion. We saw people literally being knocked off their feet by the Spirit of God . . . Others shook and jerked. Some danced, some laughed. Some lay on the floor as if dead for hours. People cried and shouted.

The first time that this experience is said to have occurred was in 1979. The recipient was South African minister Rodney Howard-Browne. He is considered to be the 'father' of what is referred to as 'Holy Laughter'. Apparently, it was during a sermon in which the minister asked God to 'touch me' or he would 'come up there and touch you'!

The general effects of this particular type of experience are:

- *Falling in the Holy Spirit* – where people fall to the ground, as they can no longer remain standing in the 'presence of God'. Some refer to being stuck to the floor by 'Holy Ghost Glue'.
- *Shaking* – part of or the whole of the body shakes 'under the power of God'.
- *Weeping* – this is said to be the result of repentance for one's sins or feeling the burden of souls not yet saved.
- *Laughter* – this 'Holy Laughter' is said to occur when the Holy Spirit comes into a person's life. Those who believe this to be a genuine form of religious experience say that laughter is an expression of the joy experienced. It is, perhaps unsurprisingly, the most controversial element of the experience.

The interesting thing about the 'Toronto Blessing' is that it is a *corporate experience* – that is, it appears to be undergone by many people at the same time. Since January 1994, it is said to have occurred to many Christians all around the world.

Something to think about

Why do you think that many religious people dispute the authenticity of the 'Toronto Blessing'? In particular, why do you think that 'Holy Laughter' is dismissed by many?

Something to think about

Rodney Howard-Browne is quoted as saying that he is the 'Holy Ghost bartender' who dispenses the 'new wine of joy', which leads to people being 'drunk in the Spirit'. What do you think he means by this? What are the implications of accepting what he is saying? How might more 'traditional' Christians respond to this idea?

If people were to exclaim 'I have had a religious experience so YOU must believe in God' one could, and arguably *should*, object because:

- As has been made very clear already, the experience cannot be corroborated empirically. This means that claiming authority on the basis of an alleged experience is highly susceptible to abuse from those seeking personal adoration or gratification.
- Partly as a result of the above point, it would appear that no one has ever been able to derive a meaningful statement from such an experience. For example, if the experience is *so* individual, how can your vision bear any relevance to my life?
- The way in which you interpret the experience may be entirely erroneous. What basis is this, then, for claiming authority?

Conclusion to this Argument

It would seem that religious experience as an 'argument for the existence of God' is only applicable for the individual concerned. As with all philosophical arguments that attempt to prove the existence of God, this argument may well do much to strengthen the existing faith of the believer. This is a point highlighted by C. S. Evans, who suggested that if believers are filled with the need for dependence on a higher being, they will probably be drawn towards the cosmological argument. If, on the other hand, they are particularly moved by the concept of order in the universe, they will probably be drawn to the teleological (design) argument, and so on.

The implication of this for the argument based on religious experience is that a believer who recognises the importance of God's *involvement* in human affairs will accept it as affirming their faith. William James points out that any criticism of the faith of a believer who has undergone such an experience will be completely in vain.

However, it is perhaps appropriate to conclude that the argument is probably of value to the non-believer only in as much as it points to another area of human life that *might* involve a divine being.

As we have seen, there is no clear answer to the question of whether one can demonstrate God's existence as a result of religious experience. What about if we were to examine religious authority, however?

You need to know

Look up the **cosmological** and **teleological** (design) arguments in Chapters 5 and 6.

Religious Authority as Evidence of God's Existence

Many of those who have undergone a religious experience are recognised as an authority within the religious tradition.

Religious authority ensures that followers of a specific faith-tradition know what they are expected to believe and how they are expected to behave according to the teachings of that faith. The authority teaches them how to live their lives and to worship. The authority establishes the basic beliefs of the faith.

The source of the authority is God or the Ultimate Reality accepted by the believers. The divine being transcends human understanding and therefore needs to communicate with the world in a form that can be understood. The form and interpretation of this differs not only between the different religions but also often within the religions themselves. As the basis of the authority comes from outside an individual or group, then different interpretations can occur. **For believers, the fact that God communicates with the world through the accepted authorities is evidence that God exists.**

In its **strongest form** the religious authority is believed to be the direct word of God in either an oral or written form. This is the scripture accepted by the faith-tradition as not created or invented but as directly from God, or as in the case of Christians, God in human form as Jesus.

In its **weakest form** the authority may be a teacher or guru that others in the faith follow because the guide helps them to interpret how they are expected to behave. Such leaders have achieved such understanding indirectly, perhaps through an oral tradition from an earlier teacher or leader. In the early development of a religion it may be directly from the founder of the faith but with the passage of time a diversity of attitudes within a religion develops. The way in which such an individual may become aware of God's message is usually through a religious experience.

The Nature of Scripture

The Bible is a collection of sacred writings in Christianity. It is not one book but a collection of sixty-six books written over a long period of time. The Bible is in two parts: the Old and the New Testaments. Christianity gives a differing status to the Old and New Testaments. The Old Testament is evidence of God's plan for the world including the Messiah. Christians regard the New Testament as the fulfilment of what was prophesied in the Old Testament with the arrival of the Messiah. Christians believe that the Messiah (Christ) is Jesus. The New Testament guides people on how to follow the example of Jesus, as Jesus is the living example of God's will.

Many theologians, such as **Brevard Childs**, consider the Old Testament to be historically produced and that it should be studied as such. Childs regards the books of the Old Testament as a set of ancient writings that were inspired by Judaism and formed the basis of that faith.

Other scholars, such as **Philip Davies**, disagree, and argue that it was not until the Middle Ages that individual writings were collected together into one single book. When this collection occurred, the historical period to which the writings referred was over. The influence on the collection was not therefore the historical period in which they were written but the period in which the collection was made. It was the historical dynamics of the Middle Ages that influenced the choice of writings. Davies argues that the Jewish writings chosen by Christianity resulted in a Canon with different religious dynamics to Judaism. Christians will interpret the Old Testament differently from Jews. Davies concludes that the Old Testament contains biblical scholarship accepted by both Jews and Christians but the authority given to these writings will be different for each faith. Davies also concludes that because there are various versions and translations of the Bible, it is not possible to speak of 'the Bible'.

All Christians believe the Bible is in some way the inspired word of God. When Christians refer to the Bible as inspired, they mean that the writers of the Bible appear to have been influenced by God. The Bible tells Christians that:

- God created the universe
- Sin came into the world because Adam and Eve disobeyed God
- God first revealed himself to the world through the history of the Jews and prophets, who foretold the coming of the Messiah
- Humans are to follow God's commands and to live as God wishes if they are to avoid God's punishment
- God planned the ultimate redemption of the world in Christ from the beginning
- Jesus Christ is the word of God made flesh
- Through the death and resurrection of Jesus Christ, those who follow Christ have the chance of salvation

Something to think about

How will the Christian interpretation of the Old Testament writing be different from that of Judaism?

What will have influenced Christians in their selection of the writings to be included in the Old Testament?

The Bible is the authority to inform Christians not only what to believe but also how to practise the faith. Christians do not agree that the Bible is the only authority, nor do they agree on the emphasis to be given to sections in the Old and New Testaments. Some Christians accept other authorities as sources of knowledge from God to explain how to live by God's laws.

Catholics, Orthodox Christians and some Anglican Christians believe that there are other authorities besides the Bible for their Christian beliefs and practices. They accept that God has also spoken through inspired individuals and traditions within the Church. An oral tradition has been passed down from Jesus, through the Apostles, to the leaders of the Church. This oral tradition is an additional source of authority to the Bible. It provides the leaders with the extra knowledge that needs to be added to the biblical message. Some would argue that it is a stronger authority than the Bible as the Church chose the books of the Bible that were to be considered authoritative. The Church leaders, especially the Popes, defined what Christians should believe about the words in the Bible.

An example of how the Church believed that it had the authority to define what Christians are to believe is demonstrated by the doctrine of the Trinity. The Old and New Testaments do not specifically teach this doctrine and yet Christians state in their creeds that they accept the belief in the Trinity. The early church councils established the belief in the Trinity.

The Council of the early Christian Church held at Nicea in CE 381 had developed a statement of Christian beliefs called the 'Nicene Creed'. The beginning of the creed stated that the part of God in the Trinity, God the Holy Spirit, 'proceeded', meaning 'came from God the Father'. Later the Western Church added 'and from the Son' as well. The doctrine that there is one God in three parts had been established. Therefore the authority for a major Christian doctrine was the early Christian church rather than scriptures.

The early Church decided which books in the Bible are authoritative and has the authority to define what Christians believe about the words of the Bible.

The Catholic view of the inspiration of scripture is that it is inspired by God but written by humans. Its words are not always self-evident in their meaning, and the Church as a whole has the authority to define and interpret its words. In

Something to think about

God the Son *God the Holy Spirit*

GOD

God the Father

The Trinity

Look at the diagram of the Trinity.

What do Christians mean when they use the term 'the Trinity'?

Something to think about

If the early Church decided which books of the Bible were authoritative then, which is the major authority for Christians, the Bible or the Church?

the Catholic tradition it is accepted that the Bible is a complex series of books that require understanding and interpretation. It is recognised that some parts of the Bible are not to be taken literally, and that the Bible consists of allegorical, symbolic, poetic and mythic as well as historical passages. The inspiration of the Bible is not to be taken literally word-for-word but depends on the assent of the Church. The Church interprets the true meaning of scripture for the laity.

This has led to other branches of Christianity rejecting Catholic traditions that are not supported by scripture. For example, the Catholic doctrine that Mary, the mother of Jesus, remained a virgin all her life and was carried up to heaven at her death (the Assumption) is rejected by many other Christian denominations as not supported by the authority of the Bible.

Some Christians do not accept that there is any other authority within Christianity than the Bible. These Christians believe that the Bible is the direct word of God and is to be taken literally.

The **literalist's view** of the Bible accepts only the Creation story in Genesis as a factual, historical account of the beginning of the world. There are sections of the Bible that say that this passage is symbolic and therefore that it may be interpreted. A literalist Christian, however, may disregard no part of the Bible. This can cause difficulties when there appears to be a conflict between biblical passages. For example, Moses gives the right of revenge in Exodus but Jesus condemns revenge in the Gospels. There are two accounts of creation in Genesis, and they are not identical. This means that an interpretation of the passages has to be made that can account for both versions. It is assumed that the second Genesis account is simply a resumé of what occurred at the time of creation as a reminder for the believer. Everyone within the denomination is expected to have the literal interpretation of scripture and to follow that teaching in their lives. The Bible is the only authority necessary for a community as it is the direct word of God.

Most Protestant Christians are not so fundamental in their approach to the Bible. These Christians believe that God inspired the Bible, and that the Bible has authority as the message is directly from God. It is the Bible, not the leaders of the Church, that is the final arbiter in any decision about belief

Something to think about

There are radical differences in belief between denominations about aspects of the Christian faith. This may appear to suggest that there are inconsistencies within Christianity. How might a non-Christian view these inconsistencies?

You need to know

Verbal inerrancy means that in the original texts, the writers of the Old and New Testaments were directly inspired by God through the Holy Spirit. As each word is from God then it is the literal truth and contains no errors.

Something to think about

What problems are likely to arise in modern society for a literalist Christian?

How could a literalist Christian address the conflict between biblical passages and modern society?

or practice. The leaders of the Church cannot add to the Bible. This is a **conservative** approach to the authority of the Bible that accepts there may be errors in the Bible because the writers were human and were influenced by the society in which they lived. Although this allows for acceptance of changes in society, it does not provide clear guidelines as to what Christians must and must not do. It allows for an individual rather than a community interpretation of passages, which may lead to friction when a society has to make moral and ethical decisions.

Some Christians are very **liberal** in their interpretation of the Bible. The liberal view of the Bible is that it records the experiences of people seriously seeking to find God in their lives. The words are those of the writers and are influenced by the lives of others and the society in which they lived, rather than directly inspired by God. This means that the Bible is not given the position of authority found in other Christian denominations. A liberal Christian would feel free to reject passages in the Bible that no longer seem relevant to today. It is the duty of individual Christians to decide for themselves which sections of the Bible are appropriate to their own lives. Individual conscience is a guide to what is right and wrong behaviour. There is no need of a total community response to all parts of the Bible, as it is how an individual interprets the Bible that counts. Interpreting the Bible in this way means that biblical teaching and scientific evidence can be matched and there is no need to worry about inconsistencies in the Bible. However, many Christians are concerned that such liberal attitudes weaken the authority of the Bible and lead to people 'doing their own thing'.

Something to think about

'In Christianity today, the authority of the Bible is not as important to Christians as the authority of religious leaders.' Explain and assess this view.

Essay questions

AS

(a) State and explain the main features of a religious experience.
(b) 'Religious experiences are no more than ordinary experiences mistakenly thought to be from God.' To what extent do you agree with this statement?

A2

(a) What are said to be the distinctive features of a mystical experience?
(b) Explain and assess the claim that such experiences can be dismissed as 'purely subjective'.

Chapter 4

The Ontological Argument for the Existence of God

Something to think about

What is your 'concept of God'? List the characteristics involved.

Before we can look at the ontological argument, it is necessary to consider what many philosophers have said in answer to the question 'What is God like'?

The Attributes of God

As discussed in Chapter 2, the very *way* in which we discuss God is open to considerable discussion. Some people have suggested that no human terms would ever be suitable to describe God, while others believe that we can know some things about God by 'proving' what He is not!

The areas to be considered here, therefore, are far from comprehensive. They are intended to provide some stimulus for general discussion and, in particular, to provide some focus for the points of view put forward in the Ontological Argument for the existence of God below.

'God is the Creator and Sustainer of All That Is'

There are three areas we can use to suggest the existence of a creator God:

Something to think about

Look up Genesis 1–3 in the Old Testament. Make notes on the way in which God is portrayed as the Creator.

- **Reason** – the Cosmological argument (see Chapter 5) shows that if there is reason behind the universe, we must suppose a self-existent being behind it
- **Revelation** – the New Testament, Qur'an and Torah clearly state that God created the world
- **Experience** – the human sense of dependence, and the apparent 'experiences' of God claimed by many (see Chapter 3)

To understand the belief of Creation, we must first understand several basic principles:

- God (the creator) and ourselves (the creature) are *ontologically distinct*. This goes way beyond the 'epistemic distance' referred to by Hick in developing Irenaeus's Theodicy (see Chapter 8). It means that we are *absolutely* distinct from God in every way. The implication here is that it is logically impossible for the creature to be or become the creator.

- Although we feel a sense of dependence on God, as mentioned above, we have a 'derived autonomy'. This means that while God created us, he gave us independence and our own principles of right and wrong. For example, the physical world around is understood in terms of natural laws and science.
- **Anthony Flew** rejects the concept of creation being compatible with free will:

> As Creator, God must be first cause, prime mover, supporter and controller of every thought and action throughout his utterly dependent universe. In short: if creation is in, autonomy is out.

H. P. Owen disagrees, claiming that God has chosen to create beings with the capacity for free will.

- God is, as mentioned, ontologically the first cause of everything. However, as far as sustenance is concerned, he operates through *secondary* causes – for example, the laws of nature, and our free will.
- Despite this, as creator, God can act to intervene in human affairs by a supernatural act, if so required. It should be remembered that this could only occur if such action is compatible with his own nature, *and that of the entities concerned*.
- God as 'Sustainer' means that he is *continuously* required to *keep* the process going. This contrasts with the views of the deists of the eighteenth century.
- God's act of creation was '*ex nihilo*' – there is no finite parallel.
- God's creation is *incomprehensible*. This is only understood when we consider *why* God created the world.

'God is Immanent'

God's immanence is the idea that He is *in the world* and, as such, wholly involved in the idea of God as Creator *and Sustainer* of all things. It highlights the key difference between Deism and Theism. Whereas deists maintain that after the single act of creation, God 'left the world to its own devices', theists believe that God is *immanent*; that is, God's creative activity is *continuous*.

How do we know this? Theists believe that God is the sustainer of life, and that we are dependent on his continuous creative power. An example of this creative power would be the laws of nature as referred to above. The Design Argument

Does the claim 'I believe that God is present in the world and involved in all things' create any philosophical problems?

for the existence of God highlights the fact that nature is perfectly suited to our survival. Those who suggest that God is immanent point to this sort of evidence to show that God *is* involved in the world all the time.

The idea of God being immanent also leads to the understanding that God is a *personal* being – but what exactly do we mean by the word 'personal'?

By personal, we are suggesting that God

- has knowledge and awareness
- performs actions
- can enter into relationships with beings other than himself

Why does God have to be personal?

Michael Peterson and others suggest that many of the finest qualities that exist – love, creativity, intelligence and moral goodness, for example – are found only within the framework of the person; therefore, if God were not personal he would be unable to possess these qualities.

If people can engage in any sort of relationship with God, then God must be personal; that is, he must have an identifiable personality. This is absolutely essential for the theist who claims that he/she can engage in conversation with God through prayer, for example.

'God is Transcendent'

'Transcendent' is an adjective incorporating three important ideas:

- God is distinct from the world – therefore not limited by time and space within the world
- God has no need of this world
- God is incomprehensible

What problems would this cause for the religious believer?

The key idea here is that God is completely outside the world and is therefore not limited by space and time. Many believers feel that this must be true, as it is further evidence of the *ontological distinction* between God and people. Others, however, oppose the idea in its strictest form, as it would appear to rule out the notion of God as personal.

Those who believe that God is impersonal might well be content to say no more than that God is utterly incomprehensible, or perhaps they would draw on Rudolph Otto's idea of 'the numinous' (see Chapter 3).

'God is Omnipotent'

In referring to God as 'omnipotent', we mean one of two things: God is the ruler over all things; or, God can do all things.

1   Obviously, if God is the infinite creator he rules over all the things he has created.
2   The notion that God can do all things is a far more common use of the term, and it is that which we must focus on.

The concept of God being able to do all things is something required by his infinity. Importantly, it means that he can do all things *that are in accordance with his nature*. This means that he cannot make $3 + 3 = 8$, nor can he make a square hole round; he cannot make charity wrong and cheating right; he cannot violate human freedom, which is a spiritual gift that he gave us in creation. All of these examples *must be the case* according to many believers, because if they were not, God's nature would become contradictory.

A problem arises here when one tries to equate the omnipotence of God with his love – if capable of all things, why does God permit evil?

'God is Omniscient'

Basically, the *omniscience* of God means that God knows all things. We are not omniscient, as we are finite beings; this means that we are ignorant beings. God's knowledge, like every other aspect of his being, is perfect. How can we know this? Theists claim that the answer lies both in the *manner* and *extent* of his knowledge.

In terms of the manner of God's knowledge, it excels human knowledge in that it is wholly intuitive; that is, it does not have to be reasoned through or 'worked out'. Obviously, there are intuitive elements of our own knowledge, but in the main our knowledge has to be reasoned out, and is largely discursive (moves from one topic to another).

> God's knowledge is not reasoned or discursive, though he knows all reasonings and processes'
>
> *Aquinas*

More obvious is the fact that God's knowledge differs from ours in terms of extent. We build up our knowledge discursively and within a limited setting (our culture, geographical area, time in history, personal aptitude, etc.), so we can never know anything completely. For the same reason,

Something to think about

How might a religious believer answer this question? If you need some suggestions, look at Chapter 8.

Something to think about

The attributes listed above are not the only ones that philosophers and theologians have traditionally claimed that God 'must have'. Try to find out more about the following ideas:

- God as *perfect*
- God as *eternal*
- God as *infinite*
- God as *simple*
- God as *impassible*

You need to know

The **ontological argument** is an *a priori* argument; such arguments use **logic** to prove an initial definition to be correct.

our knowledge is fallible; how often do we think we 'know the truth', when in fact we are in error? Theists claim that God knows all things perfectly and infallibly; why do they think so?

This idea is based on the concept of God as Creator. If God creates '*ex nihilo*', he must posses this perfect and infallible knowledge, *and* he must know all things simultaneously. If he did not, where did his knowledge of the world come from? Not from the world, as it *did not exist*. Aquinas suggested that as God knows himself he *must* know all things, as nothing can exist (in reality or theory) that did not pre-exist in his mind.

The Ontological Argument

The **ontological argument** is an example of an *a priori* argument. 'Ontological argument' as a term refers to a *number* of arguments within one school of thought. These arguments attempt to prove God's existence from the *meaning* of the word *God*.

Another example of an *a priori* argument is the **moral argument**, which is considered in Chapter 7.

The basis of these arguments depends upon one's understanding of the nature of God. The particular *type* of ontological argument that one might consider is determined by the answer to the question 'What is the concept of God?'. The argument was introduced by **St Anselm of Canterbury** (1033–1109) in his book *Proslogion*.

Anselm originated the form of the argument known as the 'Classical Argument'.

The Classical Ontological Argument

There are two principal contributors to the 'Classical Argument':

- **St Anselm of Canterbury**
- **René Descartes**

St Anselm of Canterbury

Anselm defined God as 'that than which nothing greater can be conceived'. According to Anselm, even the atheist (non-believer) *must* have a definition of God, if only to dismiss His existence.

Therefore, God (like dragons) exists in the mind.

But, God must exist *in reality* because He is 'that than which nothing greater can be conceived'.

Something to think about

What is the difference between *that than which nothing greater can be conceived* and *something greater than can be conceived*?

Is this difference important?

You need to know

By *necessary*, Anselm is referring to the **eternal** and **transcendent** nature of God. (Did you have these words in your description above?) This means that God exists *outside* our space and time, but is able to create and act *within* it. If He did not exist in this way, Anselm would say, we would not exist either.

You need to know

In this context, **perfection** means *flawless*, or lacking *any* faults.

Why is this so? Because that which exists in reality is greater than that which exists purely in the mind. *Imagine* being given £1000. It's a nice thought; but wouldn't it be better to actually *have* the money?

In the words of Anselm:

> Therefore, Lord, not only are You that than which nothing greater can be conceived but you are also something greater than can be conceived. Indeed, since it is possible to be conceived to be something of this kind, if you are not this very thing, something can be conceived greater than You, which cannot be done.

St Anselm, Proslogion

So far, Anselm has suggested a proof for God's existence. However, for God to *be* God there must be more to Him than that He simply 'exists' (after all, that would make God fundamentally similar to ourselves). In the next stage of Anselm's argument, therefore, he attempts to demonstrate that God's existence is *necessary*. But what does he mean by 'necessary'? Is he using it in the same context as in *It is necessary for me to catch the 8.10 bus, in order to get to work*?

To suggest that God is *necessary* is to suggest that there is *no possibility* of Him *not existing*. To do this, Anselm suggests that we need to know more than that He simply exists inside and outside our minds. Anselm believes that we *do* know this:

- it can be conceived that something exists that cannot be thought *not* to exist
- God *must be* such a thing if He is 'that than which nothing greater can be conceived'
- this is because something that can be thought not to exist would be inferior to that which cannot

Thus, Anselm felt that he had demonstrated not only the *existence* of God, but also that His existence was *necessary*.

René Descartes

Descartes developed Anselm's argument. His definition, that God is 'a supremely perfect being', is the basis of his argument.

From this, Descartes believes we can conclude that God exists, because existence is a **predicate** of a perfect being; therefore, God must exist to avoid being self-contradictory. Descartes says that trying to imagine God without the predicate of existence is *illogical*, like imagining a triangle without three sides!

The Modern Versions of the Ontological Argument

There have been a number of contributors to the ontological argument in more recent times. In this section, the following will be considered:

- **Norman Malcolm** (1911–1990)
- **Alvin Plantinga** (1932–)

Norman Malcolm

Malcolm considers Anselm's arguments, and concludes that the *second* section (*Proslogion* 3) is more accurate than the *first* (*Proslogion* 2). Why is this?

1   Some versions of the ontological argument are subject to a specific criticism: existence is treated as a **predicate** that things either have or lack (such as *blue eyes* or *brown hair*).
2   According to Malcolm, *Proslogion* 2 is subject to such a criticism.
3   He believes that *Proslogion* 3 *does not* treat existence as a predicate: Anselm is saying that God must exist because the concept of God is the concept of a being *whose existence is necessary*.

On the basis of this conclusion, Malcolm develops *Proslogion* 3 as follows:

> If God, a being greater than which cannot be conceived, does not exist then he cannot come into existence. For if He did He would either have been caused to come into existence or have happened to come into existence, and in either case He would be a limited being, which by our conception of Him He is not. Since He cannot come into existence, if He does not exist His existence is impossible. If He does exist He cannot have come into existence . . . nor can He cease to exist, for nothing could cause Him to cease to exist nor could it just happen that He ceased to exist. So if God exists His existence is necessary.
>
> Thus God's existence is either impossible or necessary. It can be the former only if the concept of such a being is self-contradictory or in some way logically absurd. Assuming that this is not so, it follows that He necessarily exists.

Norman Malcolm

Something to think about

Do you know what a **predicate** is? If not, look it up in a dictionary and write down the definition in your notes.

Also, try to find out about **René Descartes**.

Something to think about

- Why would God be a *limited* being if He had been caused to come into existence, or had 'happened' to come into existence?

- Is it acceptable and coherent to conclude that God exists because He has the *property of necessary existence*? Why, or why is this not, the case?

Something to think about

On the basis of the above definition, consider your own position in, say, three years time. How will your life differ if you are:

- at university?
- unemployed?
- celebrating a lottery win?
- suffering with a terminal illness?

Each of these scenarios is a possible world.

Alvin Plantinga

Plantinga developed the philosophical notion of 'possible worlds'. For example, in our world, John F. Kennedy was an American president. This, however, was not necessary; he could have made a different career choice and been an estate agent! This is an example of a possible world.

In each of the possible worlds that you have considered above, there will be many differences. That is the whole point of this philosophical notion – the possibilities are *infinite*. With this in mind, Plantinga offers a description of another possible world:

- there is a possible world, *W*, in which there exists a being with 'maximal greatness'
- a being has maximal greatness only if it exists in every possible world

This means that in every possible world one envisages, there is a being of maximal greatness. This, however, does *not* mean God!

Plantinga's argument states that to be maximally great, a being only has to be present in every possible world. He has not, as yet, accounted for the fact that in each world there may be an individual being that is more powerful, more knowing, more morally perfect, and so on, than this maximally great being. The fact that these beings may only be found in *one* possible world is irrelevant.

To deal with this, Plantinga introduces the concept of 'maximal excellence'. He states that:

- maximal greatness entails maximal excellence
- maximal excellence entails omnipotence, omniscience and moral perfection

Therefore:

1 There is a possible world in which there is a being that is maximally great.
2 It has maximal excellence (entailed within maximal greatness).
3 If omnipotent, omniscient and morally perfect, *and* maximally great, it is existent in *our* world.
4 Therefore, there *is* a God.

An estate agent?!

How Successful is the Ontological Argument?

Since the conception of the ontological argument for the existence of God, there have been a number of fairly diverse objections to its different forms.

In this section, the objections of the following commentators will be considered:

Something to think about

Try to find out about these philosophers and add any biographical information to your notes.

- **Gaunilo of Marmoutier**
- **Immanuel Kant**
- **Gottlob Frege**
- **Bertrand Russell**
- **Brian Davies**

Gaunilo of Marmoutier

Gaunilo opposed Anselm. He gave an immediate response to Anselm's *Proslogion* 2.

Gaunilo stated that if someone were to describe to you a 'most perfect island', lost somewhere and basically untouched by man, and then state that it *must* exist *because of* its perfection, you would be a fool to believe him. He is trying to criticise the process by which Anselm moves from his definition of God to his suggestion of God's existence.

However, Gaunilo's criticism is not valid in this context. Anselm never compares things of a like kind above. He speaks of God as 'that than which *nothing* greater can be conceived'. Gaunilo, on the other hand, occupies himself with a comparison between *islands*.

But let us suppose that Gaunilo had spoken of an island 'than which no greater an island can be conceived'. Would this coherently oppose Anselm's argument?

The answer would have to be 'No'. As Plantinga points out, islands have no **intrinsic maximum**; that is, an island can always be bettered (try adding another lagoon, palm tree or sandy beach!). It would seem that Gaunilo's objections do not successfully refute Anselm's argument.

Immanuel Kant

Kant opposed Descartes' version of the argument. Kant objects to Descartes' claim that denying God's existence is tantamount to denying that triangles have three sides, which is contradictory. He states that if one dismisses both the idea of the three sides (predicate) *and* that of the triangle itself (subject), one is left with no contradiction.

What does this mean?

One can define a thing as one sees fit, but whether or not anything matches that definition *in reality* is another question altogether. Therefore, it would seem that Kant has dealt with Descartes' notion of existence as a predicate.

However, in order to deal with Anselm, Kant raises a second objection.

Kant states that 'existence is not a predicate'. This means that saying *X exists* tells one nothing about *X* (whereas *X is female* or *X is tall* does).

A predicate, says Kant, must give us information about X; the statement X *is* does not. In fact, the opposite statement presents us with the following paradox.

If X *exists* tells us about a property that X has, then X *does not exist* denies that it has this property (or affirms that it *lacks* it). *But*, how can that which does not exist *lack* anything?

Gottlob Frege (1848–1925)

Frege is a more recent objector. He distinguishes between 'first-' and 'second-order' predicates.

First-order predicates tell us something about the *nature* of something – for example, *the horses are brown*.

Second-order predicates tell us about *concepts* – for example, *the horses are numerous*.

Frege's objection to Anselm and Descartes is that they both seem to use existence as a first-order predicate, whereas it is actually a second-order predicate.

Bertrand Russell

Russell is a twentieth-century philosopher. He claims that Anselm uses the word 'exist' incorrectly.

Existence cannot be a predicate. If it were, we could construct the following argument:

Men exist.
Santa Claus is a man.
Therefore, Santa Claus exists.

This is a **syllogism**.

Something to think about

Try to come up with your own examples of first- and second-order predicates.

Assess how and what each predicate tells you about the subject that it is referring to.

Something to think about

Find out what **syllogism** means. Then, write your own syllogism.

'Of course I exist'!

Russell is saying that existence is not a *property* of things, but of the *ideas* of those things.

Therefore, to say that *dragons do not exist* is to say that, of all the things that exist, none of them are referred to by the word *dragon*.

Therefore, Russell has put Anselm's argument into different terms. He states that to label and define something is to provide an *intention* concerning the object under discussion. Therefore, if I were to say that *a cow is a quadruped with udders etc.*, my intention would be to describe a cow.

The fact that a cow exists provides an *extension* to my intention. Therefore, *existence* is an *extension* of an *intention*.

When we conceive of a cow it is easy to accept its existence, because we see cows in fields. The same can be said for most 'things' that we have experienced.

Russell concludes that 'that than which nothing greater can be conceived' is simply the totality of everything that can be conceived by the human mind. That is the *intention* of the phrase; but does it have an extension?

Yes! If *any* idea can be said to exist, then 'that than which nothing greater can be conceived' must exist, as it is the *totality* of all ideas. It does not have to have physical existence, or even *be* conceived, as long as it is conceivable.

Therefore, Russell would support Anselm's claim that God is the greatest thing we can think of, but not Anselm's belief that this proves God's existence in reality.

Brian Davies

Davies is a current philosopher. He recognises Malcolm's attempt to distinguish between existence and necessity. In relation to Frege's point, we can accept existence only as a second-order predicate, but accept necessity as a first-order predicate.

Therefore, Malcolm's argument can be represented as *God is necessary; therefore God 'is'*.

Davies illustrates this point:

> A pixie is a little man with pointed ears. Therefore there actually exists a pixie.

He goes on to suggest that if one were to claim that the pixie must exist in order to have those pointed ears, one would surely find the reasoning unacceptable.

Something to think about

What about my intention of a *unicorn*, that it is *a quadruped with one horn*. Is there a problem when I add (extend) existence to my intention?

Something to think about

Why does this reasoning appear unacceptable?

Davies states that the word *is* can be used in two different ways:

1   It can be used to *define* something – for example, *a queen is a female monarch*.
2   It can be used to explain that there actually *is* something – for example, *there is such a thing as a vampire*.

Davies suggests that the first use says nothing about existence, in that it says nothing about an existent queen. The statement does, however, explain what the word 'queen' *means*.

The second use, on the other hand, while also saying nothing about existence, is not *defining* anything either. It is saying that there is a vampire, and by this statement *implicitly supposing* its existence.

From this, one can conclude that Malcolm's argument favours moving from the premise 'A pixie is a little man with pointed ears' (an example of the first use) as a definition, to the conclusion 'Pixies actually exist' (an example of the second use).

A Critique of Plantinga's Argument

Is Plantinga's claim that it is possible to have a being with maximal excellence in every world, and that therefore we actually have such a being in our world, coherent?

According to Davies, even if we accept that a being with maximal excellence is *possible*, and therefore it is *possible* that such a being exists in our world, it does not follow that such a being *actually* exists. All that we can coherently conclude from Plantinga's evidence is that maximal excellence is *possible*, and therefore God is *possible*, not *actual*.

Something to think about

Do you think that this argument is valid? Why/why not?

How does your conclusion relate to Malcolm's version of the ontological argument?

Something to think about

Overall, the ontological argument seems to be unsuccessful. This may be due to the fact that *definitions are limited*; that is, we can say what we mean about something without it actually being real (dragons, unicorns etc.).

Also, it is clearly difficult to establish a definition for God in the first place, as we are limited to finite, human terms, which may not be adequate for describing God.

Are there any other areas that you feel weaken or corrupt this argument?

Essay questions

AS
(a) Explain Anselm's two versions of the ontological argument for the existence of God.
(b) Explain and evaluate the view that the ontological argument is a weak argument for the existence of God.

A2
(a) Outline the various forms of the ontological argument for the existence of God.
(b) 'The ontological argument is only in the mind and is therefore a weak argument.' Evaluate and assess this claim.

Chapter 5

The Cosmological Argument for the Existence of God

You need to know

The term **cosmos** refers to the world or universe as a perfect and well-ordered system.

A **contingency** is something that may or may not happen. An event or condition depends on something else, which may or may not happen. Things do not contain the reason for their own existence, but depend on external causes. Objects around us exist, but they could just as easily not exist.

You need to know

Remind yourself of the difference between *a posteriori* and *a priori* argument by reading the definitions in Chapter 1 (page 6).

You need to know

Look back at Chapter 4 (page 56) to remind yourself of what the term **necessary existence** means when applied to God.

The **cosmological argument** is a classical argument for the existence of God. It is also known as the **first cause argument**. Unlike the ontological argument, it derives the conclusion that God exists from *a posteriori* premise. The argument is *a posteriori* because it is based on what can be seen in the world and the universe.

The cosmological argument is based on the belief that there is a first cause behind the existence of the universe (**cosmos**). In its simplest form, the basic cosmological argument is based on contingency and states that:

- things come into existence because something has caused them to happen
- things are caused to exist, but they do not have to exist
- there is a chain of causes that goes back to the beginning of time
- time began with the creation of the universe
- there must have been a first cause, which brought the universe into existence
- this first cause must have necessary existence to cause the contingent universe
- God has necessary existence
- therefore God is first cause of the contingent universe's existence

The cosmological argument has taken many forms and has been presented in many ways. In each form, the argument focuses upon the causes that lead to the existence of things. The argument appears to answer the questions:

- How did the universe begin?
- Why was the universe created?
- Who created the universe?

The argument pre-dates Christianity. Plato developed one of its earliest forms. He argued that the power to produce movement

You need to know

Ex nihilo means out of nothing. Most believers accept that God created the universe *ex nihilo*, out of nothing.

You need to know

Remind yourself of the philosophy of **St Thomas Aquinas** by reading the section about him in Chapter 1 (pages 3–4).

You need to know

Aquinas accepted the biblical account of creation found in Genesis. He did not accept the concept of **infinity**, because he believed in God as the necessary being who created the universe.

Something to think about

Why would the acceptance of a series of infinite causes or motion contradict the biblical account of creation?

logically comes before the power to receive it and pass it on. In order for movement to occur in the first place, there must be an uncaused cause to originate the movement. Plato termed this uncaused cause the 'First Cause' or 'First Mover'.

St Thomas Aquinas' Version

St Thomas Aquinas developed the most popular version of the cosmological argument. He developed his **Five Ways** to prove the existence of God, which he called *'demonstratio'* for the existence of God. He put these forward in the *Summa Theologica*. The first three of his Five Ways form the cosmological argument as a proof of the existence of God. The three ways that support the argument are:

- motion or change
- cause
- contingency

The **First Way** is based on *motion*. In the world there are things that are in motion, and whatever is in motion must have been moved by something else. According to Aquinas, this chain of movement cannot go back to infinity. There must have been a first, or Prime, Mover, which itself was unmoved. The Unmoved Mover began the movement in everything without actually being moved. Aquinas argued that the Prime Mover is God:

> The first and more manifest way is the argument from motion. It is certain, and evident to our senses, that in the world some things are in motion. Now whatever is moved is moved by another, for nothing can be moved except it is in potentiality to that towards which it is moved; whereas a thing moves inasmuch as it is in act. For motion is nothing else than the reduction of something from potentiality to actuality, except by something in a state of actuality.
>
> *St Thomas Aquinas, Summa Theologica*

Aquinas was speaking of motion in the broadest sense. He included *not only* movement from one place to another, *but also* movement in the sense of change of quality or quantity. According to Aquinas, an object only moved when an external force was applied to it.

He continued that objects only changed because some external force had brought about the change. He spoke of things achieving their potential through an external influence.

Potentiality refers to inherent but undeveloped capabilities, to the possibilities within someone or something for development or change.

Actuality is a state of being, the reality of something at this moment in time.

Something to think about

List examples of other objects besides wood and fire that have the potentiality to change. State their actualities as well.

You need to know

An **efficient cause** is a cause that is capable of performing an action and bringing about the desired result.

Something to think about

According to Aquinas, the chain of causes led to a specific action. List the chain of causes that led you to read this book. How far back in time do you think your chain needs to go to include all the causes that have led to this action of reading the book?

Aquinas used the example of fire making wood hot. When applied to wood, fire changes the wood to achieve its potential to become hot. In order for a thing to change, actuality is required. If it were not, a thing would have to initiate change in itself, which would require that it was both actual and potential at the same time. Aquinas considered this to be a contradiction. For example, if wood could make itself hot then it would be hot already. Wood cannot be hot to begin with; otherwise, it would not change and become hot. The fact that it is not hot already is its actuality. The fact that fire can make it hot is its potentiality. In turn, something must have made the fire change and become alight. Each change, therefore, is the result of an earlier change. Aquinas, however, did not accept that there was a series of infinite changes. He concluded that there was a point at which the first movement (or change) occurred, brought about by 'a first mover'. Therefore, according to Aquinas, 'it is necessary to arrive at a first mover, moved by no other; and this everyone understands to be God'.

In Aquinas' **Second Way**, he identified a series of *causes* and effects in the universe. Aquinas observed that nothing can be the cause of itself, as this would mean that it would have had to exist before it existed. This would be a logical impossibility. Aquinas rejected an infinite series of causes and believed that there must have been a first, uncaused, cause. This first cause started the chain of causes that have caused all events to happen. This first cause was God:

> The second way is from the nature of efficient cause. In the world of sensible things we find there is an order of efficient causes. There is no case known (neither is it, indeed, possible) in which a thing is found to be the efficient cause of itself; for so it would be prior to itself, which is impossible. Now in efficient causes it is not possible to go on to infinity, because in all efficient causes following in order, the first is the cause of the intermediate cause, and the intermediate is the cause of the ultimate cause ... Therefore it is necessary to admit a first efficient cause, to which everyone gives the name of God.

St Thomas Aquinas, Summa Theologica

Aquinas' **Third Way** identified the contingency of matter in the universe. On the basis of the fact that things come into existence and later cease to exist, Aquinas concluded that there must have been a time when nothing existed. Therefore the cause of the universe must be external to it and must always have existed. There must have been a 'necessary being', to bring everything else in to existence. Aquinas argued that *this 'necessary being' was God*. He concluded that if God did not exist, then nothing would exist:

> The third way is taken from possibility and necessity, and runs thus. We find in nature things that are possible to be and not to be, since they are found to be generated, and to be corrupted, and consequently, it is possible for them to be and not to be. But it is impossible for these always to exist, for that which can not-be at the same time is not. Therefore if everything can not-be, then at one time there was nothing in existence. Now if this were true, even now there would be nothing in existence because that which does not exist begins to exist through something already existing. Therefore, if at one time nothing was in existence, it would have been impossible for anything to have begun to exist; and even now nothing would be in existence – which is absurd . . . therefore we cannot but admit the existence of some being having of itself its own necessity, and not receiving it from another, but rather causing in other their necessity. This all men speak of as God.

St Thomas Aquinas, Summa Theologica

Something to think about

List any objections that you can think of which might count against Aquinas' version of the cosmological argument.

Something to think about

The *first part* of the *kalam* argument is an *a priori* argument. Why do you think that this first part is an *a priori* rather than an *a posteriori* argument?

The *Kalam* Version

Kalam is an Arabic term which means to 'argue' or 'discuss'. The Muslim scholars **al-Kindi** (ninth century CE) and **al Ghazali** (CE 1058–1111) developed the *kalam* argument to explain God's creation of the universe. The *kalam* argument is cosmological because it seeks to prove that God was the first cause of the universe.

William Lane Craig

Craig developed a modern version of the argument in his book, *The Kalam Cosmological Argument* (1979). The **first part** of the argument states the following:

- the present would not exist in an actual infinite universe, because successive additions cannot be added to an actual infinite
- the present does exist, as the result of a chronological series of past events
- the universe must be finite
- a finite universe had a beginning
- whatever began to exist had a cause, as things cannot cause themselves
- therefore the universe had a first cause of its existence
- this first cause was God

To say that something is **infinite** means that it is *endless, boundless* and *limitless*. For example, if there is infinite time or distance before a point Υ, then that point Υ will never be reached. This is because it is not possible to complete infinite time, or to cover the infinite distance to reach Υ.

A **potential infinite** exists if it is always possible to add one more to a series of things or events. It is possible to think of the future as a potential infinite, because more events are always being added to history.

An **actual infinite** is a mathematical concept found in set theory. It refers to sets or collections of things with an infinite number of members. It is *not* growing towards infinity, because it is infinite already. A part within an actually infinite set is equal to the whole set because it is infinite. For example, in an actually infinite set of numbered books in a library, a count of the even-numbered books is equal to a count of all the books. Some philosophers argue that *actual infinite* numbers cannot exist. This is because whether you add to, or subtract from, an actual infinite number, it would always remain the same number – infinity. An actual infinite is 'complete' at all times, and many philosophers regard this as illogical.

Craig argued that if the universe did not have a beginning, then the past must consist of a series of events that is actually – and not merely potentially – infinite. Craig cannot accept this idea because it would mean that past events form a collection of events; in which, for example, there would be just as many wars as there would be all other events together. Craig concluded that:

- the history of the universe was formed by one event following on after another event – this is successive addition
- a collection formed by successive addition cannot be actually infinite
- therefore the universe must have had a beginning in time

Since everything that begins to exist has a cause of its existence, and since the universe began to exist, we conclude, therefore, the universe has a cause of its existence . . . Transcending the entire universe there exists a cause which brought the universe into being . . . But even more: we may plausibly argue that the cause of the universe is a personal being . . . If the universe began to exist, and if the universe is caused, then the cause of the universe must be a personal being who freely chooses to create the world . . . the kalam cosmological argument leads to a personal Creator of the universe.

William Lane Craig, The Kalam Cosmological Argument, 1979

The **second part** of the *kalam* argument seeks to prove God as the *personal Creator* of the universe. If the universe had a beginning, then this beginning was either *caused or uncaused*. Either it was a natural occurrence or a choice was made to bring the universe into existence. Supporters of the *kalam* argument argue that since the rules of nature did not exist before the beginning of the universe, the universe cannot be the result of natural causes. Craig concluded that 'if the universe began to exist, and if the universe is caused, then the cause of the universe must be a personal being who freely chooses to create the world'.

The argument depends on the belief that God created the universe *ex nihilo*. If the universe was created out of nothing, then the beginning of the universe was the beginning of time. There must have been a personal agent existing outside time to start the process of creation, an agent who willed the universe into existence.

In an *actually infinite* library, the number of books with green spines and the number of books with black spines will be equal. Yet the number of books with green spines will be equal to the total number of books in the library. What do you think happens to the total number of books in this library when I borrow a book, and what happens to the total number of books in this library when I return the book?

The twentieth century began in 1900. One year after another was 'added' to the century until the year 1999 was reached. Why would Craig think it absurd to regard the history of the twentieth century as an *actually* infinite series of events?

If the universe is infinite and does not have a beginning, then is it possible to measure the passage of time in chronological order as we do at present?

Remind yourself of the philosophy of **Bertrand Russell** by reading the section about him in Chapter 1 (page 9).

How Successful is the Cosmological Argument?

A number of objections have been raised against the cosmological argument, which those who support it have had to counter.

One of the major objections to the argument is the suggestion that infinity is impossible and that the universe had a beginning. Many philosophers point out that Aquinas and Craig contradict themselves when they reject the possibility of the infinite. Both Aquinas and Craig deny the infinite and yet argue that God is infinite. Supporters of the argument point out that God is unique and that the laws of nature do not apply to God.

Anthony Kenny

In *The Five Ways* (1965), Kenny said that Aquinas' principle that nothing moves itself goes against the fact that people and animals move themselves. He continued that Newton's first law of motion, in which movement can be explained by a body's own inertia from previous motion, disproves Aquinas' argument. It is possible for objects to have uniform motion as well as to be in a state of rest. Kenny says that Newton's law 'wrecks the argument of the First Way. For at any given time the rectilinear uniform motion of a body can be explained by the principle of inertia in terms of the body's own previous motion without appeal to any other agent.'

David Hume

In *Dialogues Concerning Natural Religion* (1779), Hume asked why we must conclude that the universe had to have a beginning: 'How can anything that exists from eternity have a cause, since that relation implies a priority in time and in a beginning of existence?'

Even if the universe did begin, Hume continued, it does not mean that anything caused it to come into existence. **Bertrand Russell** supported Hume's view. Russell observed that just because humans have a mother it does not mean that the universe had to have a mother. The universe does not have to have had a beginning. It could always have been there. As Russell stated, 'I should say that the universe is just there, and that's all.'

Something to think about

Copleston's argument is based on the premise that everything can be explained. Is this a valid statement or can you think of things that cannot be explained?

You need to know

A **sufficient reason** is an adequate reason that explains the cause of an event, in this case the origin of the universe.

Something to think about

If there has to be sufficient reason for everything that exists, then why does God exist without a sufficient reason?

You need to know

Read the section on **quantum physics** in Chapter 10 to help you understand Quentin Smith's reasons for rejecting the cosmological argument for the existence of God.

You need to know

Remind yourself of the philosophy of **Immanuel Kant** by reading the section about him in Chapter 1 (page 8).

In a 1948 radio debate, Father Frederick Copleston debated the origins of the universe with Russell. Copleston argued that the reason for things can be explained. The universe is a thing and can be explained. If the universe can be explained then God exists, as God is the explanation for the existence of the universe. Russell continued to argue that the world has no explanation and it is a mistake to suggest that it can be explained.

Gottfried Leibniz (CE 1646–1716)

Leibniz accepted the cosmological argument because he believed that there had to be 'sufficient reason' for the universe to exist. He did not accept that it was uncaused. He argued as follows:

> Suppose the book of the elements of geometry to have been eternal, one copy having been written down from an earlier one. It is evident that even though a reason can be given for the present book out of a past one, we should never come to a full reason. What is true of the books is also true of the states of the world. If you suppose the world eternal, you will suppose nothing but a succession of states and will not find in any of them a sufficient reason.

Gottfried Leibniz, 'Theodicy', 1710

Leibniz rejected an infinite universe because he did not believe that it was a satisfactory explanation for its existence. He accepted that God was the first, uncaused cause on which everything else depends.

Recently, **Quentin Smith** has argued against the *kalam* version of the argument. Smith uses quantum mechanics to demonstrate the possibility of things existing without a direct cause. The universe may have had a beginning, but there is no reason to think that it is God.

Immanuel Kant

Kant examined the argument of the existence of a supreme being as a first cause of the universe. He argued that the idea that every event must have a first cause only applied to the world of sense experience. It cannot apply to something that we have not experienced. Kant did not accept any justification for the conclusion that God caused the universe to begin. Kant would not accept it as valid to extend the knowledge that we do possess to questions that transcend our experience. God would be a causal being outside space and time as we understand it. Therefore, it would be impossible for people to have any knowledge of what God created or of God Himself.

The Steady-State Theory

This theory provides a scientific explanation that would undermine the cosmological argument as it denies a beginning to the universe. Until recently, scientists have accepted the theory that energy cannot be created and that therefore the universe will always weigh the same and energy within the universe will simply be redistributed. The acceptance of the uniformity of the universe led to the theory that it should look much the same not only from the same place but also at any point in time. This is the Steady-State theory. It is the opposite view to Creationism since it teaches that there is no beginning or end to the universe, that the universe has always been there and that its appearance does not change with time. The old stars are mixed in with new ones. So although the universe is expanding, i.e. galaxies are moving apart, the theory states that new galaxies have to be created to fill in the gaps left by old galaxies. The continuous creation of new particles of matter is at a rate that is automatically adjusted by the cosmological expansion. This is at a steady rate and is always the same. 'The universe is a huge self-regulating, self-sustaining mechanism, with the capacity to self-organise ad infinitum' (Paul Davies, *The Cosmic Blueprint*, page 154). The idea was originally put forward by Herman Bondi, Tommy Gold and Fred Hoyle in the 1940s. Bondi and Gold worked on the theory from a philosophical point of view whereas Hoyle tried to put it on a scientific footing. The Steady-State theory has generally been rejected in favour of the Big Bang theory.

The Big Bang

This theory provides a scientific explanation for the beginning of the universe. Both supporters of the cosmological argument, and those who deny it, use the Big Bang theory as a proof for or against the existence of God. Scientific observation has confirmed that there was a beginning to the universe, and has provided further evidence that the universe developed a structure very early in its history. The debate rests on whether or not the cause of the Big Bang was natural or divine. Was the Big Bang caused by a spontaneous random event, or by a deliberate action by God?

Something to think about

What problems would acceptance of the Steady-State theory raise for a believer in the God of Classical Theism?

You need to know

The **Big Bang** is a scientific theory to explain the origin of the universe. The Big Bang is considered to have occurred when a single, extremely condensed state of matter exploded. The universe was formed from the gases created by the explosion. Those scientists who accept the Big Bang theory regard it as the moment at which time began.

Conclusion

Some philosophers argue that even if there was a first cause of the universe, there is no proof that it is the God of Classical Theism. The first cause could be anything. Hume argued that the first cause, if there was one, could be the material, physical world rather than God. The material world as its own cause is just as satisfactory an explanation as God.

Brian Davies

Davies takes the position that the cosmological argument cannot stand alone as a proof for the existence of God, and would have to be supported by other evidence. The design argument might be further evidence to establish the existence of God:

> As an argument for a first cause of all existing things the cosmological argument seems a reasonable one. But it does not by itself establish the existence of God with all the properties sometimes ascribed to him.

> *Brian Davies, The Introduction to the Philosophy of Religion,*
> *OUP, 1990*

Essay questions

AS

(a) Explain Aquinas' argument for the existence of God based on the apparent beginning of the universe.
(b) Explain and evaluate the extent to which it is important for religious believers to challenge the idea that the universe came into existence by chance.

A2

(a) Outline the various forms of the cosmological argument for the existence of God.
(b) Explain and evaluate the strengths and weaknesses of the various forms of the cosmological argument as a proof for the existence of God.

Chapter 6

The Design Argument for the Existence of God

The design argument for the existence of God is also called the **teleological argument**: *teleos* is a Greek word meaning 'end' or 'purpose'. The design argument is an *a posteriori* argument. It is based on observation of the apparent order in the universe and the natural world, to conclude that it is not the result of mere chance, but of design. The evidence from design points to a designer and the argument concludes that this designer is God. 'With such signs of forethought in the design of living creatures, can you doubt they are the work of choice or design?' (Socrates)

The Classical Argument for Design

The basic argument for design states that:

- the universe has order, purpose and regularity
- the complexity of the universe shows evidence of design
- such design implies a designer
- the designer of the universe is God

The argument makes the basic assumption that there is order and design in the universe, and that all things function to fulfil a specific purpose. For example, the changing seasons, the lifestyles of animals and birds, the intricate organism of the human body and the perfect adaptation of its parts to the whole appear to provide evidence that the universe was designed.

The design argument is in two parts:

- design *qua* regularity
- design *qua* purpose

Design *qua* Regularity

This aspect looks at design in relation to the order and regularity in the universe. Philosophers who support the argument consider that the order and regularity evident in the universe is evidence of a designer at work. Just as a formal garden shows evidence of a gardener because of the order, a

Something to think about

Look at **John Wisdom's** Parable of the Gardener in Chapter 2 (pages 13–14).

How do you think this parable could be used to support the argument for design *qua* regularity?

You need to know

Remind yourself of the philosophy of **St Thomas Aquinas** by reading the section related to him in Chapter 1 (pages 3–4).

Something to think about

Why do you think Aquinas believed that there is evidence of design in the universe?

lack of weeds and the arrangement of the flowers in the borders, so there is order and regularity evident in the universe; for example, the rotation of the planets and the natural laws. Philosophers conclude that this cannot have occurred by random chance.

St Thomas Aquinas

Aquinas used a form of the teleological argument in the fifth of his **Five Ways**, 'from the governance of things'. He identified that the way in which 'natural bodies' act in a regular fashion to accomplish their end provides the evidence for the existence of an intelligent being:

> Hence it is plain that they achieve their end, not fortuitously, but designedly. Now whatever lacks knowledge cannot move towards an end, unless it be directed by some being endowed with knowledge and intelligence; as the arrow is directed by the archer. Therefore some intelligent being exists by whom all natural things are directed to their end; and this being we call God.
>
> *St Thomas Aquinas, Summa Theologica*

Aquinas was arguing from design *qua* regularity. He regarded the overall order evident in the world as proof of a designer, 'this being we call God'.

Design *qua* Purpose

This aspect looks at the evidence of design in relation to the ways in which the parts of the universe appear to fit together for some purpose. The universe is compared to a man-made machine in which a designer fits all the parts together for a specific function. For example, the parts of a television are fitted together in such a way as to receive pictures and sound. If the parts were fitted together in a random manner, then the television would not function. Similarly, there are complex arrangements within nature that have been fitted together by a designer for special purposes.

William Paley (CE 1743–1805)

Paley put forward the most famous form of the design argument in his book, *Natural Theology* (1802):

> In crossing a heath, suppose I pitched my foot against a stone, and were asked how the stone came to be there, I might possibly answer, that for any thing I knew to the contrary it

Something to think about

Why does Paley conclude that a person seeing a watch for the first time would assume that the watch is designed for a purpose?

Why would not the same assumption be made of a stone?

had lain there for ever; nor would it, perhaps be very easy to show the absurdity of this answer. But suppose I had found a watch upon the ground, and it should be inquired how the watch happened to be in that place, I should hardly think of the answer which I had before given, that for any thing I knew the watch might have always been there. Yet why should not this answer serve for the watch as well as for the stone; why is it not as admissible in the second case as in the first? For this reason, and for no other, namely, that when we come to inspect the watch, we perceive – what we could not discover in the stone – that its several parts are framed and put together for a purpose, e.g. that they are so formed and adjusted as to produce motion, and that motion so regulated as to point out the hour of the day; that if the different parts had been differently shaped from what they are, or placed after any other manner or in any other order than that in which they are placed, either no motion at all would have been carried on in the machine, or none which would have answered the use that is now served by it . . .

William Paley, Natural Theology, 1802

You need to know

Remind yourself of the meaning of **analogy**, by looking back at Chapter 2 (page 17).

The **first part** of Paley's argument was *design* qua *purpose*. Paley put forward the argument for design in the form of a simple analogy. If we were to come across a watch, we would conclude that all the parts fitted together for a purpose and had not come into existence by chance. An intelligent person would infer a designer of the watch. In the same way, if we look at the world we can infer a design because of the way in which things fit together for a purpose. For example, Paley thought that a similar conclusion might be drawn from the intricate mechanisms of the human body.

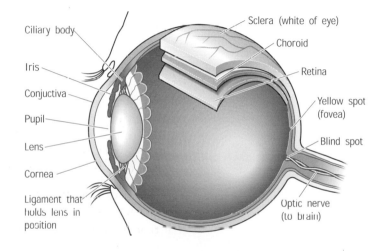

The complexities of the human eye suggest design

Paley used the example of the eye and the way in which it is adapted for sight. Its various parts co-operate in complex ways to produce sight. He believed that the eye was designed for the specific purpose of seeing, and that this complex design suggests an intelligent designer. He adds to this example the instincts of animals that aid survival; a bird's wings for flight or a fish's fins for swimming. Such evidence, Paley argued, could only be the result of a 'designing creator', which for Paley was God.

The **second part** of Paley's argument for the existence of God is *design* qua *regularity*. Paley used evidence from astronomy and Newton's laws of motion and gravity to prove that there is design in the universe. Paley pointed to the rotation of the planets in the solar system, and how they obey the same universal laws, and hold their orbits because of gravity. This could not have come about by chance. He concluded that an external agent must have imposed order on the universe as a whole, and on its many parts, and that this agent must be God.

In the twentieth century, **Arthur Brown** has supported the argument for design based on astronomy. Brown pointed to the ozone layer as evidence of design. He argued that the ozone layer's purpose, to filter out ultraviolet rays in order to protect life, could not have happened by chance. Brown argued that:

> The ozone gas layer is a mighty proof of the creator's forethought. Could anyone possibly attribute this device to a chance evolutionary process? A wall which prevents death to every living thing, just the right thickness and exactly the correct defence gives every evidence of a plan.

Arthur Brown, Footprints of God, 1943

You need to know

Anthropic means to be linked to the science and study of mankind.

The Anthropic Principle

The Anthropic Principle is a recent development of the teleological argument. The argument claims that the cosmos is constructed for the development of intelligent life. If there had been just a minute change in the values of, for instance, the strong nuclear force or the charge of the electron, then intelligent life – or any form of life at all – would have been unlikely to develop.

The 'new' design argument denies any claim that there is a chain of coincidences that led to the evolution of human life. Supporters of the argument go on to make the further claim that the best explanation is the existence of a designer, and that this designer is God.

You need to know

Conspiration refers to the act of joining together, or combining.

A **conspection** is a survey or observation of events.

Something to think about

Where does Tennant believe that the evidence for design can be found in nature?

You need to know

Aesthetic means having an appreciation of beauty.

You need to know

Natural selection is the mechanism of evolutionary change. Those hereditary characteristics of a member of any species that are good for survival and reproduction will lead to more members of the species with those characteristics passing on their genes. Characteristics that help a species to survive will be passed on to each generation until all members of the species have inherited it. In this way, species evolve and change. So, by natural selection, particular variations are favoured and effect a gradual transformation in the appearance and behaviour of any species.

The Anthropic Principle was developed by **F. R. Tennant**, in his book *Philosophical Theology* (1930). Tennant believed that there were three types of natural evidence in the world in favour of a divine designer:

- the fact that the world can be analysed in a rational manner
- the way in which the inorganic world has provided the basic necessities required to sustain life
- the progress of evolution towards the emergence of intelligent human life

Tennant believed that it would be possible to imagine a chaotic universe in which no rules applied. However, the universe is not chaotic and was designed in such a way that the evolutionary process would create an environment in which intelligent life could exist. Human life is the culmination of God's plan, or at least the current stage in God's plan:

> The forcibleness of Nature's suggestion that she is the outcome of intelligent design lies not in particular cases of adaptedness in the world, nor even in the multiplicity of them . . . it consists rather in the conspiration of innumerable causes to produce, by either united and reciprocal action, and to maintain, a general order of Nature. Narrower kinds of teleological arguments, based on surveys of restricted spheres of fact, are much more precarious than that for which the name of 'the wider teleology' may be appropriate in that the comprehensive design-argument is the outcome of synopsis or conspection of the knowable world.

> F. R. Tennant, Philosophical Theology,
> Cambridge University Press, 1930

Tennant developed not only the Anthropic Principle but also the **Aesthetic argument** to prove God's existence. Tennant argued that humans possess the ability to appreciate the beauty of their surroundings – to enjoy art, music and literature. Yet such an appreciation is not necessary for survival or for the development of life, and is therefore evidence of a divine creator. It cannot therefore be the result of natural selection.

Richard Swinburne

Swinburne accepted the Anthropic Principle and that the universe is law-governed. He recognised that the universe could just as easily have been chaotic. The fact that it is not suggests design rather than chance. Swinburne considered that it came down to *probabilities*. Which is the most probable reason for order in the universe, random chance or design?

You need to know

Probabilities quantify the likelihood of any one of a number of possible outcomes.

Something to think about

Do you think that Swinburne's points are valid?

Do you think that it is more or less probable that there is design in the universe?

If there is design in the universe, do you think that it is probable that the designer is God?

Something to think about

What evidence might be produced to support the idea that the world could be the technology project of an 'apprentice deity'?

If the world was an examination piece, do you think that this 'apprentice deity' would have achieved an 'A' or a 'U' for his or her project?

You need to know

Epicurus (BCE 341–270) was a Greek philosopher who maintained that the universe was only made up of atoms and space – nothing else. The atoms are eternal, but they move and change. All physical objects are a combination of atoms.

The sheer complexity of the universe makes it unlikely that the universe would just 'happen' to be the way it is, so Swinburne accepted that it is more probable that there is design. If there is design, then he concluded that God is the simplest explanation.

How Successful is the Design Argument?

David Hume

In *Dialogues Concerning Natural Religion* (1779), Hume emerged as a major opponent of the design argument. His main reasons for opposing the argument include the following:

- Humans do not have sufficient knowledge and experience of the creation of the world to conclude that there is only one designer. Humans have only the experience of the things that they design and create. This limited experience is not sufficient to come to similar conclusions about the creation and design of the world.
- If the human experience of design was valid, the design argument would prove that the universe has a designer, but not that the designer was the God of Classical Theism. The design could have been the work of several lesser gods or, alternatively, of an apprentice god who has moved on to create bigger and better worlds:

This world, for all he knows, is very faulty and imperfect, compared to a superior standard; and was only the first rude essay of some infant deity who afterwards abandoned it.

David Hume, Dialogues Concerning Natural Religion, 1779

- There is no evidence to support the benevolent God of Classical Theism. The very existence of evil in the world would suggest a designer who is not the benevolent or all-powerful God of Classical Theism.
- Hume argued that to try to discuss the design of the universe in human terms was not an acceptable analogy, because God transcends human understanding. If we are going to use an analogy of manufactured objects, then it is more usual for a machine to be designed and made by many hands. This analogy would suggest many gods rather than one God.
- Hume does not think that it is a good analogy to liken the universe to a vast machine. The universe is more like a vegetable or inert animal – something that grows of its own accord, rather than something made by hand.

Something to think about

Read the section related to the problem of the existence of evil for believers on pages 91ff. How does this problem support Mill's rejection of the God of Classical Theism?

Something to think about

Do you think the way in which all parts of the universe appear to function together is the result of design or of random chance?

You need to know

Evolution is the process by which plant and animal life rose from the earliest and most primitive organisms to reach its present state of development. It means that one species is descended from another species that is different from itself. A chain can be established going back through time to trace the origin of each species. Human beings, for example, have descended from a species similar to the apes. This 'ape' species descended from a species of mammal, and in turn the mammal descended from a reptile, before that from a fish, and eventually the chain can be traced back to the origin of all life-forms, a simple bacterium. One way in which this is achieved is by natural selection.

Look back to the definition of natural selection earlier in this chapter (page 77), and remind yourself of what it involves.

John Stuart Mill also challenged the idea that evidence of design in the world proves the existence of the God of Classical Theism. He argued that because there is evil and suffering in the world then the designer cannot have been all powerful, all knowing and all loving. If the designer was all-loving then the suffering of humanity would not have been included in the design. As it is then at least one of these three attributes must be missing.

The Epicurean Hypothesis

The Epicurean Hypothesis argued that, at the time of creation, the universe consisted of particles in random motion. This initial state was chaotic, but gradually the natural forces evolved into an ordered system. The universe is eternal and, in this unlimited time, it was inevitable that a constantly ordered state would develop. The stability and order is not the result of a divine designer but of random particles coming together through time to form the current stable universe.

Evolution
Charles Darwin (CE 1809–1882)

Darwin was an English naturalist who formulated the theory of natural selection in his work *On the Origin of Species by Means of Natural Selection* (1859). The book challenged the argument for design, as it revolutionised thinking about the way in which species, including human beings, developed. Darwin provided an alternative explanation for the design of the world, without reference to creation by God. He offered a mechanical explanation for the development of life on Earth, in which natural selection took place. Herbert Spencer coined the phrase 'the survival of the fittest' to explain part of the process. Darwin argued that random variations, which gave the best advantage to a plant or animal in the struggle for survival, resulted in the survival of the fittest member of that species:

> In order to make it clear how, as I believe, natural selection acts, I must beg permission to give one or two imaginary illustrations. Let us take the case of a wolf, which preys on various animals, securing some by craft, some by strength, and some by fleetness; and let us suppose that the fleetest prey, a deer for instance, had from any change in the country increased in numbers, or that other prey had decreased in numbers,

Something to think about

How does Darwin use the example of the wolf to explain natural selection?

Something to think about

Richard Dawkins titles one of his books *The Blind Watchmaker*. Why do you think he might have chosen that title?

What does the title suggest about his view of the idea that there is design in the world?

You need to know

There are more details of **evolutionary theories** in Chapter 10 (pages 140–143).

Something to think about

Why do you think that **F. R. Tennant** was able to accept Darwin's theory of evolution as part of God's design for the universe?

What other examples might Tennant point to in nature as evidence of design besides the survival of the fittest?

You need to know

Look back at Chapter 1 (page 8), and remind yourself of **Kant's** Idealism.

during that season of the year when the wolf was hardest pressed for food. Under such circumstances the swiftest and slimmest wolves would have the best chance of surviving and so be preserved or selected, – provided always that they retained strength to master their prey at this or some other period of the year, when they were compelled to prey on other animals. I can see no more reason to doubt that this would be the result, than that man should be able to improve the fleetness of his greyhounds by careful and methodical selection.

Charles Darwin, On the Origin of Species by Means of Natural Selection, 1859

The Origin of Species led many people to claim that a belief in God was no longer necessary to explain the way in which the natural world had developed. More recently, zoologist **Richard Dawkins** has written several books to support Darwinian evolution and reject God. Dawkins argues that natural selection gave the appearance of design, and that this led to the mistaken belief that there was a designer. He rejects any design in the world, and argues that the variations in the world were caused by random mistakes in the DNA molecules of any life-form.

Darwinism and the Anthropic Principle

The Anthropic Principle accepts both Darwin's evolutionary process and the existence of God. It claims that evolution is part of God's plan for the development of intelligent life. Nature produces living beings but without the 'fine tuning' that is found in the universe: life could just as easily not have developed on Earth. Supporters of the principle suggest that nature may be compared to a machine that makes other machines and, like all machines, it needed an intelligent designer.

Immanuel Kant

Kant emphasised that the design argument depended on the assumption that there is design in the universe. The design must be the independent work of a designer who imposed order on the universe. The argument is based on the assumption that there is regularity, order and purpose in the universe. Kant argued that the universe may be in chaos but, because of the way in which our minds organise our experiences, the world around us appears to be ordered. We impose the design on the world ourselves, and cannot be certain of the reality of the situation.

Something to think about

Thomas McPherson said 'How can we talk sensibly of the existence of a world independent of order, when to talk at all is to impose order?'

What do you think he meant by this statement?

How might the statement be applied to the design argument for the existence of God?

Conclusion

Whether or not there is design in the universe comes down to probabilities. Hume accepted that it was more probable that the universe was designed and that there was a designer, but there was no proof that the designer was God.

Paul Davies

Davies accepts that there is a reason for the organisation of the universe, and that someone designed it. According to Davies, this someone might be God:

> It's certainly consistent with that. This is really a question of your threshold of conviction. As the philosopher John Lesley has remarked, if every time we turned a rock over we saw the message Made by God stamped on it, then I guess everybody would have to assume that we did live in a universe of his design. It has to be a matter of personal taste whether you regard the accumulated evidence as compelling enough to want to make that leap. But inevitably it's outside the scope of science as such. Science deals with the facts of the world, religion deals with the interpretation of those facts.

> *Paul Davies, in Russell Stannard, Science and Wonders,*
> *Faber and Faber, 1996*

Essay questions

AS
(a) Explain Paley's argument for the existence of God based on the apparent order and design in the world.
(b) Explain and evaluate the extent to which it is important for religious believers to accept that there is regularity, order and purpose in the universe.

A2
(a) Outline the various forms of the teleological argument.
(b) Explain and evaluate the strengths and weaknesses of the various forms of the teleological argument as a proof for the existence of God.

Chapter 7

The Moral Argument for the Existence of God

Like the other arguments for the existence of God, the moral argument comes in different forms. All of these set out to prove God's existence from the evidence of morality in the world.

All the moral arguments work on the principle that the vast majority of people have some experience of morality. Most people feel there are certain obligations about how they should or should not behave. Moreover, most people have a broadly similar understanding of what is right and wrong, despite the cultural differences between them. For example, the vast majority of cultures strictly forbid incest.

Philosophers have given three possible explanations for these similarities:

- Morality stems from God, either through our conscience or an objective set of rules that He has built into us. This represents the view of **H. P. Owen** and **Cardinal Newman** (1801–1890).
- Morality stems from an objective appraisal of the world, which reveals that there are certain goals and values to be aimed for and upheld. This leads us to endorse some actions as good and others as bad. **Dom Trethowan** and **Immanuel Kant** infer the existence of God from this appraisal.
- Morality stems from the demands placed upon the human animal by living in societies. Rules meet the needs of a particular situation and facilitate human development in that particular context. This view explains morality without reference to God. It also suggests that moral laws can change as and when necessary.

Morality as Derived from God

H. P. Owen's Argument

Owen argued that the existence of objective moral laws suggests that there is a divine law-giver who wrote these laws. He explained:

You need to know

Morality is about understanding what is the right and wrong action in a given situation. A moral person has this understanding and then acts appropriately.

Something to think about

Imagine that you are on a tropical island with a group of people. There is no government and there are no laws.

Write a list of the rules that you still consider important for the group to follow.

Compare your list with those of others in your group. What are the similarities?

Something to think about

Look back at the list of rules you decided were important.

From where have you gained this sense of morality? List the possibilities.

An **objective law** is a law that always holds true, independently of humans.

Trethowan's version of the moral argument is given below.

The **conscience** is the inner voice that tells us how to behave. It produces feelings of guilt and shame.

It is impossible to think of a command without also thinking of a commander ... A clear choice faces us. Either we take moral claims to be self-explanatory modes of impersonal existence or we explain them in terms of a personal God.

> H. P. Owen, The Moral Argument for Christian Theism,
> George Allen & Unwin, 1965

Owen's point was that since commands and laws do not write themselves, they must either be brute facts, requiring no explanation, or put there by God. Since the fact these laws exist itself requires explanation, he concluded that they must have been put there by God. This reasoning is supported by Dom Trethowan, who described objective laws as 'far from being self-explanatory'.

Cardinal Newman's Argument

Cardinal Newman deduces God's existence not from objective moral law but from the fact of conscience:

> If, as is the case, we feel responsibility, are ashamed, are frightened at transgressing the voice of conscience, this implies that there is One to whom we are responsible, before whom we are ashamed, whose claim upon us we fear ... If the cause of these emotions does not belong to this visible world, the Object to which [our] perception is directed must be Supernatural and Divine.

> J. H. Newman, A Grammar of Assent, ed. C. F. Harrold,
> David McKay and Co., 1947

For Newman, the conscience is like an inner voice that guides our behaviour and produces feelings of guilt and shame. Newman takes the view that the conscience is the voice of God within us, the point at which the human meets the divine in everyday life. From the conscience, Newman infers the existence of God.

Morality as Objectively Pointing Towards God

Dom Trethowan's Argument

Trethowan developed a version of the moral argument that rejected the use of logic to establish God's existence. Instead, he interpreted morality as a religious experience, which points towards God. Every time we make a moral decision, we choose between possible courses of action. A sense of obligation guides us to make this choice. Trethowan traces this obligation to the fact that each person has value. A sense of value thus underpins each moral decision. If we accept that people have intrinsic value, then there must be a source to this value. Trethowan takes this to be God:

> We have value because we receive it from a source of value. That is what I mean, for a start, by God. That is why the demand upon us to develop ourselves is an absolute, unconditional demand.
>
> *D. I. Trethowan, Absolute Value, George Allen & Unwin, 1970*

The value instilled by God in His creation thus explains the obligations that we feel. The moral experience, with its sense of obligation, is thus an indirect experience of God.

Immanuel Kant's Argument

Kant presented a distinct form of the moral argument. In fact, it cannot strictly be termed an argument, since Kant believed that God's existence could only be established through faith, as opposed to logic.

Kant's enquiry into the relationship between religion and morality begins with him considering his own beliefs about the nature of morality. He reasoned that in a perfect world, behaving morally should lead to happiness, since happiness should be the natural reward of virtue. In our world, however, as this rarely happens, Kant considered that there must be another answer.

He reasoned that there must be something else that motivates people to behave morally, other than the possibility of immediate happiness. Instead, he argued that people must be subject to an objective sense of obligation, which compels them to behave in a certain way, regardless of the consequences. Kant argued that there were certain, rationally discoverable laws which we are duty bound to follow. Kant calls these laws **categorical imperatives**.

Kant moved on to consider whether any further conclusions could be drawn from his discovery that morality is a matter of applying rational thought to discover categorical imperatives. Effectively, he was asking 'If I experience this sense of objective obligation, what else must I implicitly be accepting to be true?' Kant's *Critique of Practical Reason* argued that there are three such assumptions: *freedom*, *immortality* and *God*. Kant called these the **postulates of morality**.

Something to think about

Imagine that you came upon a drowning child and felt an absolute urge to save that child. Can you trace this urge to the inherent value that this child possesses?

If so, from where do *you* think this value has come?

Something to think about

List some examples of where good people have been made to suffer.

If being good does not lead to a reward, *why do people continue to make the effort to live a moral life?* There may be more than one reason!

You need to know

A **categorical imperative** is a law that is binding in *all* situations, regardless of the context. An example would be *Treat others as you would have them treat you*.

A **deontologist** is somebody who believes that morality stems from a sense of duty. The moral person is the one who follows his or her sense of duty. Kant was a deontologist.

A **consequentialist** is someone who believes that the only guide as to whether an action is right or wrong is the consequences that the action produces. A good action is one that results in good consequences, while a bad action one that results in bad consequences.

In practice, many people use a combination of deontology and consequentialism to help them judge the moral worth of a certain course of action.

A **postulate** often means nothing more than a *suggestion*. Kant used the term in a stronger sense, to denote the idea of *something which is required to be the case*. The **postulates of morality**, for example, denote the assumptions that must be made by anyone who accepts an objective morality.

Rational thought had led Kant to establish the categorical imperatives, or objective laws. Further rational thought led Kant to establish the *summum bonum*, or highest good, as the goal of that law. The goal is a state of absolute morality combined with absolute happiness for, as we have seen, it seemed logical that morality should lead to happiness. However, Kant did not believe it possible for anyone to attain the highest good through their efforts alone, on account of the imperfect world in which we live.

The first postulate, freedom, may seem obvious: if we feel obliged to fulfil a certain duty, then we must have the freedom to fulfil it.

Kant's argument can be summarised into three main stages. They involve Kant's concept of the highest good.

The three stages of Kant's argument proceed as follows:

- morality demands us to aim for the highest good
- we cannot attain this unless there is a God to assist us
- God must exist to ensure that we can achieve that which we are duty bound to do

Let us look at these three stages in greater detail:

- The first point is a natural extension of Kant's concept of objective law. If it is our unconditional duty to follow this law, it must also be our unconditional duty to aim for the goal of this law: 'We should seek to further the highest good.'
- The second step relies upon simple empirical evidence combined with logic. Since we are not the 'cause of the world and of nature itself' we do not have the power to bring about the highest good. Even if we were able to achieve perfect morality, we would not be able to ensure the 'necessary connection' of perfect happiness that should follow. Humans do not therefore have enough power to bring about the highest good.
- For Kant, these two points formed a contradiction; if we are to aim for the highest good, this 'must at least be possible'. To Kant, it seemed illogical that we could be required to aim for an impossible goal. This deadlock led Kant to postulate the existence of God and immortality. If we are unable in our present life to attain this goal, there must be someone else who can ensure that we can attain it in a future life.

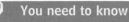

You need to know

Remind yourself of the meaning of the word **empirical** by referring back to Chapter 1 (page 4).

God, as the 'cause of the whole of nature', has the necessary power. God, the 'highest original good' is both the ground for the moral law and that which can enable us to achieve its goals. Hence we reach Kant's conclusion: 'Therefore it is morally necessary to assume the existence of God.'

How Successful is the Moral Argument?

As with many of the arguments for the existence of God, the moral argument may strengthen aspects of the existing faith of believers. Those who already believe in a God concerned with morality will quite reasonably trace their notion of right and wrong back to that God. Newman's argument, for example, may appeal to those who already worship the God of the Bible. The Bible presents a God who is very much in control of His world. He 'writes his covenant upon our hearts'. If this is the case, then, our own consciences may appear to stem back to God. Those moral arguments based upon objective laws might appeal to those who already accept such unconditional, *a priori*, laws. As **John Hick** explains:

> To recognise moral claims as taking precedence over all other interests is, implicitly, to believe in a reality of some kind, other than the natural world, that is superior to oneself and entitled to one's obedience . . . This is at least a move in the direction of God.

John H. Hick, Philosophy of Religion, 4th edn, Prentice-Hall, 1990

The problem, however, is that for those who do not accept God's existence, or that of objective law, the moral argument would be unlikely to kindle belief. This judgement arises from the four major criticisms:

- Morality can be explained without the need for God. The inconsistencies within morality – such as the clashes of opinions upon war and abortion, for example – would tend to support this view. This criticism counts against all forms of the argument.
- The concept of the objective law has been vigorously challenged. This counts against the versions of Owen, Trethowan and Kant.
- Even if objective law is accepted, God may still not be necessary. This counts against the same three versions.
- Proof of the existence of God is beyond the scope of all of the moral arguments. The most that they could possibly establish is the existence of a being who makes laws.

We shall explain these criticisms one by one in greater depth.

Non-religious Explanations for Morality

The first major criticism affirms that there are many alternative explanations for morality which have nothing to do with God. We noted at the start of the chapter that some philosophers argue that morality is a man-made tool that helps us meet the needs of life in society. Against Newman, then, the conscience can be understood as a product of the brain, activated by the demands of living in close proximity with others. This interpretation is supported by the concept of **cultural evolution**.

This concept supports a non-religious origin for the conscience, because it is seen as a safety mechanism that restricts behaviour and prevents needless and life-threatening clashes with others.

Kant's apparently objective duty can likewise be traced back to a combination of social conditioning and human nature. **Sigmund Freud** supports this general approach, regarding the conscience as a product of the unconscious mind or super ego. The super ego continues the work of the parents in limiting the behaviour of the child. It develops in accordance with the conditioning received by the growing human being.

You need to know

Cultural evolution, supported by Richard Dawkins, affirms that the evolutionary process that ensures the best fit between the individual and his or her environment extends to cultural characteristics as well as purely physical ones. Cultural institutions, such as marriage and law-making, have developed over the generations.

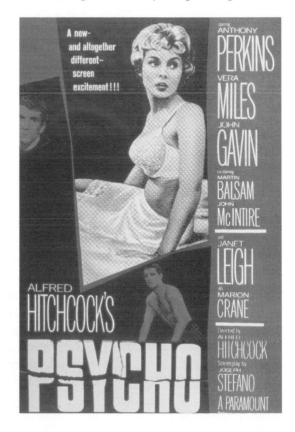

Was this a film about the voice of God?

Support for a psychological background to conscience and laws includes the varieties within these entities. If the conscience was the voice of God, we should expect its message to be consistent. This is far from the truth. Voices in the mind of the notorious Yorkshire Ripper led him to commit murder, apparently in the name of conscience. There are too many variations from individual to individual for the conscience to be the voice of God. A belief that it is may not only be mistaken, but also highly dangerous. The same criticism can be applied against the concept of objective law. The fact that no one can establish the exact rules of this law calls its objectivity into question, thus supporting a human as opposed to divine origin.

Difficulties with the Concept of Objective Law

The concept of an objective law has been attacked in many other ways. One attack consists of the claim that this concept is morally untenable.

Many philosophers argue that morality is far more than a simple matter of obeying an objective duty. **Joseph Fletcher**, for example, devised the system known as **situation ethics**.

Followers of situation ethics argue that a system of morality based upon obeying rules is callous and unsatisfactory, because it pays no attention to the individual case. Few people would wish to go as far as Fletcher, by rejecting *all* rules, but it does seem that the consequences of an action need at least to be taken into account before we decide whether it is good or bad.

If the law is truly objective, then there can be no room for consequences. For as soon as we take into consideration other principles, the law ceases to be our objectively binding duty. If the law is no longer our objective duty, there is no need for a God to underpin the system (against Trethowan and Newman). Nor is there need for God to help us attain the highest goal of that law, since this goal is no longer our absolute duty (against Kant).

Kant's moral argument, then, only has a possibility of working as long as we accept Kant's world-view, which contains an *a priori* objective moral law. The same is true of the arguments of Owen and Trethowan.

You need to know

If a law is **objective**, then it operates independently of human actions. This means that it holds in every possible situation: there can never be any exceptions to the rule. This, in effect, is what Kant upholds.

You need to know

Situation ethics works on the principle that, in any moral dilemma, the only reliable principle is to act in the most *loving* way. There are no absolute rules, since how one acts always depends on the situation.

Something to think about

Look back at the list of laws that you felt would be required if you were placed on a tropical island. Can you conceive of any situations in which it may be justifiable to break these laws?

If so, what makes it justifiable to break them?

You need to know

In Chapter 9, we shall see that **C. G. Jung** believed that it is impossible for a human being to know anything about objective reality. This is because human thoughts are necessarily limited to the subjective world of the human mind. On this basis, the objective law could simply be a notion dreamed up by the mind. Read the section on Jung (pages 119ff.).

Non-religious Explanations for Objective Law

Yet even if we accept the objective law, there may still be no grounds for concluding that God exists. Regarding Kant's argument, objective law requires God because only God could ensure that its goal is met. He thinks it illogical that we should be required to aim for something outside our reach. But **Brian Davies** questions this line of thinking. Sometimes it is not illogical to aim for something even if it is possible that we may never attain it (such as a grade 'A' in a philosophy exam).

Failure of the Argument to Prove God as the Basis for Morality

Something to think about

List some examples of situations in which you have been required to aim for something that you did not, in fact, attain.

Would you have continued to aim for them if you had known in advance that you were going to fail? If so, *why*?

The final criticism consists of the claim that even if we accept all these premises to the moral argument, it could never in fact point us to the existence of God. If we accept that morality points us to belief in a law-giver and belief in a source for our conscience, all we have established is that there is a law-giver of some description. It does not establish the existence of the omnipotent, omnibenevolent God of Classical Theism. This is because the concept of God as law-giver is only one aspect of the traditional view of God. It does not require all the others. As a result, Brian Davies suggested that Kant's argument might only point to the existence of a being who devises laws; a 'Kantian-minded angel', for example.

Conclusion

The moral argument for the existence of God cannot be used to provide proof of the existence of God. For those who already believe – either in God or in an objective law – there may be grounds for strengthening aspects of these beliefs. For example, the existence of morality may reinforce the view that God is interested in morality.

The unbeliever, however, would not be persuaded to take up religious belief solely on the grounds of the argument. This is because the moral argument is based on a logical error. For while the existence of a moral God would indeed suggest the existence of moral laws, the existence of a moral laws in one form or another cannot point us back to the existence of God.

Essay questions

AS

(a) Explain Kant's argument for the existence of God.

(b) Explain and evaluate the extent to which it is possible to prove the existence of God based on morality.

A2

(a) Outline the various forms of the moral argument for the existence of God.

(b) Explain and evaluate the strengths and weaknesses of the various forms of the moral argument as a proof for the existence of God.

Chapter 8   Evil and Suffering

Introduction

The major argument used by non-believers against God's existence is the presence of evil and suffering in our world.

The Nature of Evil

When we describe something as evil, we often mean that it is morally wrong. Hence, we describe the action of Jack the Ripper as evil. In philosophical terms, however, we must distinguish between **moral evil** and **natural evil.**

The consequence of evil is **suffering**. The Lisbon Earthquake of 1755 caused the suffering and deaths of some 4000 people; the Holocaust, some 6 million. Suffering often involves mental anguish and depression as well as physical pain. These effects can be very long-lasting; the participants in the two world wars have never recovered from their ordeals. In addition to the pain that it causes, suffering is often unjust. It does not discriminate as to whom it strikes, with the result that innocent victims are often caught in its path.

The Problem of Evil for Believers

The devastating effects of evil leave us in no doubt that evil is unpleasant for everyone. For religious people, however, it poses an additional challenge to their faith. The philosophical discussion about the *problem of evil* concerns this challenge of how an all-powerful and all-loving God can allow His creation to suffer, without coming to its rescue and putting an end to the torment. This challenge is an oft-quoted reason for being unable to believe in God. For, it is argued, either God does not exist or, if He does, He is not a God worthy of our worship. Here, we shall set out this argument in stages.

The problem of evil is a problem specifically for upholders of the God of Classical Theism. Other religious outlooks, which accept the presence of a variety of gods of assorted character and authority, do not have the same problem, since the existence of evil can be attributed to the tensions between the

What are the different ways in which this earthquake caused suffering?

Something to think about

List the concepts of the **God of Classical Theism**. If you're unsure, look back at Chapter 4 (pages 51ff).

different gods. Followers of the God of Classical Theism, however, acknowledge the existence of one God only, who is the all-powerful Creator of the universe. This leads to the following dilemma:

- Since God alone created the universe out of nothing, He has total responsibility for everything in it. If He is all-powerful, then He can do anything that is logically possible. This means that He could have created a world free from actual evil and suffering, and free from the possibility of ever going wrong. It also means that, should He ever have allowed it to come about, He could end all evil and suffering.
- Since God is omniscient, He has complete knowledge of everything in the universe, including suffering and evil. He also knows how to stop it.
- If God is omnibenevolent however, He would wish to end all evil and suffering. Any sense of love, as we understand the word, would wish to stop the multiple horrors heaped upon the millions of innocent people over the years. No all-loving God would allow His creation to suffer physical and mental torment for no reason and to no avail. Since God is omnipotent, He could carry out immediately His desire to step in and stop the suffering.
- Yet evil and suffering continue to exist, so either (1) God lacks omnipotence or omnibenevolence or (2) He does not exist.

David Hume set out this dilemma famously in his *Dialogues Concerning Natural Religion*. Upon examining the qualities of omnipotence, omnibenevolence and evil, he concluded that only two out of the three can exist alongside each other. Therefore, *either:*

- God is not omnipotent, *or*
- God is not omnibenevolent *or*
- evil does not exist

Something to think about

Imagine that you have toothache and are trying to describe it to a friend who has no idea what it feels like.

How could you convince your friend that you are in pain?

Would your friend be unreasonable to doubt the truth of your claim?

While the existence of evil has been questioned by some, Hume considered that its effects are felt too widely, and its presence attested too vividly for it to be dismissible. Therefore, accepting that evil exists, he concluded that God must either be impotent or malicious. Either way, this entails the death of the God of Classical Theism. Hume therefore concluded that God does not exist.

This position is supported by an argument that is found in Aquinas' *Summa Theologica*, which suggests that God's existence in the face of evil is *logically* impossible:

> It seems that God does not exist: because if one of two contraries be infinite, the other would be altogether destroyed. But the name of God means that He is infinite goodness. If, therefore, God existed, there would be no evil discoverable; but there is evil in the world. Therefore God does not exist.

> *St Thomas Aquinas, Summa Theologica*

Since, for Aquinas, the concept of infinite goodness is an essential part of God's nature, any proof against God's goodness being infinite will constitute proof that God does not exist. The existence of even the tiniest quantity of evil precludes the possibility of infinite goodness. We, as witnesses to the evil in our world, are thus witnesses to proof against the existence of God.

Aquinas differed from Hume, however, in that whereas Hume, as an atheist, accepted this conclusion, Aquinas went on to reject it. Despite drawing attention to the apparently insurmountable contradiction between God and evil, Aquinas remained one of the most famous Christian thinkers of all time.

This is possible because Aquinas' logical argument only works if we accept its two premises:

- the concept of infinite goodness is part of the definition of God
- in talking about God's *goodness*, we are referring to the same thing as human goodness

It can be argued, however, that God's goodness is a very different concept from our own, and that His goodness might allow Him to tolerate the existence of what we consider to be evil as a temporary part of His plan. If this be the case, there can be no logical contradiction in supposing that God is all-loving, all-powerful *and* has a reason for allowing what we call evil to exist. For this reason, numerous religious thinkers have constructed **theodicies** to explain what this reason is.

Theodicies tend to argue that God is just in allowing the existence of evil and suffering, because they are in some way necessary and essential. In this chapter, we shall consider the following:

- Augustine's theodicy
- Irenaeus' theodicy
- the freewill defence
- process theodicy
- monism

Augustine's Theodicy

St Augustine (AD 354–430) based his arguments on the Bible, especially the accounts of the Creation and the Fall in Genesis. His influential theodicy rests upon two major assumptions:

- evil did not come from God, since God's creation was faultless and perfect

- evil having come from elsewhere, God is justified in allowing it to stay

Augustine's Argument in Brief

- God is perfect. He made a world free from flaws.
- God cannot be blamed for creating evil, since evil is not a substance but a deprivation, and it makes no sense to say that God created a deprivation.
- Evil comes from angels and human beings who chose deliberately to turn away from God.
- The possibility of evil in a created world is necessary. Only the uncreated God Himself can be perfect; created things are susceptible to change.
- Everyone is guilty because everyone was seminally present in Adam.
- Therefore everyone deserves to be punished.
- Natural evil is a fitting punishment and came about because the human action destroyed the natural order.

- Therefore God is right not to intervene and put a stop to suffering.
- That God saves some through Christ shows that He is merciful as well as just.

Augustine started from the assumption that God is wholly good, and that God created a world free from defects. Following the teaching in Genesis 1, Augustine emphasised that 'All God has made pleased him.' Suffering and evil were therefore unknown.

He made the logical point that it is not possible for God to be responsible for evil, since evil is 'not a substance'. Instead, evil refers to what is lacking in a thing; it is a 'privation of good'. Augustine used the analogy of blindness, which is not an entity in itself but an absence of sight.

If God cannot have created evil, Augustine traced its origin to those entities within the world that have free will; namely, angels and human beings. These abused God's gift of freedom and chose wilfully to turn their attention away from God, the supreme good, and to idolise instead 'lesser goods'. In keeping with the story of the Fall in Genesis 3, he argued that the desire for power proved too much for Adam and Eve, who were tempted by Satan, a fallen angel, to break God's command and to eat the forbidden fruit.

Having explained the origin of evil, Augustine went on to show that all suffering is a fully deserved consequence of human sin. **Natural evil** originated from the loss of order within nature following the first sin. This destroyed the delicate balance of the world. It also, however, caused the world to become distanced from God In this new and damaged environment, remote from God, **moral evil** flourished and spread.

Both types of evil are interpreted as a punishment: 'All evil is either sin or the punishment for sin.' Augustine made the essential point that *all* humans, including supposedly innocent babies, deserve to suffer because *all* humans were present 'in the loins of Adam'. This reflects the ancient belief that every generation was seminally present in Adam, and therefore that every generation is guilty because they inherit his guilt for disobeying God.

Augustine concluded his theodicy with a reminder of God's grace: if God were simply just, everyone would go to their rightful punishment in Hell. Through his grace, however, God sent his son to die on the Cross so that some might be saved and go to Heaven. This shows that God is merciful as well as just.

How convincing do *you* find Augustine's response to the problem of evil?

List both positive and negative features.

How do *you* know that certain laws should not be broken?

What is the problem with holding that, in a world which has no knowledge of good or evil, God uttered the command not to eat a particular fruit?

Critique of Augustine's Theodicy

Augustine's theodicy has had considerable influence. Certain features about it have retained appeal. **Brian Davies**, for example, supports the claim that evil cannot properly be called a substance; rather, it is 'a gap between what there is and what there ought to be'. Any criticism of God would need to be based along the lines that God should somehow have created *more* than He has – which seems rather strange. For example, it is unclear *how much* more He should have created.

Augustine's argument that evil is the result of free will is another feature of the theodicy that – to some extent, at least – we can uphold. The extent to which we do so depends upon how important the gift of free will is considered to be, and whether this gift *necessarily* entails the possibility of suffering. We will consider these issues in greater detail below (see The Freewill Defence).

Despite certain advantages, Augustine's theodicy has been severely criticised for containing:

- logical error
- scientific error
- moral error

The logical problem has been expressed by **F. D. E. Schleiermacher** (1768–1834). Schleiermacher argued there was a logical contradiction in holding that a perfectly created world has gone wrong, since this would mean that evil has created itself out of nothing, which is logically impossible. Whether or not evil is a deprivation, it is still a real feature of the world, as is the suffering that it produces. As such, evil must somehow be attributed to God. Either the world was not perfect to begin with or God enabled it to go wrong.

Augustine's appeal to the freewill defence poses a logical difficulty within the specific framework of his theodicy. It is hard to see how, in a perfect world where there was no knowledge of good and evil, there could possibly be freedom to obey or disobey God, since good and evil would be unknown. The fact that God's creatures chose to disobey Him seems to suggest that there was already a knowledge of evil, which could only have come from God.

The scientific difficulties stem from Augustine's reliance upon the Genesis Creation and Fall stories. As a result, much of the argument rested upon ancient and scientifically controversial

Judaeo-Christian theology. This dependence led to two major criticisms:

- One problem is Augustine's idea that the world was made perfect by God and then damaged by humans. This contradicts evolutionary theory, which asserts that the universe has continually been developing from an earlier stage of chaos. Essential to evolution, moreover, is the innate and selfish desire for survival. This renders the Genesis concept of blissful happiness in the Garden of Eden still less easy to accept. Yet if God's world contained flaws at the outset, God must bear responsibility for evil.
- The second major weakness concerns Augustine's assumption that each human being was seminally present in Adam. This theory must be rejected on biological grounds, which means that we are not in fact guilty for Adam's sin. This means, of course, that God is not just in allowing us to suffer for someone else's sin.

One moral difficulty within Augustine's theodicy concerns his concept of Hell. Hell appears to be part of the design of the universe. This means that God must already have anticipated that the world would go wrong – and have accepted it.

Finally, although Augustine argued that God's selection of some people for Heaven shows His mercy, others would argue that it displays irrational inconsistency, further questioning God's goodness.

As a result of these criticisms, we need to conclude that, taken as a whole, Augustine's theodicy does not work.

Irenaeus' Theodicy

Central Features of the Theodicy

- God's aim when He created the world was to make humans flawless, in His likeness.
- Genuine human perfection cannot be ready-made, but must develop through free choice.
- Since God had to give us free choice, He had to give us the potential to disobey Him.
- There would be no such potential if there were never any possibility of evil. If humans were made ready-perfected, and if God policed His world continually, there would be no free will.

Something to think about

Hell is a place of complete separation from God. It is often thought to involve eternal, and therefore pointless, suffering. This marks the very opposite of the good world that God created.

If God's plans have been turned upside down in this way, what might that suggest about His omnipotence?

You need to know

Irenaeus (AD *c*.130–202) *followed* Augustine in tracing evil back to human free will. He *differs* in that he admits that God did not make a perfect world and that evil has a valuable role to play in God's plan for humans.

Irenaeus has removed the logical problem of evil appearing from out of the blue by accepting that God's world was not perfect.

What problem(s) does Irenaeus now face?

Can evil or suffering ever be valuable?

Consider some examples, perhaps where *you* suffered. Are there any occasions where, looking back, you are *glad* that you experienced suffering?

So far, Irenaeus has established that the *potential* for evil is essential to God's plans. What of *actual* evil?

Why does God not simply remove it, should it ever be chosen?

- Therefore, the natural order had to be designed with the possibility of causing harm, humans had to be imperfect, and God had to stand back from His creation.
- Humans used their freedom to disobey God, causing suffering.
- God cannot compromise our freedom by removing evil.
- Eventually, however, evil and suffering will be overcome and everyone will develop into God's likeness, living in glory in Heaven. This justifies temporary evil.

Unlike Augustine, Irenaeus admitted that God is partly responsible for evil. His responsibility extends to creating humans imperfectly, and making it their task to develop to perfection. This idea is based upon Irenaeus' interpretation of Genesis 1:26, where God said, 'Let us make man in our image, after our likeness.' Irenaeus concluded that at first, humans were made in God's *image* and only later would develop into his *likeness*. For Irenaeus, being in God's image involved having intelligence, morality and personality, yet it lacked completion. Completion would only be gained upon transformation into God's likeness. It was Irenaeus' claim that evil was an essential means to effect this transformation.

Irenaeus' biggest challenge, of course, is to explain *why* evil is necessary and *why* God did not simply create humans perfectly to begin with. We shall see that Irenaeus' supporters have added their own answers to these questions. Irenaeus' own explanation, however, was that attaining the likeness of God requires the 'willing co-operation of human individuals'. Irenaeus was effectively saying that absolute goodness could not be bestowed upon humans by God, but had to be developed by humans themselves through willing co-operation. Willing co-operation requires genuine freedom; we cannot willingly co-operate with something if we are being forced into it. Genuine freedom requires the possibility of choosing evil instead of good. God's plans therefore require the genuine possibility that our actions might produce evil.

Irenaeus explained that humans *did* choose evil, which is why the Fall occurred. But although evil clearly makes life difficult (it 'multiplies the perils' that we face), it nevertheless is beneficial in that it enables us to understand what good is:

> How, if we had no knowledge of the contrary, could we have instruction in that which is good?

Irenaeus, Against Heresies iv, xxxix.1

Imagine that you are free to choose good or evil, but every time you choose an evil deed, God intervenes and prevents any harm resulting from it.

How would the knowledge that God will always stop harm from resulting change the way you live your life? Would you *like* to live in such a world?

Why might Irenaeus say that in some way you are no longer human?

He further argued that those who say that God should never allow evil to happen are in fact saying that God should take away their humanity. For being human entails having freedom; yet if God were to intervene each time an evil act is committed, there would not in fact be any freedom to commit evil:

> If anyone do shun the knowledge of both kinds of things . . . he unaware divests himself of the character of a human being.

Irenaeus, Against Heresies iv, xxxix.1

Having explained the necessity of both potential and actual evil, Irenaeus looked ahead to Heaven, where everybody will have completed the development into God's likeness, and where the sufferings on Earth will have been long forgotten. It is important to note that under Irenaeus' scheme, it is vital that everyone attains this stage, thus marking the completion of God's creation.

Modern Additions to Irenaeus' Theodicy

We mentioned earlier that Irenaeus' line of thought has been taken up by other philosophers and developed. One major point explained by such philosophers is why God needed to allow humans to develop themselves, rather than doing it for them.

John Hick, for example, explained that goodness that has been developed by free choice is infinitely better than the ready-made 'goodness' of robots. If God wanted humans to be genuinely loving, He had to give them the opportunity to develop this quality for themselves. Were we to have been created in such a way that we would automatically always love God and obey Him, we would have been automatons and our love would have been valueless. **Peter Vardy** has clarified this through the analogy of a king who falls in love with a peasant girl. Although he would have the power to force the girl to marry him, he instead chooses to win her round of her own accord, since love cannot be created by compulsion. In the same way, God had to allow humans to develop for themselves, if their love of God was to be genuine.

If human perfection must be created by development, three things are required to enable this development to take place:

- humans had to be created imperfect
- humans had to be distanced from God
- the natural world could not be a paradise

Consider why *you* are studying philosophy of religion.

Why do your teachers not simply answer the exam questions for you, and give you a copy of the answers?

What is the difference between this situation and Irenaeus' argument that the omnipotent God needed to allow humans to develop for themselves?

Humans had to be created imperfect so as to be free to go against God. A perfect being who was already in God's likeness would never disobey Him.

They had to be created at a distance from God so that they could decide for themselves whether or not to follow His laws. John Hick called this distance an '**epistemic distance**', or a distance in the dimension of knowledge. The argument is that were God's presence to be too imminent, humans would be overwhelmed by knowledge of God's expectations. In practice, therefore, they would obey God not because they had chosen to upon their own volition, but because He was overlooking their every move.

Relating to this is the point that if the world were a paradise, in which there was no possible chance of ever causing any kind of harm, then humans would not in fact be free. They would not be free because every possible human action would result in happiness. Evil would be indistinguishable from good, since both would result in the same outcome. Consequently, humans would in effect be robots and not, in fact, humans. A further and related argument for the presence of real, actual evil is that without such evil, everyone would follow God's laws because there would never be any difficulty in doing so. Qualities such as courage, honour and love would all be impossible. As a result, there would be no opportunity to develop into God's likeness – since these qualities are essential to such development.

In this case, the counterfactual hypothesis establishes that God's purpose would not be possible in a world completely free from suffering and evil. So, while it may not be possible to demonstrate the need for every example of suffering, the world must contain natural laws that can produce some suffering. Therefore, Hick concluded that while our world is not

> designed for the maximisation of human pleasure and the minimisation of human pain, it may nevertheless be rather well adapted to the quite different purpose of 'soul making'.

John H. Hick, Philosophy of Religion, 4th edn, Prentice-Hall, 1990

In this way, Irenaeus' theodicy can be developed to explain further why at least *some* natural evil is essential, as well as moral evil.

Finally, we shall consider *modern developments* of Irenaeus' belief that Heaven must be the goal of everyone. There are three main reasons:

- The challenges of the world do not always result in genuine human development. Often, they result in horrific suffering. If life were to end at death, God's original purpose, the creation of beings in his likeness, would have been frustrated.
- Only a supremely good future in Heaven can justify the magnitude of the suffering.
- Many apparently 'evil' people are in fact nothing more than 'victims of the system'; people who perhaps have been brought up badly and who cannot be held responsible for their actions. It is therefore essential for God's justice that no one is overlooked.

Something to think about

Why do you think many people find Irenaeus' theodicy more credible than that of Augustine?

Critique of Irenaeus' Theodicy

Irenaeus' theodicy allows room for the modern concept of evolution and avoids Augustine's stumbling block of evil appearing from nowhere. It has, however, attracted other criticisms:

- the concept of Heaven for all seems unjust
- the quantity and gravity of suffering is unacceptable
- suffering can never be an expression of God's love

Let us look at these in turn.

Something to think about

If you had known, at school, that *no matter what you did with your time* you were going to gain the top grades in every exam, how would your behaviour have differed?

If this had been the case, clearly you would have been unpopular with friends.

Why might you *yourself* not have benefited from guaranteed success?

The Concept of Heaven for All Seems Unjust

Irenaeus' view that everyone will go to Heaven has attracted criticism because it does not seem fair and therefore calls God's justice into question. Religious people object to it because it contradicts religious texts, including the Bible and the Qur'an, which promise punishment for the unrighteous. It also makes moral behaviour pointless: If everyone is to be rewarded with Heaven, what is the point of going out of our way to do good? We are left with no incentive to make the development that Irenaeus regarded as so important.

The Quantity and Gravity of Suffering is Unacceptable

We might accept from the counterfactual hypothesis that the process of soul-making could not take place in a paradise. Does our world, however, need to contain the extent and severity of suffering found in events such as the Holocaust? Would it not have been sufficient for 4 million Jews to die instead of 6 million?

Can this be an expression of God's love?

Suffering can Never be an Expression of God's Love

The third problem is a more fundamental one. It consists of the concern that love can never be expressed by allowing *any* amount of suffering, no matter what the reason. **D. Z. Phillips** argued that it would never be justifiable to hurt someone in order to help them. When we consider the magnitude of suffering in our world, this problem is all the more serious.

Irenaeus' theodicy cannot, therefore, be accepted wholesale without difficulty. Yet, as with Augustine, its emphasis upon the importance of free will has proved a popular defence in recent times. We shall now consider this part of the theodicy separately.

You need to know

The **freewill defence** comes in several forms. All of them need to establish that:

• it was necessary for God to give us free will

• free will necessarily entails the possibility of evil

The Freewill Defence

Both classical theodicies contain the argument that evil was a tragic consequence of human free will. More recently, this line of thought has been separated and developed into a theodicy in its own right, known as the **freewill defence**.

The Basic Argument

The world is the logically necessary environment for humans – the type of place that enables humans to be humans – for the world provides true freedom in the form of real choices which produce real goodness or real harm. Without such choices, we should not be free – and nor, therefore, should we be human.

Richard Swinburne has supported this defence and has helped to counter some of the criticisms that are often levelled against it. One such criticism asks why God needs to allow the scale of suffering witnessed in the Holocaust, for example. Swinburne answered:

> The less he allows men to bring about large scale horrors, the less the freedom and responsibility he gives them. [We are] ... asking that God should make a toy world, a world where things matter, but not very much; where we can choose and our choices can make a small difference but the real choices remain God's. For he simply would not allow us the choice of doing real harm ... He would be like an over-protective parent who will not let his child out of sight for a moment.
>
> *Richard Swinburne*

Something to think about

Swinburne used the analogy of God as a good parent who allows an older child greater freedom in order to grow up.

Does this analogy work? What quality does God have that human parents do not have?

In other words, a God who intervened to prevent the large-scale horrors would compromise the gift of freedom and remove human responsibility, thus preventing genuine human development.

Swinburne took the example of death, and argued that, despite the suffering it causes, it is nevertheless essential to the freewill defence. This is because death means that life, and the chances that each life contains, are limited. This is essential because only in a limited lifespan can we have genuine responsibility for our actions:

> A situation of temptation with infinite chances is no situation of temptation at all. If there is always another chance there is no risk. There would not be overriding reasons not to do a bad act, if you are always preserved from its consequences ... If you cannot damn yourself no matter how hard you go on trying, your salvation will be inevitable ... A God who wishes that all men shall be saved is a being of dubious moral status.
>
> *Richard Swinburne*

In other words, if we were immortal there will always be another chance for us to make amends. The world therefore needs to contain natural laws that can cause death, however painful this may be. The freewill defence therefore renders death explainable.

Critique of the Freewill Defence

The freewill defence adds to the work of Augustine and Irenaeus, giving further explanation as to why some evil and suffering may be necessary. However, it attracts some of the criticisms that we have already considered; especially the concern that divine love cannot be expressed through such suffering.

It also does not explain *why* people chose to turn away from God. This, in turn, prompts the interesting question as to whether God could have created a race of genuinely free beings who, nevertheless, would never in fact have chosen to commit evil. While a majority of philosophers have argued that this guarantee could never be made with genuinely free beings, **J. L. Mackie** provides a challenge:

> If there is no logical impossibility in a man's freely choosing the good on one, or on several occasions, there cannot be a logical impossibility in his freely choosing the good on every occasion. God was not, then, faced with a choice between making innocent automata and making beings who, in acting freely, would sometimes go wrong: there was open to him the obviously better possibility of making beings who would act freely but always go right. Clearly, his failure to avail himself of this possibility is inconsistent with his being both omnipotent and wholly good.

> *J. L. Mackie, 'Evil and omnipotence', Mind, April 1955*

If this challenge holds true, it entails the death of not only the freewill defence but also the theodicies of Augustine and Irenaeus. For Mackie is effectively arguing that God's gift of freewill is in no way an excuse for the existence of evil. God should simply have made free beings who would never in fact have chosen to sin.

All we can say on the matter here is that there is disagreement upon this issue. **John Hick**, for example, argued that while humans might have appeared to be freely choosing the good on all occasions, in relation to God they would not be free, because God would have made them in such a way that He knew they would never choose evil. From God's point of view, therefore, such humans would be no more satisfying than robots, because their actions would have already been concluded when they were made. The issue becomes extremely complex when we relate it to the concept of free will and determinism. For if God knows in advance what His creation will do in any case, does this not suggest that He has preordained evil? And yet if He had no idea what they would do, does this not suggest that evil rather took God by surprise, thus questioning His omnipotence? At this point, it is fitting for us to conclude our discussion on the freewill defence!

Alternative Counters to the Problem of Evil

Other philosophers have argued for the existence of God by offering more radical alternatives. Some have denied God's omnipotence, while others have questioned our understanding of evil. Here, we shall consider **process theodicy** as an example of the former, and **monism** as an example of the latter.

You need to know

The **process theodicy** rests upon the assertion that God is not omnipotent.

Process Theodicy

Process philosophy is a distinctive world-view developed by **A. N. Whitehead** (CE 1861–1947). During the twentieth century, **David Griffin** developed a theodicy based upon the process format. Given the complexities of the theory, our examination here must necessarily be brief. John Hick's *Philosophy of Religion* gives a fuller account.

Since God is not omnipotent, He did not create the universe. The universe is an 'uncreated process which includes the deity'. In other words, God is part of the world and is bound by natural laws. God's role in creation was limited to starting off the evolutionary process. Since this process has led to the development of humans who exert their own influence on the world, God no longer has total control, since humans are free to ignore God. Moreover, they have a very limited knowledge of God's will, since He did not fashion them after His own likeness: 'It is necessarily the case that God cannot completely control the creatures.'

An important feature of process theodicy is that God suffers when evil is committed. This follows naturally from the fact that God is part of the world – affected by it, yet unable to control it. Whitehead therefore described God as the 'fellow sufferer who understands'.

Although God is not powerful enough to stop evil, He nevertheless must bear some responsibility for it, since it was God who started off the process of evolution in the knowledge that He would be unable to control it. In Griffin's words:

> God is responsible for evil in the sense of having urged the creation forward to those states in which discordant feelings could be felt with greater intensity.

D. Griffin, God, Power and Evil: a Process Theodicy,
Westminster Press, 1976

The theodicy needs to explain satisfactorily why God took such a risk. It does this by arguing that the universe has produced enough quantity and quality to outweigh the evil. In other words, given a choice between the universe we live in and no universe at all, the former is preferable. This, it is argued, justifies God's work.

Critique of the Theodicy

To its adherents, process theodicy does bear several advantages:

- It removes the stumbling block of why, if God is all-loving and all-powerful, He simply does not put an end to all suffering. It removes it with the simple answer that He cannot.
- For religious believers, the fact that God suffers may be encouraging, since people realise that God can understand what they are going through.
- Within the process scheme, there is no certainty that God will triumph in the end. The theodicy may therefore encourage some believers to join in the fight against evil and secure victory. It is not a theodicy that encourages inertia, for such would result in disaster for all.

Despite these benefits, however, there are severe criticisms. One is the argument that it is not in fact a theodicy at all. This term, we recall, refers to a justification of God in the face of evil. Since process philosophy removes the concept of omnipotence from God, it does not in fact justify him at all. It actually denies the God of Classical Theism. This conclusion is simply unacceptable to many, both on religious and on philosophical grounds. It is uncertain, for example, whether a being with such limited power is worthy of worship.

While, for some, the uncertainty of the future could encourage a valiant effort, for others it might simply fill them with despair. If God cannot guarantee anything, what is the point of human efforts? Finally, the theodicy has justified God's initiation of evolution on the grounds that good has outweighed evil. It is unlikely that this justification would appeal to those who have actually borne the suffering! Since there is no promise of Heaven, there is no certainty that the suffering of the innocent will ever be rewarded. For example, the fact that nature has produced a Leonardo da Vinci hardly makes up for the suffering and deaths of those involved in the Lisbon Earthquake!

Something to think about

Imagine you are about to play a football match. It is an important event and you have prepared well. *You know that your opponents are good players.*

How would this affect your attitude and the way you would play?

Something to think about

List the reasons why you would not be willing to worship a God with limited power.

If your life were to contain a lot of suffering, how much of a comfort would it be that your limited God was suffering alongside you?

Monism

If process theodicy alters the concept of the God of Classical Theism, monism alters instead the concept of evil by arguing that, in fact, evil is not a reality. For if everything is *good*, evil must be a mere illusion in our minds. Monists argue that we would recognise it as good if only we could see the whole picture.

Something to think about

Identify an occasion on which your *first* experience of something or someone was unpleasant, but subsequent experiences made you realise you had been mistaken.

Could our experiences of suffering in the world likewise be mistaken?

One of the challenges facing monism is to explain why we suffer the illusion of evil.

Baruch Spinoza (1632–1677)

Spinoza said that it is because we make two mistakes when assessing things:

- First, we assess things in terms of their usefulness to ourselves. This bias means that we often do not recognise the real value of things.
- Second, we assume that there are general norms to which humans and animals conform. As a result, we consider both a shrivelled tree and a sinful man to be defective.

Spinoza argued, however, that if we considered the universe objectively, we should accept that each thing has a unique value:

> All things are necessarily what they are, and in Nature, there is no good and evil.
>
> *Baruch Spinoza*

Gottfried Leibniz

Leibniz, in his work *Theodicy*, supported the monist idea by arguing that evil *must* be an illusion, since this world must be the best of all possible worlds. This is because God, in His infinite wisdom and goodness, could never have chosen any other. In this way, Leibniz moved from his definition of God to a definition of the world, suspending his empirical judgement in the process. For those who question why God should allow the illusion of suffering, Leibniz explained that the world could not have been made truly perfect, since only God, the uncreated being, can be perfect.

Mary Baker Eddy

Baker Eddy, from the Christian Science movement, upheld the monist line by arguing that evil is a mere matter of the mind: 'The only reality of sin, sickness and death is the awful fact that unrealities seem real to human, erring belief.' A boil, for example, 'simply manifests, through inflammation, and swelling, a belief in pain and this belief is called a boil'.

Critique of Monism

Monism is not, however, widely supported. It denies the reality of evil, which contradicts not only empirical evidence but also religious belief. The Bible repeatedly demonstrates the genuine reality of evil. From a philosophical point of view, however, it does not matter, in fact, whether or not evil is an illusion. For even if it is illusory, it is real enough for those who believe that it is making them suffer. For those so afflicted, it is as unpleasant as if it were real. The theodicy fails even to its adherents, since it does not explain why God allows people to suffer from their 'beliefs'.

Perhaps most seriously, it is a very dangerous theodicy, since it trivialises the concept of evil, making it seem unimportant. If the world as a whole is good and if illusion is not real, why should we try to be good and avoid evil? More to the point, if so much of what we believe to be the case is illusory, how can we be sure what behaviour we should be trying to uphold and what to reject?

Conclusion

We have now considered a variety of responses to the problem of evil. Some of these responses adjust the nature of God and the nature of evil. Others attempt to harmonise evil with the existence of the God of Classical Theism. We have seen that although each theodicy has its strengths, each is also beset by weaknesses.

At the start of this chapter, we said that the problem of evil was a major argument against the existence of God. Since we have in fact been unable to resolve it with any certainty, does this then mean that its force against God's existence is conclusive? The answer will generally depend upon the beliefs of the subject.

For those who already feel that the existence of God is improbable, the problem of evil will merely strengthen this conviction.

To those who already have faith in God, however, the response will be rather different. Reference may be made to God's goodness to humanity, evidenced in gifts such as His messengers, or eternal life and the like. The problem of evil itself will be dealt with quickly by what is sometimes known as the 'eternal cop-out clause'; the argument that we, being human, cannot understand the ways of the divine, and that God, in His infinite wisdom and purpose, must have some deep and unavoidable purpose for the existence of evil. And since there is no logical inconsistency here – since it is not logically impossible that the God of Classical Theism could have some use for evil within His plan – the position of the faithful is unassailable.

In **John Hick's** words:

> Our 'solution', then, to this baffling problem of excessive and undeserved suffering is a frank appeal to the positive power of mystery. Such suffering remains unjust and inexplicable, haphazard and cruelly excessive. The mystery of dysteleological suffering is a real mystery, impenetrable to the rationalizing human mind.

John H. Hick, Evil and the God of Love, Macmillan, 1978

Something to think about

We all accept that certain things, such as the law of gravity, exist, even if we are unable to explain them fully. Surely it is no more unreasonable, therefore, to accept the existence of God, even though we cannot explain suffering?

Essay questions

AS

(a) Outline the problem of the apparent existence of evil for a believer.

(b) Explain and evaluate the answers which a believer gives to account for the apparent existence of evil in the world.

A2

(a) 'God is the omnipotent wholly good creator of all things.' 'There is evil in the world.' Explain these two statements and show why they are said to be contradictory.

(b) Explain and assess the extent to which **three** theodicies seek to remove the contradiction.

Chapter 9　Religion and Psychology

You need to know

Look back at the meaning of
empirical on page 4.

Introduction

In this chapter, we look at the contribution of psychology to the understanding of religious behaviour. The majority of the arguments for the existence of God rely on the premise that God is an objective reality whose existence can be proved by logical or empirical means. The God of Classical Theism is understood to be the Creator of the world, who stands apart from it and yet is able to intervene in it. The psychological study of religion leads to the very different conclusion that the God worshipped by believers is first and foremost a construct of the human mind. Instead of attempting to prove or disprove the existence of God, psychologists ask instead 'What makes people religious?' Examining the mental processes involved in religion, they conclude that, under certain circumstances, the brain is stimulated into a religious outlook. The stimulus can be emotionally, socially or physically based. This is not to say, incidentally, that psychologists are asserting that God cannot exist. What they do say is that religious belief can be explained without requiring God, and that the primary reason why people adopt a religion is because their psychological structure encourages them to.

In this chapter, we shall consider the work of the two giants in this field:

- **Sigmund Freud** and
- **Carl Jung**

Freud's Theory of Religion

You need to know

The term **illusion** here does not mean *error* or *mistaken belief* but, rather, *a belief derived from human wishes.*

At its simplest, Freud's argument is that *religion is an illusion based on human wishes*. It is created by the mind to help us overcome:

- inner psychological conflict
- stress, which stems from the structure of society
- fear of the dangers of the natural world

What Freud was saying is that in certain circumstances, the human mind will create beliefs and images to satisfy its most

Freud and Jung in 1909

Something to think about

You may have a desperate desire that England will, one day, win the World Cup again. As such, on the basis of Freud's definition, this belief is an illusion. It will, however, hopefully be perfectly true.

basic longings and desires. It is this idea to which the term 'wish fulfilment' refers.

Given what Freud meant by the term 'illusion', when he applied it to religion, he did not mean that religion is necessarily false or that there can be no God, but that it answers the inner needs of the person.

Whether or not an illusion is true depends upon whether there is any grounding in hard evidence for its claims, or whether it is picked out of the air by the mind to answer its needs. In the case of religion, it is Freud's argument that practically *all* of its features – including the apparent evidence in its favour – can be explained in terms of the mind's wish-fulfilment. We shall therefore consider in more detail Freud's three arguments as to the psychological purpose of religion.

Religion as an Aid to Overcome Inner Psychological Conflict

This forms the main body of Freud's work on religion. We shall start with a summary (which will necessarily seem unbelievable to the uninitiated!):

- religion is a form of neurotic illness
- it stems from the unconscious mind
- it results from incompletely repressed traumatic memories
- the trauma is invariably sexual in nature
- therefore religion is an illusion resulting from sexual difficulties

Freud believed that the construction of the mind and the development of the human personality led to deep inner conflicts, invariably sexual in nature. The mind's solution to such trauma is to lock it away in the unconscious mind. Such 'locking away' is unsuccessful, and the trauma re-emerges later in the form of religion. We shall begin our more detailed study with some background information.

Freud's work with patients who were suffering from hysteria led him to conclude that, in addition to the conscious areas, the mind also contains unconscious parts which we cannot normally access.

It was Freud's work on hypnosis and his studies of dreams which led him to realise that the unconscious mind comprises a vast store of information about events that we consider long forgotten.

In his work with patients suffering from hysteria, he was able to demonstrate that unpleasant memories that are trapped in the unconscious can surface later in the form of hysterical behaviour. This often takes the form of compulsive–obsessional disorders, such as compulsive hand-washing.

The link with religion was made when Freud noticed close similarities between the behaviour of his patients in relation to the source of their obsession and that of religious people in relation to the object of their worship. He noticed, for example, that both involve highly specific ritual behaviour. In both cases, this behaviour is filled with symbolic meaning for its followers, while at the same time it appears completely meaningless to the uninitiated. In both cases, failure to perform a particular act results in severe guilt, which is inexplicable to others, and in both cases the object of attention is regarded with ambivalence.

From this, Freud concluded that religion was a form of neurotic behaviour, caused, as in the case of other hysterias, by traumas buried deep within the psyche. The central, and perhaps most startling, feature of Freud's argument was his belief that the trauma in question was invariably *sexual* in nature:

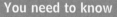

You need to know

A **neurotic illness** involves physical symptoms (pain, compulsive behaviour, etc.) which – unlike, for example, a broken leg – have no physical cause, but are rooted in the *mind*. Hysteria, obsessions, anxieties and phobias are all neurotic symptoms.

You need to know

The **conscious** mind contains our present thoughts and accessible memories.

The **unconscious** mind contains basic drives, such as breathing, and forgotten memories.

You need to know

The **psyche** is the technical term for the *mind*. The term is understood to include all the conscious and unconscious components of the mind.

At the bottom of every case of hysteria there are one or more occurrences of premature sexual experience, occurrences which belong to the earliest years of childhood.

Sigmund Freud, The Aetiology of Hysteria, 1896

This was because, for Freud, the sexual drive, or **libido**, was the body's most basic urge and, as such, the one most capable of causing psychological problems within the development of the individual.

The trauma that lies behind neurotic behaviour results from problems in the sexual development of the child. The major problem concerns what Freud termed the **Oedipus complex**.

Putting this simply, the sexual development of the child results in trauma. Whereas the suckling child was used to having its mother's sole attention, when the libido is transferred to the sexual organ, there is an already present rival in the form of the father. The acute feelings of jealousy and hatred combine with the respect and fear previously felt for the father. The father is thus viewed with ambivalence. This desire to possess the mother and the ambivalence towards the father is the Oedipus complex. Freud goes on to say that 'In the conditions of our civilisation it is invariably doomed to a frightening end.' As a result, the child represses the conflict deep into the unconscious mind.

The mechanism of repression, however, is only partially effective. While the repressed event or desire may *appear* to be long forgotten, the mind continues to struggle to prevent it from re-emerging into the conscious. As a result of the conflict, the event is channelled out in the form of neurotic symptoms. One of these symptoms is religion which, as such, is termed the 'universal obsessional neurosis of mankind'.

You need to know

For Freud, the sex drive involves far more than the desire to have sex. It represents the body's general, subconscious desire for satisfaction (**libido**), which stems from the unconscious. In babies, for example, the libido centres upon the mouth, and the desire to suckle from the mother. This changes as the child develops and is gradually transformed to the mature desire among adults to reproduce.

You need to know

Repression is the name given to the process whereby the mind subconsciously takes unpleasant memories and locks them away in the mind.

Support for Freud's Theory of Religion

It is unsurprising that Freud's arguments caused uproar when they became known. To some, they were deeply offensive; to others, merely bizarre. As the father of psychoanalysis, however, Freud was a respected figure in various branches of psychology and his considerable work with patients claimed to provide support for his theories. We shall now consider the evidence upon which Freud's claims rest.

If Freud's theories are to have any chance of success, it is clear that two things at least must be established:

- that the Oedipus complex is a universal sexual trauma
- that buried trauma can reappear in the form of religion

Support for the Oedipus Complex

Freud used the work of Charles Darwin to speculate that in primitive societies, the social unit was something called the **primal horde**. Hordes were groups of people arranged around a single dominant male who had total authority over the group and who held claim over all the females. Over time, the resentment of the younger males grew, until they grouped together to kill him.

This resulted in **ambivalent** feelings towards him – hatred on the one hand, combined with veneration on the other. The strength of these feelings was so great that the father became idolised and transformed into the totem of the group. (This will be explained later.)

This shows that the Oedipus complex is not simply a personal trauma, but one that has affected all society at a historical level. It helps to explain why religion is universal and why the concept of God is such a powerful one (because it stems from a historical experience that still affects us). Freud believed in some kind of psychological mechanism whereby guilt for the original crime is passed on genetically.

How does Religion Result from Sexual Guilt?

Freud provided a complicated argument to show that the natural reaction of the psyche was to control feelings of guilt by transferring it away from itself and on to surrounding objects and people.

The first stage of the development is **animism**. Freud believed that, when suffering from extreme guilt, the mind's defence mechanism is to create idols (or totems). This involves investing stones, trees or animals with spirits. Having done this, the mind can redirect the feelings of guilt on to the idol and can make amends through prayer and sacrifice, for example. The mind is therefore able to control the feelings of guilt.

In effect, the idol or totem is a transformation of the father. And just as the father was regarded with ambivalence, so too is the totem. Freud's case studies (such as 'The Wolf Man') demonstrated that people suffering from the Oedipus complex frequently transferred their fear on to animals. Freud drew further historical support from the primal horde. He observed that as veneration of the father grew, the veneration was transferred on to a totem animal. The totem became the symbol of identity of the group. *The ambivalence, note,*

You need to know

Freud provided five major case studies to illustrate the effects of the Oedipus complex. One of them, known as 'The Wolf Man', concerned a young man, Sergei Pankejeff, who had a phobia of animals.

After much hypnosis, Freud traced the phobia back to the time when the young Pankejeff witnessed sexual acts between his parents. Freud reasoned that, over time, the repressed trauma resulted in the fear of wolves *and* of God.

remained – for while it was generally forbidden to harm the animal in any way, once a year there would be a ritual killing and eating of the totem animal.

The second stage of the development is into **religion.** As time passed, the animist emphasis on the totem proved unsatisfactory. As longing for the father grew, so did his reputation. Eventually he took on divine significance and became transformed into the gods of religion. Freud points out that the gods of religions are regarded with the same *ambivalence* as was the original father figure, proving that there is a connection. A favourite example concerned the Christian God who, generally speaking, is venerated and treated with great reverence. Every now and then, however, he is ceremonially killed and eaten in the Communion Feast. This example provides an exact link with the animist ritual killing of the totem.

Religion is therefore an illusion created by the mind to help us come to terms with the powerfully ambivalent emotions suffered during sexual development. It is a means of resolving this inner conflict. At the start, however, we noted that there were two other reasons why the mind created the illusion of religion.

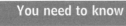

Something to think about

Identify some examples of the conflict between your own, selfish, desires, and the laws and constraints by which society limits them.

What would happen if your innate tendencies were *not* limited?

You need to know

Sublimation is the process by which the sexual instinct is redirected into other activities, such as culture and art.

Religion as an Illusion to Overcome the Conflict between our Natures and Civilisation

Freud demonstrated how the nature of our society is at conflict with our most basic desires. We have seen one such conflict, in the form of the Oedipal desire to kill the father and possess the mother.

Were conflicts such as that of Oedipus unbridled, society would not be able to operate. Society depends upon structure and order; those who have responsibility to govern must have authority and this will inevitably conflict with the desires of each individual.

The essential point is that religion provides a *reason* to submit to authority. It explains our suffering in terms of the need to obey an omnipotent God. It promises reward for suffering in the afterlife and makes society bearable.

Religion therefore provides the necessary motivation for sublimation to occur. The most natural outlet being forbidden, it forces our libidos into other areas. Having so motivated the believer, it provides ample scope for sublimation in fields such as religious art, music or charity work.

Something to think about

List some fears that religion helps people to overcome.

Religion as an Illusion to Help us Overcome our Fear of Natural Forces

This last point is perhaps the simplest. Freud's point is that the natural human response to being confronted by natural forces – including death – is one of panic and helplessness at our defencelessness and solitude.

Religion helps by creating the belief that the natural forces are no longer impersonal, and that we are no longer powerless; for through religious devotion we believe we can control them:

> Everything that happens in the world is an expression of the intentions of an intelligence superior to us, which in the end, though its ways and byways are difficult to follow, orders everything for the best – that is, it makes it enjoyable for us.

Sigmund Freud, Civilisation and its Discontents, 1930

Religious belief provides for the adult a father figure who can protect just as the father protected the child. To the 'strange, superior' powers of nature, the adult 'lends . . . the features belonging to the figure of his father; he creates for himself the gods'.

Freud's Conclusion Regarding Religion

At the outset we explained that Freud does not provide any logical proof against the possibility of religion. Strictly speaking, he admitted that his arguments prove nothing, since God could exist objectively anyway. In practice, however, he pointed out that beliefs that are derived from basic psychological needs turn out to be false. The beliefs of obsessional neurotics, for example, invariably have no grounding in fact. Freud therefore argued that in the absence of any other evidence for religion, we are justified in concluding that it is false. He does not leave things here, but goes on to support a complete rejection of all things religious. Towards the end of *The Future of an Illusion*, Freud creates a conversation with an opponent to his beliefs about religion. This opponent raises two points on the importance of religion.

First, *without* religion, civilisation would turn into anarchy:

> If men are taught that there is no almighty and all-just God, no divine world order and no future life, they will feel exempt

from all obligation to obey the precepts of civilisation. Everyone will follow his asocial, egoistical instincts . . . and chaos will come again.

Sigmund Freud, The Future of an Illusion, 1927

Secondly, depriving people of religion seems needlessly cruel: 'Countless people find their one consolation in religious doctrines and can only bear life with their help.'

In his reply, Freud admitted that religion has performed 'great services for civilisation'. He also accepted that if religion were entirely positive, it would indeed be cruel to deprive people of it, illusion though it may be. He went on to argue, however, that religion is *not* in fact beneficial. It does not prevent people from rebelling against the restrictions of society. Moreover, many believers abuse religion for their own purposes, to justify social immoralities. He gave the example of penance: 'One sinned, and then one made a sacrifice, and then one was free to sin once more.' Religion has all too often been used as a tool against the oppressed, to keep them oppressed. Freud argued that we have been 'over-rating its necessity for mankind'.

Freud's suggested alternative is to replace religion with a scientific, rational understanding of the world. This, he argued, would make people *more* willing to obey the demands of civilisation, because they would see them as being for their own personal good. He believed it possible that humans can be educated to make their unruly passions subservient to their wills. Although many would see this as unrealistic, Freud argued that the pain of removing religion would be more than justified by the benefits.

A Critical Appraisal of Freud's Work

We cannot deny that Freud had a brilliant intellect, nor that he has had a great influence on the Western understanding of the mind. There are few today, however, who accept his theories wholesale. For as **Michael Palmer** argues, in *Freud and Jung on Religion*, 'almost all the evidence that Freud presents has been discredited in one way or another'. The following areas in particular have been attacked:

* the historical and anthropological evidence regarding the primal horde
* the psychological evidence regarding the Oedipus complex

- Freud's dependence on a narrow selection of evidence
- Freud's conclusion that religion should be overthrown

Historical and Anthropological Evidence Regarding the Primal Horde

This has now been discredited. The whole theory of the horde was based on Darwin's mere speculations. It is not now accepted that people were grouped exclusively in hordes. Instead, it is likely there was much greater variety. Not all societies had totem objects that they worshipped, and there is no evidence for the ambivalent attitude towards the totems that was demonstrated by the totem meal; **E. E. Evans-Pritchard** doubts that this ever happened. The idea that guilt is handed down from generation to generation has likewise been discredited.

This criticism damages Freud's claim that religion is guilt-based, because it removes the major source of guilt. The primal crime never happened – and could not transmit guilt even if it had taken place. It also weakens the Oedipus complex theory, since the primal crime was an important illustration of its effect on society.

Psychological Evidence Regarding the Oedipus Complex

This has been attacked, the major critic of Freud's theory of the Oedipus complex being **Bronislaw Malinowski**, in his book *Sex and Repression*. We remember that Freud first needed the complex to be universal, for it to be the cause of all religion, and secondly needed it to be caused by our natures for it to precede religion and be the cause of it. Malinowski attacked both these points. First, he pointed to the Trobriand race, where the role of the father is more that of a weak nurse. In this race there is no evidence of the complex. Their religion, therefore, must have originated elsewhere. Secondly, looking at the animal world, he found nothing inherent in the nature of animals that could cause such a complex. The role of both father and mother is one of support. Malinowski argued instead that the complex is caused *by* the strict rules of religion – rather than being the cause *of* them.

This attack on the Oedipus complex leads to the conclusion that sexual guilt is not in fact the cause of religion. As a result, Freud's attack upon religion does not contain the force that it was once believed to have.

A Narrow Selection of Evidence

The third criticism concerns Freud's dependence on a narrow selection of evidence. His theories relied on the importance of the *father figure*, which is developed by the mind into the *male God* of Judaism or Christianity. They therefore failed to take account of religions based upon female deities, such as the Egyptian Isis cult, or religions which do not have any single dominant object of worship, such as Buddhism. They also failed to take account of societies such as the Trobriand race, where the father played an insignificant role in the development of the child. In societies such as these, the Oedipus complex could not be attributed to tensions with the father, since no such tensions occurred.

Freud can therefore be criticised for constructing a theory to explain the societies and religions with which he was familiar, and ignoring those of others. In a similar way, we can criticise the way in which he generalised the results of his five case studies, assuming that the Oedipus complex that he detected in those instances at work was in fact at work everywhere.

The Overthrowing of Religion

Freud's conclusion that religion should be overthrown constitutes the fourth major criticism. **Donald Winnicott**, for example, has argued that religion is an essential buffer between the mind and external reality. Religion is useful in that it helps humans adapt to their environment by providing a source of comfort and familiarity. The role and value of religion are similar therefore to those of art and music.

Finally, **Ana-Maria Rizzuto** has argued that religion is no more of an illusion than science. Both disciplines require us to interpret data and impose order on the world. Freud's assumption that science has the sole claim to the truth is therefore unacceptable. Rizzuto has therefore argued that Freud has not so much removed the illusion of religion but, rather, replaced religion with an illusion.

Jung's Theory of Religion

Carl Gustav Jung (1875–1961) spent part of his life working alongside Freud. The first conversation that the two had together is reported to have lasted for over 13 hours. Yet although Jung was at first influenced by Freud, this did not prevent him from pursuing his own ideas. These ultimately led him to reject many of Freud's conclusions, and especially those concerning religion. Although he accepted that religion was a psychological phenomenon, he objected to Freud's conclusions that:

- religion is a neurotic illness caused by sexual trauma
- religion is a dangerous entity, to be exposed and overthrown

Jung replaced Freud's conclusions with the following observations:

- religion is a natural process that stems from the *archetypes* within the unconscious mind
- it performs the function of harmonising the psyche
- as such, it is a beneficial phenomenon
- the removal of religion would lead to psychological problems

The Background to Jung's Work

Jung's theory of religion stems from his own unique understanding of psychology. Two features of this are essential in order to understand Jung's work:

- Jung's concept of neuroses and the libido
- Jung's concept of the mind

Jung's Concept of Neuroses and the Libido

Jung's work with patients suffering from schizophrenia led him to reject Freud's view that neuroses were caused by repressed sexuality; for although schizophrenia was a neurosis, it had no obvious sexual component. He concluded that the complete loss of self-awareness from which schizophrenics suffer is something far greater than mere sexual disturbance. He was also unconvinced by Freud's view that the suckling of a baby was a sexual act. From these observations, he concluded that religion, as another 'neurosis', in no way depended upon a sexual trauma. He also concluded that the libido, as the cause of neuroses that affect the whole personality, was something more complicated than a mere sexual drive.

Jung noted how people who were dreaming, or suffering from psychic disorders, were often preoccupied with similar ideas and images. The schizophrenic Miss Miller, for example, had a dream in which her desire for God was compared with a moth's desire for light. Jung noted how this parallel between God and light can be found in countless religious

You need to know

Jung viewed the **libido** as the source of *psychic energy*. If its flow was interrupted, neuroses would result.

The rejection of the sexual basis of the libido constitutes Jung's greatest split with Freud.

Something to think about

With the other members of your group, identify any similarities in the types of thing you have dreamt about. Many people, for example, have dreamt that they are being chased by something.

If there are any common features, how would *you* account for them?

traditions. The Aztec preoccupation with the Sun and the Christian view of Jesus as 'Light of the World' are two examples. Jung provided the more precise parallel between a male schizophrenic's delusion that there was an erect phallus on the Sun and an ancient religious text in the work of Alberecht Dieterich, which spoke of a tube hanging from the Sun.

To account for the similarities in mental images, Jung postulated a further division of the unconscious mind, into the **personal unconscious** and the **collective unconscious**.

The collective unconscious is the oldest part of the mind. It contains the blueprints for a whole range of ideas and images. According to this theory, the fantasy of Miss Miller and the likeness drawn by religions between light and the deity are all derived from this collective unconscious; for each one of us is born with the tendency to conceive similar kinds of primordial images. One effect of this tendency is that similar images will be produced in dreams. We shall see that Jung believed that the God concept is one of these primordial images. The collective unconscious means, therefore, that many of our ideas about God will be shared with other people.

Jung gave the technical name **archetype** to the part of the psyche that creates these images.

One of the reasons why Jung's concept of the archetypes has come under fire is because it has sometimes been misunderstood. Jung was *not* saying that the experiences of our ancestors are somehow handed down to us in the form of a set of mental pictures with which we are born. He was saying that the mind contains structures which, when combined with the knowledge gained through our experiences, construct uniform images. In Jung's words, in his book *Symbols of Transformation*, it is not 'a question of inherited ideas, but of a functional disposition to produce the same, or very similar, ideas'.

Two of Jung's archetypes are the **persona** and the **shadow**. The persona is the tendency to put up a front to cover our true natures, for the benefit of society. The shadow denotes the disposition to portray the darker sides of our characters. In dreams, the persona may manifest itself in images of ourselves trapped inside a heavy coat of armour, or appearing at a party in a disguise. The shadow, on the other hand, may reveal itself in the form of personifications of evil; for example, Satan, monsters or even a mother-in-law!

You need to know

The **personal unconscious** contains the forgotten memories of the individual.

The **collective unconscious** is common to all human beings. It is inherited and does not depend on the personal experience of the individual.

You need to know

The **archetypes** can be seen as 'image generators'. They are distinct from the actual images that they generate.

Something to think about

Consider the difference between the hunger drive and the desire to eat a roast dinner. You are born with a disposition to feel hungry. You are not born with the innate knowledge of roast dinners.

Through the experiences of your life, however, the feeling of hunger combines with your knowledge of food and manifests itself in the desire for a particular food.

God as an Archetype

Concerning religion, Jung's central claim was that our images of God are themselves archetypal. In other words, each of us is born with the tendency to generate religious images of gods, angels and other religious phenomena. The same principles apply here as with the other archetypes. That is, the actual images that we have of God are picked up through our own experiences in the world. The disposition to generate them is, however, innate.

One final point to make here is that Jung argued that in a sense, *any* images or thoughts that are derived from the archetypes can be considered to be religious.

As such, Jung argued, in *Psychology and Religion*, that 'the numinosum – *whatever its cause may be* – is an experience of the subject independent of his will'. He stated that a religious experience is always 'due to a cause external to the individual'. He added, however: 'The numinosum is either a quality belonging to a visible object or the influence of an invisible presence that causes a peculiar alteration of consciousness.' Upon this understanding, *any* experience which is archetypal in origin can be classed as religious, since it involves an invisible presence, independent of the subject's will, which causes the required 'alteration of consciousness'. As with the traditional religious concept of God, Jung affirmed that God, *along with the images generated by all the other archetypes*, is ineffable, since He comes from a part of the mind about which nothing concrete may be known.

Jung's Conclusion as to the Existence of God

If belief in God stems from structural components of the psyche, does this mean that God does or does not exist? Jung's answer is similar to Freud's; that is, there is no proof either way. Jung states:

> We simply do not know the ultimate derivation of the archetype any more than we know the origin of the psyche. The competence of psychology as an empirical science only goes so far as to establish, on the basis of comparative research, whether for instance the imprint found in the psyche can or cannot be termed a 'God-image'. Nothing positive or negative has thus been asserted about the possible existence of any God.

C. G. Jung, Psychology and Alchemy, 1944

You need to know

Jung's definitions of the words *religion* and *religious* rely upon **Rudolf Otto's** understanding of the religious or numinous experience.

Look back at Chapter 3 (pages 23 and 25) to remind yourself of the meanings of **numinous** and **ineffable**.

All that can be asserted is that God, and the whole entity of religion, exists as a psychic reality; that is, to those who experience the effects of the archetypes, God is real. However, nothing can be proved about his existence or nature outside the mind.

Here, then, we have a point of similarity between the approaches of Jung and Freud. What Jung makes of his conclusion, however, is completely different. For whereas Freud thought that religion was a neurotic illness and a dangerous illusion that needed to be overthrown, Jung argued that it performs the role of maintaining the balance of the mind and *preventing* neuroses. To explain this, we need to return briefly to Jung's concept of the libido.

The libido, we recall, can be described as a flow of psychic energy. To maintain health, all of the features of the personality need to be balanced. For example, there needs to be a balance between the unconscious mind and the unconscious. There also needs to be a balance among the different archetypes. It is the failure to maintain this balance that is the main cause of mental disorder and neurotic illness.

Someone who has, for example, an excess of mental energy concentrated upon the unconscious will appear to be detached from their surroundings, since they will chiefly be aware of the images generated by the unconscious.

Jung argued that the balance of the libido and the ensuing mental health of the individual are governed by an innate process that he terms **individuation.**

By this, Jung meant that it results in a psychically balanced personality, through the integration of the various archetypes into the conscious personality.

Briefly, Jung argued that whereas the first part of a person's life involves a coming to terms with the outer environment with its challenges – through work, friendships and relationships – the emphasis in the second part, from middle age onwards, is to come to terms with one's own personality. Faced with declining opportunities, energies and possibly health, the individual must find new purpose and meaning in life through assimilating into one's conscious mind the numerous unconscious components. This is the process of individuation. An acceptance of the various parts of the personality is all part of the individuation process. Although

Something to think about

Given that the **persona** is the archetype that governs the covering up of one's true nature, what sort of behaviour would you expect from someone whose libido was channelled excessively in this direction?

You need to know

Individuation is a spontaneous process that involves 'becoming one's own self'.

Consider, for example, the archetype of the **shadow**. What benefits to one's own personality and one's behaviour could there be in coming to terms with the unpleasant, darker features of one's own nature?

Consider, for example, how knowledge of your own weaknesses could help you to relate to others who also have such flaws.

You need to know

The design known as a **mandala** or **magic circle** is one based on a perfectly balanced circle, whose centre is emphasised. This design is traditionally understood to represent balance and wholeness.

ultimately beneficial, it can be difficult, for it involves accepting parts of one's personality that one may prefer to leave undiscovered!

Individuation and its Relationship with Religion

We have established the importance of the individuation process. All that remains is to explain what it has to do with religion. Here, two points need to be made.

First, individuation as an innate process is one which is governed by the archetype known as the **self**. More precisely, the self is the innate disposition to become whole.

We have already seen that, upon Jung's understanding of religious experience, any process or attitude that is governed by archetypes may be termed religious. Upon this basis, individuation is a religious process.

Jung provided a second and stronger basis for associating religion with individuation. This is that the self aids the process of individuation by generating *images of wholeness*. The most famous example of these images is the mandala, or balancing circles. Another major example, however, is the religious images of God. In other words, the images created by the God archetype are one and the same as those images created by the self archetype. It makes sense, therefore, to say that it is through religious images that the personality achieves its goal of integration. In Jung's words, 'The symbols of divinity coincide with those of the self: what, on the one side, appears as a psychological experience, signifying psychic wholeness, expresses on the other side the idea of God.'

As a result, Jung was saying that the religious images are used by the mind to individuate the personality. The value of religion now becomes clear. For if one rejects religion, one is at the same time rejecting a substantial part of the individuation mechanism. Those who reject religion are therefore less likely to individuate successfully, and therefore more likely to experience neurosis as a result of the remaining psychological tension. For this reason, Jung can conclude that religion is a valuable entity.

A Critical Appraisal of Jung's Work

Although Jung's theories are perhaps less sensational than those of Freud, they have nonetheless been seriously criticised, and not merely by supporters of Freud. The criticism has centred upon four main areas:

- Jung's methodology
- the theory of the archetypes
- Jung's concept of religious experience
- the role of religion within individuation

Regarding Jung's methodology, it has been pointed out that his rejection of the possibility of ever knowing whether God exists rests upon the assumption that nothing can be known of any entity outside the psychic world. The question of God's existence is therefore unanswerable, since this would involve searching beyond the psychic world into the world of reality. Many, however, reject this starting point, but Jung refused to allow any evidence to count against him. He had set up a necessary truth and hence safeguarded it from ever being refuted by empirical evidence. In this, however, he had no justification.

Jung's theory of archetypes is also criticised. It is not the concept of these instincts that is attacked but, rather, that such a concept is simply not required to explain the 'evidence' – namely, the common tendency to construct uniform images. **Geza Roheim**, for example, states that since all humans share broadly the same experiences, it is hardly surprising that we develop myths along similar lines. The common experiences of birth and dependence upon parents and the Sun explain, for example, common ideas about rebirth, parent gods and Sun gods. It has also been pointed out that the fact that many religious myths, such as the Mesopotamian legends, respond to the social concerns of a particular community makes it hard to accept that they come from an impulse which is common to the whole of mankind. Upon these grounds, it is argued that Jung is not justified in postulating an archetypal 'instinct for God' from the evidence that people believe in God.

A further point that rendered Jung's concept of the archetypes less acceptable is the fact that *many people do not believe in God*. Jung offered an answer to this criticism, but it is not one that should necessarily be accepted; for he said that atheism is itself a form of religion. The methodology here should again be questioned. Again, we see him apparently making a judgement on the basis of empirical evidence, but then manipulating any conflicting evidence to his advantage, thus precluding any possibility of his judgement ever being falsified. His judgement hence becomes a necessary truth – but without justification.

You need to know

Remind yourself of **Martin Buber's** definition of a religious experience in Chapter 3 (page 24).

Jung's theory of religious experience is often criticised. Martin Buber, for example, was not convinced that an experience that stems from the mind and, as such, is in no way external to the subject can properly be termed religious. In particular, Jung's argument that *any archetypal image* may be described as religious has come under fire. The problem is that if a vision of being trapped in armour is as religious as a vision of God, Jung has failed to preserve the uniqueness of religious experience. He has also failed to explain why this type of experience is so distinctive in the minds of the subject.

For the same reason, the definition of individuation as a religious process may be questioned. If it is governed by the self archetype, then it may be argued that it has nothing to do with God. The image of Christ, for example, is only significant for Jung inasmuch as it is a symbol of wholeness that can help to balance our minds. Religious believers, however, would argue that Christ is more than just a symbol for something else but, rather, is important in his own right, as a historical person and the Son of God. Again, then, there is an extra dimension in religious practice which Jung fails to explain.

Conclusion

Having examined the light shed upon religion by Freud and Jung, it is appropriate to ask what contribution they can make. Our answer depends to a considerable degree upon the extent to which we accept their theories as true. Whatever our judgement here, there is no proof either way that God either does or does not exist.

In all probability, those who are already committed atheists will feel confirmed in their judgements on the grounds that so many new possibilities have been revealed which account for religion without the need for a God. Committed believers, on the other hand, may also be strengthened in their beliefs. For they may argue that the work of Freud and Jung demonstrated anew the depth and complexity of God's creation, thus providing support for a possible design argument. Or, it could be claimed, their work reveals something about the way in which God makes His presence known to humans. Upon Jung's theory, we could argue that God made humankind in His image by placing a very blueprint of Himself in our minds. Followers of Freud, meanwhile, could follow **John Hick's** *Philosophy of Religion* and argue that 'in his work on the father figure, he may have uncovered one of the mechanisms by which God creates an idea of the deity in the human mind'.

Hick's conclusion regarding Freud could apply equally effectively to Jung:

> Again, then, it seems that the verdict must be 'not proven'; . . . the Freudian theory of religion may be true but has not been shown to be so.

John H. Hick, Philosophy of Religion, 4th edn, Prentice-Hall, 1990

Essay questions

AS

(a) Outline Freud's argument that 'religion is an illusion based on human wishes'.

(b) Explain and assess the extent to which a believer would agree with Freud's view.

A2

(a) Describe and explain the main features of Freud's and Jung's teachings about the function of religion.

(b) Explain and assess the claim that God only exists in the mind.

Chapter 10   Religion and Science

Changing World-views

Science and religion share the common purpose of providing a means of research and discussion on the most basic issues regarding:

- how we understand the world in which we live, and our place in that world
- how the traditional concerns and beliefs of religion and philosophy can be related to scientific understanding
- how the joint reflections of scientists, philosophers and believers can contribute to the welfare of humans

In the present century, the two disciplines of religion and science are often in opposition with each other in the understanding of these basic issues, and the way in which the truth behind them might be discovered. *Modern scientific thought* is based on *observation* and *experiment* to test out theories and to reach a conclusion as to what is the literal truth. New theories may replace older ones if there is a greater weight of evidence in their favour. *Religious thought* is usually based on *reflection* and *abstract ideas*, and is concerned with values and beliefs rather than facts. Religious beliefs are based on faith, and scientific principles may be rejected when there is conflict with the basic tenets of the faith.

In the past, religion and science were in much closer agreement with each other, as it was out of the work of theologians and philosophers that science was born. Until the sixteenth century, the philosophers and theologians *were* the scientists. The early theologians and philosophers tried to understand the world in which they lived, and asked scientific questions such as:

How was the world made?
What holds the world up?
Why does the Moon not fall down?

The religious and scientific world-views agreed with each other because the scientific explanation included reference to God. The beginnings of modern science in the sixteenth

Something to think about

In the modern world, is it possible to be both a believer and a scientist?

You need to know

Remind yourself of the philosophies of **Plato** and **Aristotle** by reading Chapter 1 (pages 2–3).

century led to a change in the way in which people understood God's place in the universe and His relationship with humans. This change resulted in a gradual separation of science and religion, so that it became possible to accept scientific principles without reference to God.

The Ancient Greek World-view

The *ancient Greek philosophers* based their understanding of the development of the world on reason, and on philosophical explanations. The ancient Greeks did not possess the technology to make detailed visual observations of the stars and planets. Their findings were based on mathematics and on observation with the naked eye.

Plato

Plato sought to find answers to how this world could be changing and yet the reality behind it could remain constant. He divided the world into 'reality' and 'appearance'. Humans live in a world of space and time in which nothing lasts and nothing stays the same. The world we see is not the real world. The true world is beyond the senses, and contains the truth of ideas such as Beauty, Truth and Justice. Plato called these the 'Forms'. He stated that these Forms were eternal, changeless and incorporeal (not in a physical form). According to Plato, these Forms are the source of moral and religious inspiration. They are imperceptible, and can only be known through thoughts. We only have an image of the realm of these unobservable and unchanging Forms, which are in fact the reality. We can recognise beauty but not the reality of Beauty. The highest form of all is Good. This is the unifying principle of the universe. Later philosophers identified the ultimate Form of Goodness as God, although Plato had no place for God in his philosophy. Plato believed that people needed to transcend the physical world to achieve the ideal and the eternal. He regarded things in this world as pale, imperfect reflections of the universal ideals, the reality of which was to be found only in the realm of pure Forms or ideas. He believed that mathematics was the expression of pure thought, and it could explain the pure Forms.

Mathematics and observation of the universe led to the belief that the heavens were an expression of perfect reality and truth. Plato pictured the physical universe as a vast finite

Something to think about

Why do you think Plato believed that mathematics was an expression of pure thought?

Would you agree with Plato's philosophy of the Forms?

You need to know

The term **geocentric** refers to the belief that the Earth is at the centre of the universe, and all of the other bodies in the universe revolve around it.

You need to know

An **epicycle** is a circle whose centre moves round the circumference of another larger circle.

sphere, 100 million miles across, with the spherical Earth at its centre. Plato laid down the principle that the motion of heavenly bodies was circular, uniform and constantly regular. Plato's model of the universe was to last – with only minor modifications by later astronomers – for nineteen centuries.

Aristotle

Aristotle developed Plato's ideas. Aristotle's cosmological system was an infinite geocentric universe consisting of a series of concentric circles. He stated that there were eight concentric spheres revolving around the stationary Earth. The spheres were crystalline and invisible, and embedded on each were the Sun, the Moon, the stars and the five planets known at that time. The circles moved in perfect circular motion round the Earth. Each body was attached to its own crystalline sphere, which was made of an incorruptible, unchanging substance, called quintessence. This substance was not found on Earth. The Earth was made up of the four elements of earth, water, fire and air. Aristotle believed that there were two regions in the universe, each with its own set of laws. The region above the Moon was ethereal, perfect and unchanging. The Earth was changeable and corruptible, and therefore could have a history. On Earth, movement was unnatural, as the natural state of objects was to be at rest. When a force was applied, an object moved in a straight line, according to the natural tendency of the particular element. Air and fire rose upwards, away from the Earth, whereas water and earth moved towards the Earth's centre.

Ptolemy (CE c. 100–170)

Ptolemy was a Greek astronomer who – on the basis of observations – put forward an influential theory to explain motion in the universe. He retained a geocentric universe. However, it had been observed that Aristotle's model did not give a satisfactory explanation for some of the planetary movements. At times, planets appeared to go backwards. If they were attached to spheres going round the Earth, how was this possible? Ptolemy developed the idea of epicycles to account for the observed motion of the planets. He concluded that each planet moved in a small circle on the circumference of the sphere to which it was attached. As it circled round the Earth and in an epicycle, a planet would at times appear to be going backwards. Ptolemy's explanation was accepted for over 1000 years.

The Medieval World-view

In the Middle Ages, Christian philosophers combined Aristotle's and Ptolemy's models of the universe with Christian teaching to produce the medieval world-view. Any scientific reasoning had to be in line with the Christian faith. Therefore, it was accepted that God created the universe. The medieval interpretation of the biblical account of the Creation found in Genesis was based on Aristotelian and Platonic physics and philosophy. God controlled everything in the world and was the Prime Mover of all that took place.

God had placed humans on Earth, at the centre of His creation, with dominance over the animals. God controlled the universe and his representative on Earth was the Pope. The Christian Church taught that a person's present existence was of little concern. That person's eternal fate after death was all that mattered. The scholars were theologians, who were more concerned with how to achieve Heaven than how the universe functioned. Consequently, there was little interest in finding out more about the world in which people lived.

St Thomas Aquinas

Aquinas wrote commentaries on Aristotle, and concluded that Aristotle's 'unmoved mover' was God. Aquinas rejected Aristotle's assertion that the world was eternal.

The God of the Old Testament was much more personal and involved in the creation of the universe than Aristotle's unmoved mover. God had created the universe at a fixed time in the past and, on the sixth day, had placed human life at the centre of His creation. The world in which God had placed humans was corruptible and changing, and could be spoilt by sin. Above the Earth was the incorruptible realm of God, in which the heavenly bodies moved in perfect circles.

In the Middle Ages, the accepted structure of the universe continued to be based on observation and mathematics. Scholars were aware that planetary movements were erratic when compared to those of the Sun and Moon, but any irregularities observed in the movement of the heavenly bodies were explained away. The accepted world-view was that the Earth was flat and motionless, and at the centre of the universe. Jerusalem was the centre of the world and beneath

You need to know

Remind yourself of **St Thomas Aquinas'** contributions to both the cosmological argument (Chapter 5, pages 65–67) and the design argument (Chapter 6, page 74) for the existence of God.

Something to think about

Aquinas' world-view owed much to the writings of Aristotle, but was adapted to avoid conflict with Christian teaching. Why was it necessary for Aquinas to reject Aristotle's belief that the world was eternal and that there was little chance of personal immortality?

Find out more about these **five stages** and how they form the basis of Christian teaching.

Why would Christians in the Middle Ages have regarded it as important that the Earth was at the centre of the universe?

the city was Purgatory. There was no concept of natural laws, since everything that happened was explained in terms of the will and purpose of God. God was the first and final cause of everything, and His presence was immanent within the world because, at all times, He was commanding things to go to their rightful places. Christianity had taught that the Earth was a special creation of God, as the stage on which the drama of man's redemption was enacted. It was to Earth that God had come in the person of Jesus Christ. The incarnation of Christ on Earth was central to the Christian faith. The Earth's main purpose was to provide the environment in which God's five stages – of Creation, covenant, Christ, Church and consummation – could be worked out.

The Earth, on which things were constantly changing because of growth and decay, contrasted with the heavens, which were perfect and incorruptible. Outside the boundary of the heavenly spheres was the realm of God, Heaven. Below the Earth was another hierarchy of inverted circles, descending down to Satan. Everything in the universe was ranked up to God or down to Satan, according to whether it was good or evil. There was a perceived harmony between the cosmic and social orders that integrated mankind into the universe. In the Middle Ages, people's experience of space and time was ordered by religious ideas. The world-view was seen in religious terms; unlike today, when the world is seen in terms of mechanisms, mathematics and natural causes.

It was believed that the Church could best explain the universe. Everything happened for a purpose and the priest could help to explain this purpose in religious terms. The hierarchy of the universe was echoed in the hierarchy of the Church. All knowledge was subject to the Church's control, and anything that challenged the Church was challenging the very foundations of society. The authority of the Bible was regarded as final for most Christians, and it was interpreted to support a geocentric philosophy. For example, the line in Psalm 93, 'He spreads out the heavens like a tent', was accepted to refer to the heavens that revolved daily above the Earth.

Towards a Scientific World-view

Aristotle had failed to account for the known irregularities in the movements of the five planets (Mercury, Venus, Mars,

Jupiter and Saturn) without losing the idea of the simplicity of creation. Towards the end of the Middle Ages, deficiencies became evident in the Aristotelian universe. A changing attitude to learning had developed. Ideas were no longer accepted simply because that was the way it had always been. The hold of the Church on ideas and politics was breaking down, as large parts of Europe, including England, broke free of the control of Rome in religious matters. Questions were asked and the new learning included a revival of interest in astronomy and science.

By the sixteenth century, the Church needed an accurate calendar. The calendar in use was that introduced by Julius Caesar in the first century CE. It set the length of the year at 365 days, with a leap year of 366 days every fourth year. This was not totally correct, as each year was 11 minutes short, and as the centuries passed this led to the calendar being a day out every 128 years. By the beginning of the sixteenth century, the accumulated results of these errors were creating problems for the Church in accurately fixing the date of festivals such as Easter.

Nicolaus Copernicus (CE 1473–1543)

Copernicus was an astronomer employed by the Church to produce an accurate calendar. He set about measuring the altitudes of the heavenly bodies and recording his observations. Copernicus realised that to solve the problem of the calendar, he needed to solve the laws of motion of the Sun and the Moon. Because of his work, the Gregorian calendar was introduced, according to which ten days were omitted from the year 1582 (this did not happen in England until 1752). To keep the calendar in line, one leap year was omitted three times every four centuries. *The most significant result of Copernicus' mathematical observations was his conclusion that the Sun was at the centre of the universe.* In other words, the universe was **heliocentric**: the Earth went round the Sun along with the other planets, and only the Moon revolved around the Earth. Copernicus published his theories in *De Revolutionibus*. He had placed the Sun at the centre of the universe, but he still accepted that the heavenly bodies travelled in perfect circular orbits and epicycles.

You need to know

A **heliocentric** universe has the Sun at the centre, and all of the planets travel round the Sun.

Not everyone immediately accepted Copernicus' system, but scientific advances led others to use mathematics and observation to work out the shape of the universe.

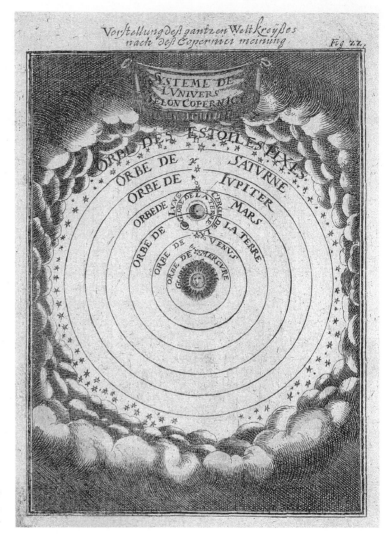

A representation of the heliocentric picture for the planets known in the time of Copernicus

Something to think about

Why do you think that many Christians in the sixteenth century could not accept Copernicus' hypothesis that the Earth was not at the centre of the universe?

Tycho Brahe (CE 1546–1601)

Brahe provided a further model of the universe as a rival to that of Copernicus. He made accurate measurements of the position of stars and the movements of the planets. By getting rid of unnecessary complications, Brahe helped astronomy to move forward. He produced a star catalogue, which was useful in removing many of the problems of earlier observations. *One important area of work was on comets.* Comets appear to move in straight lines and it had been assumed, therefore, that they occurred in the sphere below the Moon. Brahe's work would change this long-held view.

Brahe demonstrated that comets moved across the orbit of planets. This raised the question of how they could move through the crystalline spheres. In 1572, he discovered a new

Something to think about

Why did astronomers in the Middle Ages assume that comets only existed in the region below the Moon?

Something to think about

Which do you think the medieval Christian Church would prefer; Copernicus' model of the universe, or the model put forward by Tycho Brahe?

star (a supernova) in the constellation of Cassiopeia. He had demonstrated that objects moved in straight lines *above* the Moon, and that as something new had appeared in the heavens, they were *not* unchanging. Brahe did not accept Copernicus' model and retained the Earth at the centre of the universe. He suggested that the Sun and Moon orbited around the Earth, and that the other planets orbited the Sun. Brahe's work paved the way for important developments by his pupil, Johannes Kepler.

Johannes Kepler (CE 1571–1630)

Kepler was a pupil of Tycho Brahe. He discovered the three laws of planetary motion that helped to lead Isaac Newton to universal laws of gravity. As with the earlier astronomers, Kepler based his model of the universe on mathematics, particularly geometry. He maintained that the physical universe was laid out according to a mathematical design that was simple and accessible to human intelligence. Kepler developed three laws of planetary motion:

- planets move in elliptical orbits, with the Sun at one end of the ellipse
- if one were to imagine that a line joined the centre of a planet to the centre of the Sun, then if one viewed the orbit from along this line, the planet would be seen to move faster at the end of the orbit closest to the Sun
- the square of the true period of the orbit (measured relative to the fixed stars) is proportional to the cube of the planet's average distance from the Sun

Kepler's predictions now matched astronomers' observations of the universe.

Kepler's Christian beliefs convinced him that he would find order in the universe, as it was evidence of God's design. He did not accept that his new model of the universe would undermine the Christian faith. Kepler considered that his observations of the complex design of the universe added to the proof of God's existence.

From the Medieval World to the Scientific World-view

Galilei Galileo (CE 1564–1642)

Galileo did not try to discover the final causes of the universe. He wanted to explain what had led to the events observed in the natural world, which he believed were based on mathematical laws. Galileo was the first astronomer to make systematic *observation of the universe through a telescope*. When he observed the Moon, he discovered that it had mountains and craters. He saw that the Moon was not a perfect sphere, as his ancestors had believed. He realised that we did not live in a closed, Earth-centred universe, but an immeasurable space. Jupiter had moons and Venus had phases. This evidence disproved the existence of crystalline spheres orbiting the Earth. Galileo's observations supported a heliocentric universe in which the heavenly bodies were not made of a substance superior to the Earth. He observed sunspots, which proved that the heavens were not unchanging or infinite. He proved that the movement of the planets was natural and was not the result of a Prime Mover. His findings were published in *Dialogue Concerning the Two Chief World Systems* (1632). This work led to a general acceptance of Copernican theories. Galileo continued to distinguish between celestial and terrestrial laws. He was not anti-Christian. He argued that Scripture must be metaphorical, but still accepted that to study the universe was to find out more about God:

> Philosophy is written in that great book – I mean the universe – that forever stands open before our eyes, but you cannot read it until you have first learned to understand the language and recognise the symbols in which it is written. It is written in the language of mathematics and its symbols are triangles, circles, and other geometrical figures without which one does not understand a word, without which one wanders through a dark labyrinth in vain.
>
> *Galilei Galileo, Dialogue Concerning the Two Chief World Systems, 1632*

The Catholic Church imprisoned Galileo as a heretic and banned his works.

Something to think about

Galileo believed in God, so why did the Catholic Church declare him a heretic?

Why did Galileo's books remain banned by the Catholic Church until the second half of the twentieth century?

Isaac Newton (CE 1642–1727)

Newton brought about the final break with Aristotelianism, with its universe proceeding according to different laws above and below the hypothetical sphere of the Moon. He shared Kepler's view that there is order in the universe. Newton based his findings on his Christian world-view. He believed that because man was made in the image of God, he had a perception of God's creation. This was why he was able to understand his discoveries of the universal laws of gravity and motion. Newton demonstrated that the same physical laws that we know on Earth are applicable throughout the whole universe. His **universal law of gravity** states that the force of attraction between any two masses, anywhere in the universe, is proportional to the product of the two masses divided by the distance between them:

> With such a fundamental, simple framework in place, it did not take much of a leap for Newton's successors to imagine planets confined forever to totally predictable, orderly orbits around the sun. Such a perpetual clockwork would never need rewinding or adjusting. This mathematical machinery, by encapsulating completely the solar system's past, present and future, in principle seemed to leave no room for the unforeseen.
>
> *Ivars Peterson, Newton's Clock: Chaos in the Solar System,*
> *W. H. Freeman, 1993*

Something to think about

Why did the work of Galileo and Newton result in the destruction of the medieval world-view?

Newton developed a new kind of reflecting telescope, and essentially invented the modern techniques of scientific investigation, in which ideas are tested and refined by comparison with experiments, instead of being plucked out of the air as more or less wild flights of fancy. Science no longer depended on observation alone, and on fitting these observations to the accepted facts. Now, any hypothesis had to be supported by evidence and data as well as observation.

The Scientific World-view

You need to know

A **paradigm** is a model or pattern that serves to represent a group or collection of things or events.

Scientific developments had proved that the planets orbited the Sun according to strict patterns and according to comprehensive laws. This pattern was seen to be a paradigm for the whole universe. Everything seemed to be governed by a set of unbreakable natural laws, which could be discovered by the process of scientific inquiry. If phenomena were investigated in an impartial, open-minded manner, then the truth could be found. Mathematics was an essential investigative tool, and the universal laws could be expressed in mathematical terms. Experiments, rather than philosophy, became the final arbitrator of truth. Many believers were able to accept what became known as the 'New Philosophy' without losing their faith, while others saw the new discoveries as a reason for abandoning religious beliefs and basing their world-view on reason alone. There was a different world-view from that of the medieval period. Religion and science began to separate. Scientific findings were to have some significant consequences for religious belief:

- The universe was now seen as a 'machine', with all parts working together, rather than as a living creation of God

Each part of this machine affected the behaviour of another part, and resulted in movement. It was no longer necessary to believe that God caused the movements in the universe. The geocentric view had been explicitly religious: the Earth was the stage on which the drama of man's redemption was enacted when God came in the person of Christ. A heliocentric view put man in a different relationship to God. Mankind was no longer the centre of everything, but inhabited a tiny planet that circled the Sun. Human life was no longer regarded as unique, because there was the possibility of other universes. God might have created the world and moved on.

- Scientists no longer had to refer to God in order to explain the way in which the physical world worked. The Christian faith no longer had control over all branches of knowledge. Kingship, religion and moral order could no longer claim the cosmic backing that they had previously had. For many, religion now became the explanation for those things that were still not understood by science, a philosophy that became known as '**God of the Gaps**'.

- God was no longer regarded as immanent and as the controller of everything. The new scientific world-view developed the acceptance of a world that was a machine that ran itself. The clockwork analogy did not seem to leave room for the spiritual soul. This led to the development of **Deism**, the belief that once God had set things going, He could not intervene in His creation. Science dealt with the everyday tick-tock of the cosmic clock, and religion dealt with first beginnings and last ends, with God and the soul. The universe was not a living organism, but consisted of material particles moving in infinite space, in accordance with strict mathematically precise, universal laws.

- The medieval world-view had been proved wrong. This resulted in many taking a sceptical approach to Scripture, and viewing the Church as fallible. Many scientists came to dismiss religion altogether. Newton had been unable to explain why two or more planets orbiting the Sun were not upset by the extra gravitational influence and sent tumbling out of their orbits. He had said that the hand of God might be needed from time to time, to nudge the planets back into position. **Pierre Laplace** (1749–1827), a French mathematician and astronomer, was able to solve this problem, by showing that these lapses are largely self-correcting. When Napoleon commented that there was

Something to think about

Is it possible to accept that this world is God's creation, and at the same time accept the scientific accounts of the structure of the universe?

no reference to God in Laplace's work, Laplace replied 'I have no need of that hypothesis'. He believed that God was irrelevant. To Laplace, everything in the solar system was determined (caused). Laplace thought that eventually all the natural laws of the universe would be known and that everything would be explained in scientific terms.

The physicist **Stephen Hawking** claims that Laplace is wrong in his assumption that there is no need for science to include God in the explanation of the laws of the universe. Hawking argues that:

> In the last 300 years, more and more regularities and laws were discovered. The success of these laws led Laplace at the beginning of the nineteenth century to postulate scientific determinism, that is he suggested that there would be a set of laws that would determine the evolution of the universe precisely, given its configuration at one time. Laplace's determinism was incomplete in two ways. It did not say how the laws should be chosen and it did not specify the initial configuration of the universe. These were left to God. God would choose how the universe began and what laws it obeyed, but he would not intervene in the universe once it had started. In effect, God was confined to the area that the nineteenth-century science did not understand.

Stephen Hawking, A Brief History of Time,
Bantam Press, 1992

Something to think about

Read the quote from Stephen Hawking.

Why does he believe that Laplace's view of determinism was incomplete?

Why does Hawking think that Laplace had left room for God in the scientific view of the universe?

The Religious Response

Many believers felt that the conflict between science and religion was over superficial points. If the biblical accounts of the universe were not taken literally, then science was regarded as revealing the laws by which God created the universe. A movement developed in theology that stressed how God was revealed through nature. The scientific laws proved that the universe was the result of a skilled designer, and this designer was God. In the Middle Ages, if scientific observations conflicted with the biblical account, then it had been accepted that science was wrong, and the laws of science had been adjusted accordingly. By the eighteenth century, however, the opposite was true. If the biblical account was contrary to the findings of science, then it was accepted that the Bible was wrong. The Bible had to be reinterpreted in the light of the scientific world-view. The result was the development of Deism and of the 'God of the Gaps' philosophy, which we have referred to in the previous section.

Other believers realised the dangers of adapting religious truths to fit scientific laws. They argued that the Bible as the word of God must contain revelations about God. It came from God and must therefore be perfect. The events in the Bible, they insisted, are historical events, events that actually happened, including the account of the Creation. As science progressed, it became harder to accept a literal interpretation of the Bible, especially when evolutionary theories were put forward to explain the origin of life on Earth.

You need to know

Remind yourself of the meaning of the terms **evolution** and **natural selection** by looking back at Chapter 3 (pages 79–80).

The Creation Model for the Origin of Life

The model for the origin of life based on the Genesis account of the Creation accepts that:

- life was created by the actions of a creator
- the basic plant and animal species were created with their characteristics complete at the time of creation
- any varieties of species were limited within each kind at the time of creation
- there was a sudden appearance of the great variety of life-forms found on Earth at the time of creation
- the characteristics of each species were complete at the time of creation
- human life was the last form to appear, and human characteristics were complete at the time of creation

The Evolutionary Model for the Origin of Life

Various theories have been proposed to explain how new species develop. The model for the origin of life based on evolutionary theories accepts that:

- life had evolved by naturalistic mechanistic processes
- the first life-form of a single organism arose from inanimate matter
- all life-forms originated from this simple organism
- there was a gradual development of increasingly complex life-forms
- there is unlimited variation in nature, and evolution is continuing

Something to think about

In what ways do the creation model and evolutionary model conflict with each other?

Is it possible to accept both models?

The two most well known evolutionary theories were proposed by:

- **Jean-Baptiste Lamarck**, and
- **Charles Darwin**

Jean-Baptiste Lamarck (CE 1744–1829)

Lamarck was a significant figure in the development of evolutionary theories. He believed that organisms change to meet their needs according to their changing environment. He believed that organisms were at various stages of evolution. At the bottom of the evolutionary 'ladder' were microscopic organisms and, from these simple organisms, increasingly complex life-forms had developed until, at the top of the 'ladder', human life was reached. Lamarck's theories included the following ideas:

Something to think about

List other examples of changes in species that you are aware of that would support Lamarck's theories.

• The organs that a life-form uses increase in size and strength to meet the needs of the species. Those organs that are no longer needed for survival will grow smaller, until they eventually disappear.

• Any genetic changes are inherited by the species' offspring. For example, the long neck of the giraffe was the gradual result of many generations of stretching to reach the leaves high up on trees. Each generation inherited the 'longer' neck of their ancestors.

Charles Darwin (CE 1809–1882)

Until Darwin put forward his evolutionary theories, religious thinkers had been able to challenge atheists by asking how chance alone could create such an intricate world – and the atheists had no good answer. Darwin's theory was to provide atheists with a coherent and credible mechanism by which life could conceivably arise without the necessity of a creator or life-giver being postulated. Charles Darwin published his evolutionary theories in *On the Origin of Species by Means of Natural Selection* in 1859. Darwin's observations led him to conclude that organisms produce more offspring than can survive. The offspring are not identical: variations exist within them. Depending on the environment, some of these variations will help some of the offspring to survive better than the others. The offspring that survive will produce more descendants than those who do not survive. Over time, this will increase the number of offspring with these particular variations. Therefore, these variations will assist the survival of the species. Darwin called this **natural selection**:

Something to think about

What do you understand by the term **natural selection**?

As each species tends by its geometrical ratio of reproduction to increase inordinately in number; and as the modified descendants of each species will be enabled to increase by so much the more as they become more diversified in habits and structure, so as to be enabled to seize on many and widely different places in the economy of nature, there will be a constant tendency in natural selection to preserve the most divergent offspring of any one species. Hence, during a long-continued course of modification, the slight differences, characteristic of varieties of the same species, tend to be augmented into the greater differences characteristic of species of the same genus. New and improved varieties will inevitably supplant and exterminate the older, less improved and intermediate varieties; and thus species are rendered to a large extent defined and distinct objects. Dominant species belonging to the larger groups tend to give birth to new and dominant forms, so that each large group tends to become still larger, and at the same time more divergent in character.

Charles Darwin, On the Origin of Species by Means of
Natural Selection, 1859

Darwin's theory of evolution undermined the biblical account of creation for a number of reasons:

- He showed how living things developed in small steps, and how this development could be the result of chance. Darwin thus demonstrated that life-forms were not in their final form at the time of creation, and might not be the work of a designer.
- Evolution showed that things changed to fit in with the environment rather than the environment being shaped for their needs. This conflicted with the biblical account that God had created the environment for the benefit of the various life-forms.
- Nature 'red in tooth and claw' did not match the idea of a gentle and kind deity, as the exponents of natural theology deemed God to be.

In 1871, Darwin published his findings as to human origins in *The Descent of Man*. He accounted for all human characteristics by natural selection from other life-forms, and concluded that humans descended from apes.

Modern Evolutionary Theories

New evolutionary theories have developed based on those of Darwin. Darwin proposed a gradual change of species, but recent theories have suggested that the process is not gradual. A theory has developed to suggest that evolution goes through 'jumps', as well as relatively slow changes. These 'jumps' result in sudden changes that happen at certain times,

Something to think about

Why were many Victorians upset by Darwin's suggestion that they had evolved from apes?

Darwin had attacked the Christian concept that humans were unique and made in 'God's image'. Christians believed that humans had a spiritual soul, which distinguished them from animals. God put the soul there – but if mankind developed from animal origins then where did Darwin's theories leave this idea?

Were humans soulless beings like the animals? Darwin had cast further doubt on the biblical account of the Creation, especially the story of Adam and Eve.

Something to think about

Creation scientists accept that there was an intelligent designer, God, who created our universe. They believe that creation was a one-time event. These scientists believe that the Bible and science are in harmony with each other. What will these scientists need to do to be able to continue to accept their world-view?

Does the discovery of **punctuated equilibrium** support or oppose the idea of a divine creator?

Something to think about

Is human life still evolving?

If it is, what changes might one expect to see in the human species at some future date?

You need to know

Creationists reject the theory of evolution. They believe that God created the world through miracles. They base their views on the Genesis account of the Creation.

Something to think about

What do you think Ernest Lucas meant in the statement quoted above?

Do you think it is possible to accept both evolutionary theories and the belief that God created the world?

but it is not certain why this happens. These 'jumps' are termed **punctuated equilibrium**.

The study of genetics has explained how natural selection occurs. Genes are also used to explain human behaviour.

Evolution versus Creation

There are several reasons why creationists oppose the various theories of evolution:

- in the fossil records that have been found, there are gaps – therefore there is no direct evidence that the evolutionary process took place
- natural selection is incapable of advancing an organism to a higher life-form
- scientists have never found the evidence of the supposed link between the apes and humans

Other Christians believe that it is possible to accept evolutionary theories without rejecting their faith. They believe that evolution is the mechanism through which God's creation took place. They see the Bible's account of creation as

> a form of narrative, but one in which truth is put across in a symbolic way, because it was dealing with the big questions of life – the questions of meaning and purpose. I think these are more powerfully put across in story form.
>
> *Ernest Lucas, former biochemist, in Russell Stannard, Science and Wonders, Faber and Faber, 1996*

Pierre Teilhard de Chardin (CE 1881–1955)

Teilhard de Chardin accepted that evolution was part of God's plan. He put forward his theories in *The Phenomenon of Man*, which he claimed was 'a scientific treatise'. The work begins with a description of the creation of the Earth, and of the evolution of life-forms, culminating in the emergence of humans. The first life-form developed from a single-celled organism, and each life-form in turn has been increasingly complex, until the higher life-form of humans developed. The higher the life-form, the more intelligent it is, and on a higher level of consciousness. Evolution has not ended, and humans are evolving on to higher levels of achievement and understanding. At some future time, which Teilhard de Chardin refers to as the **Omega Point**, everything will become integrated with Christ. Evolution is part of God's plan for the ultimate fate of mankind.

Are there any similarities between Teilhard de Chardin's 'Phenomenon of Man' and **process theodicy** as considered in Chapter 8 (pages 105–106)?

Science and Religion Today

Newton was convinced that he would find order in the universe, and indeed he did. Newton's laws of gravity and motion gave science the certainty that it would be possible to discover all the laws of nature and predict all events without any need to refer to God. Two major scientific theories of the twentieth century:

*   Einstein's theory of relativity
*   quantum theory

have brought about further changes in the scientific world-view, and had an impact on the relationship between religion and science. These two theories have cast doubt that science can discover all the laws of nature.

The Theory of Relativity

Albert Einstein (CE 1879–1955)

Something to think about

Einstein's theories proved that the universe is constantly changing. What are the implications of his findings for religion?

Einstein developed both the **special theory of relativity** and the **general theory of relativity**. Until he developed his theories, it had been accepted that time and space were separate.

The **special theory of relativity** provided a description of the relationships and interactions between moving objects. The theory only applied to objects moving at constant speeds in straight lines, but proved that the speed of light remained the same whatever the speed of the source, and whatever the position of the observer in relation to the moving object. He demonstrated that matter was not solid and could release energy. This led to the general theory of relativity.

The **general theory of relativity** dealt with the acceleration of objects and with gravity. Einstein proved that time, space, energy and mass are related to one another. Time and space are not fixed. Time depends on where one is and how fast one is moving:

Something to think about

What would happen to time if it was possible to travel faster than the speed of light?

Would you be able to see anything if you were travelling faster than the speed of light?

> Space and time are now dynamic quantities: when a body moves, or a force acts, it affects the curvature of space and time – and in turn the structure of space–time affects the way

Something to think about

You are reading the first chapter of a detective novel. The criminal has been identified in the final chapter of the book, but you have only just started reading the book, so you do not know who did it. How could you cheat and know what happened?

Is this the way in which God knows the outcome of what we are going to do?

Something to think about

Remind yourself of the details of **process theodicy** in Chapter 8 (pages 105–106).

What problems would there be in reconciling the theory of relativity with process theodicy?

Other philosophers argue that God has foreknowledge because it is part of God's divine being to have such knowledge. They do not accept that the theory of relativity adds anything to the human understanding of God. God is outside time and space, and therefore any understanding of time does not help us to know more about God. Do you agree or disagree with this view?

in which bodies move and forces act. Space and time not only affect but also are affected by everything that happens in the universe. Just as one cannot talk about events in the universe without the notions of space and time, so in general relativity it became meaningless to talk about space and time outside the limits of the universe.

Stephen Hawking, A Brief History of Time, Bantam Press, 1992

Einstein demonstrated that time slows down the closer a moving object gets to the speed of light. This means that people in relative motion may have differing perceptions of time. For example, a person travelling in a spaceship at close to the speed of light might regard events as being in the present which, for someone travelling more slowly, are long since in the past. However, the theory of relativity overcomes this paradox by saying that everything exists at the *same* time. There is no distinction between past, present and future.

Einstein's theory of relativity might explain how it is possible for God to have foreknowledge of future events and for us to retain free will. God knows about future events because He is in a different time frame relative to ours. He knows the future, even though we have not yet made up our minds. He does not influence or decide those choices, but He knows the future:

> Our own human experiences are that tomorrow hasn't yet come and yesterday's gone. But the mathematics of physics is quite different. If you look at the mathematics of Einstein's theory, you find that you are presented – whether you like it or not – with a single thing called the 'space–time continuum'. There's then a natural tendency to jump from this to saying that the whole of space and time therefore exist, in some way, as a single block entity.
>
> *Chris Isham, in Russell Stannard, Science and Wonders, Faber and Faber, 1996*

Quantum Theory

The understanding of Newtonian physics was that bodies obey fixed laws. There was an assumption that it was possible to predict their behaviour in every situation. Matter was considered to be solid and predictable, and all the laws of the universe could be discovered eventually. There was no need for reference to God, as science could provide all the answers. This certainty was lost with the development of **quantum theory**.

You need to know

Quantum theory is the set of physical laws that apply primarily on the very small scale, for entities the size of atoms or smaller. At the heart of quantum theory lie the linked concepts of uncertainty and wave–particle duality. In the quantum world, every entity has a mixture of properties that we are used to thinking of as distinctly different – waves and particles. For example, *light*, which is often regarded as an electromagnetic wave, behaves under some circumstances as if it was composed of a stream of particles, called *photons*.

John Gibbin, Companion to the Cosmos,
Weidenfeld & Nicolson, 1996

Something to think about

Remind yourself of the belief in Deism on page 138.

Why does quantum theory undermine Deism?

Werner Heisenberg

Heisenberg's **uncertainty principle** demonstrated that the smallest component parts of matter are subject to unpredictable fluctuations. These appear to be spontaneous events. The uncertainty principle limited the scientists' power of prediction. If the mechanical processes are not as predictable as once thought, then the concept of Deism is undermined.

Quantum theory raises the following question: Was the origin of the universe a spontaneous quantum event, or does it prove that there was a divine being who planned the development of the universe?

Was God responsible for setting up the laws of physics so that the universe began?

We are not at the centre of the universe, but we circle round an insignificant star in a spiral galaxy similar to the one in the picture

Conclusion

Einstein's theory of relativity and the development of quantum theory have demonstrated that space, time, energy and matter are interconnected. The universe is more complex than scientists of the eighteenth and nineteenth centuries thought. The main aim of modern physics is to find a complete unified theory, which will link all four together. Einstein said that 'God does not play dice.' He meant that there are laws in nature, rather than a series of random, chance events. Quantum mechanics has shown that Laplace's hopes of determinism are not realistic, as sought-after universal theories may well remain beyond the scope of human understanding. Modern science is able to describe the *what* of the universe, but it is not able to answer the *why* of the universe. The why could be God:

> However, if we do discover a complete theory, it should in time be understandable in broad principle by everyone, not just a few scientists. Then we shall all, philosophers, scientists, and just ordinary people, be able to take part in the discussion of the question of why it is that we and the universe exist. If we find the answer to that, it would be the ultimate triumph of human reason – for then we would know the mind of God.

Stephen Hawking, A Brief History of Time, Bantam Press, 1992

Essay questions

AS

(a) Describe and explain two different scientific theories of the creation of the universe.

(b) Evaluate the view that reference to God is no longer needed to explain the origin of the universe.

A2

(a) Outline the Big Bang and Steady-State theories for the origin of the universe.

(b) 'Genesis is the only true account of creation, and any scientific account that contradicts this account must be dismissed by a believer.' Examine and assess the claim that scientific accounts of creation that contradict Genesis 'must be dismissed by a believer'.

Chapter 11   Religion and Humanity

In the last chapter, we examined how an individual's world-view affects his or her understanding of life and any meaning that might be behind it. In this chapter, we will highlight the difference between a religious perspective and a non-religious perspective of the world.

A Religious Perspective

A 'religious perspective' of the world principally involves the belief in a specific reason and meaning for life. In most cases, this belief manifests itself in the concept of a divine being – a 'God' or 'gods'. Some sort of communication with such a being or beings is usually deemed necessary. Virtually all religious traditions maintain a fundamental belief in judgement of some sort; this varies from beliefs about reincarnation to the immortality of individual souls, residing in Heaven or Hell.

A Non-religious Perspective

A 'non-religious perspective' of the world asserts that there may well be no specific reason behind life at all. Perhaps we are simply the result of the chance mutation of genes. For some, we are no more than a natural accident. When we die, those who advocate a non-religious perspective of the world suggest that we simply re-enter the complex cycle of nature as our bodies are broken down. There is no doubt that we *do* live forever, in that the atoms and molecules that make us simply change their form constantly – physical death is seen as just another transformation.

Human Purpose and Destiny

The differences that you will have discussed are fundamental to the way in which an individual lives his or her entire life. To put this into a practical context, a person's perspective of the world and their role within it will determine what they might achieve in life, how successful they might be, how they measure success, whether and who they marry, whether they have children, how those children are educated and so on –

Something to think about

Look at the meaning of **the immortality of the soul** and **reincarnation** in Chapter 13.

Something to think about

Discuss in small groups the ways in which you think a person's life will differ if they accept the religious perspective of the world as opposed to the non-religious perspective. You might wish to focus on:

- morality
- personal relationships
- careers
- leisure activities
- your own examples

Compare your ideas with those of the rest of the group.

the list, quite literally, is endless. The significance of this perspective, therefore, cannot be overstated. Many different philosophers have attempted to categorise and develop different ideas in relation to perspectives of the world. In the previous chapters, we have discussed many of the features of a religious perspective of the world. Arguments to demonstrate God's existence, suitable language with which to talk about God, first-hand experience of God and the theodicies in Chapter 8 – all are responses from individuals who share this particular perspective.

Most of this chapter will be dedicated to a consideration of theories that are generally thought of as 'non-religious', particularly:

- **humanism**
- **Marxism**, and
- **existentialism**

These three theories, although similar in some respects, are all distinctly different. However, the most important factor that they share is that they are all concerned with the quest for the true meaning of human nature.

It is very difficult truly to understand any of these schools of thought/perceptions without some knowledge of the others. It could be suggested that they have developed historically almost as one, each adding its own distinctive flavour to the question of the meaning of life. As such, it is necessary to examine each position.

Something to think about

Try completing the sentence 'The meaning of life is . . .'. When you have done so, look at the chart in the revision section for this chapter to see if your opinions are similar to any of the schools of thought featured.

Humanism

According to Konstantin Kolenda, humanism is not a school of thought; it is a general perception from which the world is viewed. This view would appear to be in accordance with those of most humanist scholars. To understand the ethos and *raison d'être* of humanism, we must consider it from between the two conflicting world-views that have fought for the allegiance of mankind for two centuries – science and religion:

Religion	Science
Humanity is completely dependent upon a divine being	Humanity is part of the natural order and is the same as other organisms, all have evolved

Humanism

Humanity is made up of beings with unique capabilities which should be recognised, nurtured and rejoiced in, *for their own sake*

Find out more about the work of **Aristotle** and **Plato** in Chapter 1 and other sources. In *The Republic* (Chapters 4, 8 and 9), Plato considers human reason and emotion, whereas Aristotle, in his ethical works, focuses upon happiness brought through human virtue.

The Development of Humanism

The term **humanism** was not used until the nineteenth century, when it was probably brought into being by **Friedrich Immanuel Niethammer**, who was looking for a way to describe a school or university curriculum based on the 'humanities' (literature, history, languages and philosophy). However, it is clear that the seeds of humanism had been sown centuries earlier than the term was adopted.

The 'classical' writings of Plato, Aristotle and others celebrated man's capabilities and achievements. These writings were clearly a great inspiration to many of the artists and scholars of the Renaissance period.

At this time, the use of Latin (traditionally used for all written documents, because of Church influence) was forsaken in favour of the use of poets' and authors' national languages, representing a shift from obedience to the religious powers of the day to a celebration of human development and achievement.

If one considers the work of **Michelangelo**, one can see that although he is often depicting religious scenes, his work emphasises the grace, dignity and power of man.

The French **philosophes** of the eighteenth century deepened and enriched the budding humanist tradition. **Diderot**, **Rousseau** and **Voltaire** all emphasised the capability and importance of man. They helped to fuel the 'Enlightenment', as it became known, which in turn led to an absolute shift in the culture, politics and life of Europe (largely through revolution).

Other European and American figures further developed the humanist perception of the world. In Britain **Bentham** and **Hume**, in Germany **Lessing** and **Kant**, and in America

Michelangelo showed the power of man through the power of God

Something to think about

Find out about the eighteenth-century movement known as the 'Enlightenment' – its cultural impact shaped humanism considerably.

Franklin and **Jefferson** all spoke of equality, freedom, tolerance and (to some degree) secularism, as being necessary values for human progress.

Humanism as a World-view

There is a great dispute within humanism as to whether or not it is a *religious* world-view. Those who see it as philosophy are known as *secular humanists*, whereas those who see it as religion are *religious humanists*. The dispute is fairly old and culminated earlier this century when, out of the two conflicting traditions, *modern humanism* was born. The fact that there is a dispute over the *nature* of the world-view does not detract from the fact that both groups share it. This was indicated in 1933 with the signing of the Humanist Manifesto I and in 1973 with the signing of the Humanist Manifesto II. Both groups advocated the contents of both documents.

Religious Humanism

The definition of religion used by religious humanists is functional – religion serves the personal and social needs of groups of people who share the same world-view. In serving personal needs, religious humanism attempts to offer a basis for morals and values, and an overall sense of purpose.

This does not mean that religious humanists are suggesting that all personal and social needs are met through traditional religious belief and practice. Rather, they stipulate that if an individual cannot satisfy his or her needs within the context of *traditional* religion, they should try to do so within the context of *non-traditional* religion.

According to **Frederick Edwords**, Executive Director of the American Humanist Association, '. . . the true substance of religion is the role it plays in the lives of individuals and the life of the community'.

What this means is that religious humanists make sure that any doctrine they advocate or support is *never* allowed to subvert the higher purpose of meeting real human needs. This is demonstrated in humanist wedding ceremonies, which are geared to the special needs of the couple and their community, while humanist memorials focus on 'those left behind' and how they are coping with their loss, rather than earnest attempts to save the soul of the departed.

Religious humanism is also seen as 'faith in action':

Humanism teaches us that it is immoral to wait for God to act for us. We must act to stop the wars and the crimes and the brutality of this and future ages. We have powers of a remarkable kind. We have a high degree of freedom in choosing what we will do. Humanism tells us that . . . ultimately the responsibility for the kind of world in which we live rests with us.

Kenneth Phifer, 'The faith of a humanist'
(Phifer is a Unitarian-Universalist church minister)

Secular Humanism

Secular humanists often refer to religious humanists as 'humanists not yet out of the church habit'!

Something to think about

What do you understand by the secular humanists' description of the religious humanists?

Something to think about

Salman Rushdie's book led to outrage in the Islamic community, as it was seen as blasphemous in questioning the authority of the Qur'an.

Look again at his comments above. What is he trying to say about organised religion in this statement? Why might a member of such a religious tradition object to these remarks?

The most renowned example of the secular humanist worldview in modern times is that of the author **Salman Rushdie**. When he was interviewed in February 1989 regarding his highly controversial novel, *The Satanic Verses*, he said:

> [My book says] that there is an old, old conflict between the secular view of the world and the religious view of the world, and particularly between texts which claim to be divinely inspired and texts which are imaginatively inspired . . . I distrust people who claim to know the whole truth and who seek to orchestrate the world in line with that one true truth. I think that's a very dangerous position in the world. It needs to be challenged. It needs to be challenged constantly in all sorts of ways, and that's what I tried to do.

Salman Rushdie, ABC's 'Nightline', 13 February 1989

The secular humanist tradition is one of defiance, which dates back to ancient Greece. There are even examples of this in Greek mythology, the best being that of Prometheus.

Prometheus stands out because he was idolised by the ancient Greeks as the one who defied Zeus. He stole the fire of the gods and brought it down to Earth. For this he was punished, yet he continued his defiance while he was tortured. This is the root of the humanist challenge to authority.

Humanists defend this rather defiant nature in their character from the perspective that much human progress has been made through the defiance of religion and, indeed, of other authorities.

For example, we lessen the effects of a so-called 'act of God' when we clear a town before a hurricane strikes, or a volcano erupts. Furthermore, from a political point of view, the defiance of religious and secular authority has led to democracy, human rights and environmental protection, amongst a great many other things. Humanists openly maintain and take great pride in their **'Promethean defiance'**.

In addition to defiance, there is another important aspect of secular humanism: **scepticism**. In this, secular humanists look to **Socrates** for their example. This is because, unlike Jesus, Muhammad, Buddha and Moses, Socrates did not claim to know the *absolute truth*; rather, he claimed to know *absolutely nothing*! Whereas the others attempt to derive sets of values and laws, Socrates' legacy was the *methodology* that he left to enable people to question those rules and values.

Both religious and secular humanism totally reject the notion of sin and any attempt to place guilt on the shoulders of an individual as a result of that sin. In the words of **Hannah Arendt** (German-born US philosopher/historian, 1906–1973):

> It is quite gratifying to feel guilty if you haven't done anything wrong: how noble!

Before moving on to examine a specific area that has developed from a basic humanist philosophy – Marxism – it is worth recognising the beliefs that are shared by both religious and secular humanists. This list is a summary put forward by Frederick Edwords, but is by no means exhaustive:

- Humanists do not claim to have transcendent knowledge.
- Humanism rejects 'blind' faith, authority and revelation; it supports reason and science in the pursuit of knowledge.
- Humanists place great emphasis on the importance of imagination; intuition, flashes of inspiration and emotion can be useful means to find solutions to problems, if rationally assessed.
- Humanists do not regard human values in the context of a 'life after death'; what matters is here and now.
- Humanism supports the work and approach of modern science.
- In the words of Frederick Edwords:

> Humanism is a philosophy for those with a love for life. Instead of finding solace in prefabricated answers to the great questions of life, Humanists enjoy the open-endedness of a quest and the freedom of discovery that this entails.

Frederick Edwords, 'What is humanism?', 1989

Something to think about

Which aspects of humanism do you find appealing, and which aspects would you reject? Why?

To conclude, it seems to be important as to whether humanism is secular or religious only from certain perspectives. It would appear that although the world-view is the same for both groups, the implications of that view are different. For the religious humanist, humanism manifests itself in the world as a functional body that serves the greater good of mankind. For the secular humanist, it is not appropriate to associate the good name of humanism with the word religion – it bears too many trappings of the notion of 'divine truths', which they emphatically reject.

Marxism

Karl Marx (1818–1883)

Marx has often been referred to as a 'humanist'. This is because he saw the answer to the question of the meaning of life as being very human indeed. His philosophy was a historical examination of the way in which people exist and interact.

When Marx entered the University of Berlin to read law in 1836, the philosophy of Hegel was dominant in Germany. Much of his early writing would be a response to Hegel and a consideration of the implications of his work. In addition to this, Marx was clearly influenced by Ludwig Feuerbach. As such, it is important to understand the central claims of both of these men.

G. W. F. Hegel (1770–1831)

Hegel wrote in an era in which 'subjectivity' was the concept that was enthralling academic circles all over Europe (particularly in France and Germany). After centuries of 'blind obedience' to Church and state (based on the notion that everyone *must* act and believe in the same way), people had found their freedom in the writing of Fichte, Schleiermacher and others.

These writers challenged the 'objective' view of religion. They declared that while a 'faith' in God was a powerful and important thing, it should not be seen in the terms put forward by the churches of the day. For **F. D. E. Schleiermacher** (1768–1834), God was not to be found in creeds, rituals and set formulas (prayers), but through religious experience, and through encountering the divine at a spiritual level.

Of course, this also meant that ethical understanding was changed. Sin was no longer seen as breaking some divine law, but as a reflection of the human desire to be free of any command, even God's.

Hegel was clearly unhappy with this state of affairs. From the very beginning of his intellectual career, his focus and inspiration was to determine the status of religious belief – in as empirical a fashion as was possible.

He was clearly influenced by Kant's notions of universalised ethical belief, which was the idea that we are all bound by the same *objective* laws and expectations. He would eventually put forward his famous system.

Hegel's system stated that there was a universal plane to which we all had access. He spoke of an 'absolute spirit' (*Geist*) which passed through a whole series of experiences and situations in order to find *true fulfilment*.

For example, he stated that (from a historical point of view) this spirit was to be found in successive societies and could be traced.

As societies became more humane, civilised and fair, the spirit could be seen getting nearer to 'fulfilment'. But what *is* this spirit?

Hegel says that the spirit is our innermost self. As history has progressed we have sought out ways of making life more appropriate to what we believe to be fair, just, correct and meaningful. It is *this*, therefore, which is the evidence of this spirit in action.

The main implication of this, as far as we are concerned, is that it means that there is a *common, universal truth* that we are all in search of; an objective truth, therefore. Hegel says that this truth can be found in Christianity – the 'absolute religion'.

Ludwig Andreas Feuerbach (1804–1872)

For Feuerbach, Hegel was wrong: it was not the case that God progressively realises himself in history – rather, ideas of religion are produced by men because they are dissatisfied or 'alienated' in their practical lives; therefore they *need* to believe in the 'fantasy' of religion.

Religion, said Feuerbach, is an 'expression of alienation'. The only freedom from this for mankind was to be through the realisation of *human* destiny. It was this idea which inspired

You need to know

Feuerbach, along with many other philosophers, makes frequent use of the term **alienation**. He, like Heidegger and Sartre after him, uses the term to mean 'separation'. Therefore, if people are said to be 'alienated', it suggests that they have lost sight of the true meaning of their existence and are 'separated' from any chance of personal fulfilment. Obviously, such separation is seen as harmful to the individual.

Marx's atheistic tendencies (he was born a Jew, but his family later converted to Christianity). Indeed, Marx was to describe religion (in one of his most famous phrases) as 'the opium of the people'.

Something to think about

Look again at the above paragraph and at the 'You need to know' panel. Why do you think Marx described religion as the 'opium of the people'?

Marx's Ideas

Marx was forced out of Germany in 1843, going first to Paris and then, in 1845, on to Brussels. During this transitory period, he formulated his 'Materialistic Theory of History'. This stated that 'alienation' is neither metaphysical nor religious, but really social and economic.

Marx developed what he claimed was a *scientific* method for analysing human history, and the impact that different societies have had on that society. From this, he concluded that there were individual *laws* behind historical change; laws that were *universal* and that could therefore be used to predict the future.

Marx agreed with Hegel that each period in history has its own culture and character. Therefore, laws that were truly universal *had* to be laws that considered and accounted for the development from one stage to the next.

His conclusion:

> *Ancient society* gave way to *feudal society*, which gave way to *capitalism*, which would give way to *communism*.

Does Marx's Idea Work?

There is a problem in suggesting that 'laws' can be used to predict future social development, even if these 'laws' are based on proven historical fact. The problem lies in the fact that human history is *unique*, and people are not inanimate objects.

We know that if we have a row of dominoes standing vertically at a certain distance apart and we flick the first one, they will all fall in order. This is basic 'cause and effect' and can be proven using basic geometry and physics. However, Marx's 'cause and effect' theory is not comparable to this. Marx would

Something to think about

What is the difference between a *law* and a *trend*? Illustrate your answer to this with specific examples.

have us believe that societies function like the dominoes, in that the effects and actions of one will directly and predictably affect the next. This is not so. Could we be *sure* that the dominoes *would* fall if they were free and intelligent beings, with consciences, morals, emotions and senses? Probably not.

Therefore, at best we can suggest that Marx has identified a *trend*, not established a *law*.

Marx dismissed 'academic' philosophy (for example, the 'metaphysical' question) as 'mere speculation'. He was and is referred to as a **materialist**. This term focuses upon his concentrating on matters of the material and historical world.

As a consequence of this position, Marx dismissed any notion of 'life after death', seeing it as a fantasy dreamt up by religion. Everything about the individual person was determined, stated Marx, by the material conditions of his life.

Marx has endeavoured to account for man, asking 'What is he?'. Essentially, he says, man is a social being. Everything, apart from biologically necessary factors such as eating, is determined by the society we live in.

Therefore, people in one society at one time will differ from those in another. Even the **way** in which the necessary elements of life take place is socially conditioned!

In Marx's words:

> . . . it is not the consciousness of men that determines their being, but, on the contrary, their social being determines their consciousness.

> *T. B. Bottomore and M. Rubel (eds), Karl Marx: Selected Writings in Sociology and Social Philosophy, Penguin, 1963*

Finally, Marx argued that man is an active, productive being and that he fulfils all his needs through productivity. Furthermore, the kind of life that is *right* for men is one of 'productive activity'. Indeed, *alienation* is the result of a lack of fulfilment in industrial labour.

This led to Marx's insistence that the coming communist era would enable each individual to fulfil his or her talents, which is why Marx is often referred to as a humanist. This idea, although considered by many to be unrealistic, stems from Marx's basic altruism. He believed that it is always wrong to treat a human being merely as a means to an economic end – and this meant *all* human beings.

Something to think about

Find out about **Materialism** in Chapter 13.

Something to think about

Consider the basic features of everyday life, such as eating. Are there any of these which are universal and objective? How do you think that society influences individuals in carrying out the most basic functions in life?

You need to know

Altruism is a term used to describe actions taken *purely* for the good of others, often with no regard for one's self.

Something to think about

What do you think Durkheim means by his comparison of our feelings about the sacred with those for the famous? Look at Rudolph Otto's suggestions about 'numinosity' in Chapter 3 for some ideas.

Something to think about

Durkheim asked, 'What essential difference is there between an assembly of Christians celebrating the principal dates of the life of Christ, or the Jews remembering the exodus from Egypt . . . and a reunion of citizens commemorating . . . some great event in the national life?'

What sort of occasions is Durkheim comparing religious practice to here? What are the similarities and differences between such occasions and religious activities?

You need to know

Secularisation describes the process of a group or society becoming less religious.

Something to think about

List some examples that show how an understanding of science and technology have replaced older religious beliefs.

Other Sociological Perspectives

Two other commentators who attempted to find a secular explanation of religion were Emile Durkheim and Max Weber.

Emile Durkheim (1858–1917)

Durkheim believed that religion was no more than a reflection of the human need to be part of a community. He suggested that all societies needed to reaffirm their collective unity at times, and that the worship and rituals of religion provided an effective context in which to do so.

He suggested that our natural instinct was to distinguish between the 'sacred' (religious) and the 'profane' (secular). Further to this, Durkheim believed that our feelings towards the sacred could be compared to our feelings towards royalty or famous people, for example.

Durkheim believed that certain aspects of religious activity provided important facilities for people. For example:

- *Symbols* provide a focus for an outpouring of emotion or belief. Examples might include the Christian cross or the Ka'bah in Makkah for Muslims.
- *Rituals*, such as the Catholic Mass or the Orthodox Divine Liturgy, provide the context for a community to share experiences.

Max Weber (1864–1920)

Like Durkheim, Weber also sought to 'explain away' religion without reference to the sacred. His approach was to focus on why religion had seemingly lost the impact and influence it had once enjoyed.

Weber believed that a process of 'desacrilisation' had occurred. This meant that there was no longer the need or requirement to rely upon supernatural explanations about the world that had existed in previous eras. He believed that people had become 'disenchanted', meaning that most people had lost the innocence that led them to believe in magical or mystical occurrences like, for example, the Virgin Birth.

Weber believed that secularisation was due to the dawn of the scientific age (see Chapter 10 for examples). He called this a wider process of 'rationalisation', suggesting that people were becoming increasingly able to view and affect the world through their understanding of science and technology.

Existentialism

Fundamentally, any philosophy that claims to be 'existentialist' must focus upon the unique nature of the *individual human agent*. There are many different theories regarding the formation and, in particular, the development, of this school of thought.

While most people credit **Jean-Paul Sartre** with its modern form, its origins are far more difficult to pinpoint. Most scholastic opinion, however, names **Søren Kierkegaard** as the 'father of existentialism'.

Søren Kierkegaard (CE 1813–1855)

Kierkegaard was one of the foremost thinkers of the nineteenth century. He wrote widely on religion, psychology and literature.

His life was one of enormous personal suffering and anxiety, his career filled with controversy. He started life as a dedicated Christian (the son of a prominent Protestant father), but he would eventually turn his back upon and dismiss organised religion.

In order to understand Kierkegaard's impact upon the philosophical climate since his lifetime, it is essential to examine the context in which he worked, and the ideas that he was responding to.

One the main inspirations for Kierkegaard was his fundamental objection to the work and ideas of Hegel.

How/Why does Kierkegaard Object to Hegel?

There is no doubt that Kierkegaard saw Hegel's view of the world as invalid. He despised the way in which Hegel accounted for *everything* through reason. For Kierkegaard, religion was not an organised body that functioned through rules, set formulas, politics and statesmanship. There is no doubt that both the Catholic Church and the Lutheran Church, of which he had been brought up a member, were such organised bodies. Rather, religion was a '**leap of faith**' (see Chapter 3). It could not be *reasoned through*, but simply believed in. In Kierkegaard's words:

> How often have I shown that fundamentally Hegel makes men into heathens, into a race of animals gifted with reason. For in the animal world 'the individual' is always less

important than the race. But the peculiarity of the human race is that just because the individual is created in the image of God, 'the individual' is above the race.

This can be wrongly understood and terribly misused ... But that is Christianity. And that is where the battle must be fought.

> R. G. Smith (trans.), *The Journals of Søren Kierkegaard, Harper and Row, 1965*

Kierkegaard accused Hegel of looking at humankind too generally, with no regard for the individual. Any notion of truth according to Hegel, therefore, seemed impersonal and dispassionate.

This seemed to Kierkegaard to conflict with the inherent nature of religion – indeed, with the Christianity he believed could yet fight its way free of church *reason* and *bureaucracy*.

For Kierkegaard, truth was to be found in *subjectivity*:

It is perfectly true, isolated subjectivity is, in the opinion of the age, evil; but 'objectivity' as a cure is not one whit better. The only salvation is subjectivity, i.e. God as infinite compelling subjectivity.

> R. G. Smith (trans.), *The Journals of Søren Kierkegaard, Harper and Row, 1965*

This means that religion is a subjective choice, not based on historical facts and/or reason.

How Successful was Kierkegaard?

While he was alive, Kierkegaard was ridiculed, heckled and disowned by all his friends, and ended up a recluse before dying at the age of 42. However, his influence on twentieth-century philosophy has been enormous. It is clear that his focus upon subjectivity can be seen in the work of Neitzche, Heidegger and Sartre.

However, there were problems with his philosophy – the most notable being that he left reason out of decisions concerning religion, existence and truth *altogether*.

Something to think about

Remind yourself of the implications of **Kierkegaard's** ideas in relation to organised religion, by looking back at Chapter 3.

Friedrich Wilhelm Nietzsche (1844–1900)

Nietzsche was a German philosopher/literary critic who specialised in classical (Greek and Roman) philosophy.

For many years, he saw composer Richard Wagner as a friend and inspiration for his work, but later fell out with him, because he came to see him as representing the fundamental problem that concerned him. This coincided with Wagner being closely associated with the movement that supported Aryan supremacy in Germany – the embryo of the Third Reich.

But what *was* that fundamental problem? Nietzsche saw the *world's* problem as a crisis of culture and, therefore, of meaning. He later characterised this in terms of 'the death of God'. He described the process as **nihilism**.

In *The Birth of Tragedy* (1872), Nietzsche suggested that the inspiration of philosophy and the arts *could* renew human meaning, as it had lost the 'consolations of religious faith' and the 'confidence in reason and science as substitutes for it'.

Between 1883 and 1885, Nietzsche produced the four parts of *Thus Spoke Zarathustra*. In these volumes, he arrived at a conception of human life and meaning. He saw a time of nihilism approaching as a result of the decline in traditional religious belief and values, which distressed him enormously.

Nietzsche was convinced that God and religion were not a tenable means of explaining our existence. He saw the challenge of philosophy as being to reinterpret life and the world in a far more tenable way than God and religion could ever provide, and also to overcome nihilism.

It seems that there were two ways of viewing Nietzsche:

As a 'radical nihilist'	As providing a serious attempt to overcome nihilism
Dismissing all that had gone before him, including religion, philosophers and codes of morality. Those who view Nietzsche in this way see his sweeping, negative comments as reducing *all* attempts to account for our existence to fiction and speculation	A more positive way of interpreting Nietzsche's work. This view demonstrates his *concern* over the speculated consequences of nihilism

Nietzsche emphasised the **perspectival** character of all thinking. This rejects the notion that there exists 'absolute truth or knowledge' regarding our existence. Therefore, for Nietzsche, there is no 'truth' regarding being; no knowledge that is absolute and certain. He calls this philosophy *fröhliche Wissenschaft* ('cheerful science').

Nietzsche saw the 'God hypothesis' as 'unworthy of belief'. He claimed that its invention was due to error and 'all-too-

Something to think about

By 'the death of God', Nietzsche was referring to the demise of Christian and moral interpretations of God and the world.

What do you think the problems of this demise could be? How could it affect the question of the meaning of life from the point of view of the religious believer?

Something to think about

Consider Nietzsche's point that nothing is objective or absolute. Do you agree? Illustrate your view with examples.

human need'. He also dismissed associated concepts, such as the 'soul', as ontological fictions.

Instead of this, Nietzsche conceives the world as being an interplay of many different forces. In terms of human existence, he calls the most significant concept the 'will to power'.

You need to know

By the 'will to power', Nietzsche meant that life can be viewed as a succession of power struggles and relationships, an idea that he shared with Darwin. He felt that the meaning of human life was to fulfil our potential. We can only do this by struggling and, as with any struggle, the strongest individuals will 'win'. Nietzsche attempted to re-interpret all human values in this context, and spoke of the *ubermensch* ('superman'). This is not to be confused with Nazi racial propaganda: the term referred to a person who *truly* recognised the human condition – that there was no God. Love (agape) and compassion were therefore seen as weaknesses. For Nietzsche, morality could only be built upon *strength*.

You need to know

The term **agape** is used frequently by St Paul in his letters. It refers to 'self-giving love', or love for our fellow man. It is not to be confused with **philos** (friendship) or **eros** (sexual love).

The implications of Nietzsche's views in relation to the question of human purpose and destiny are considerable. He asserts the immediate recognition that there is no God and that we as human beings must actualise our own potential for one reason only – *our own happiness, comfort and convenience*.

Martin Heidegger (1889–1976)

The work of Martin Heidegger can be divided clearly into two parts – the earlier and later works. It is his earlier work that to a certain extent inspired and influenced existentialism's most famous advocate, Jean-Paul Sartre.

Heidegger's most important piece of work was *Sein und Zeit* ('Being and Time', 1927). Published while he was teaching at Marburg University, the book focused on the classic metaphysical question, 'What is the being of entities in general?'. Drawing mainly on the work of Kierkegaard, but also recognising Nietzsche among others, Heidegger rejected what were seen as 'traditional' theories.

You need to know

Metaphysics is the philosophical study and investigation of reality. It includes questions regarding the origin of the universe, the existence of God and the nature of causation.

Heidegger claimed that philosophers since Plato had tried to answer the 'question of being' by viewing 'being' as a property or essence that is present in everything. He tried, therefore, to ask the question 'What is the *meaning* of being?'

In an attempt to answer the question, Heidegger undertook an analysis of *Dasein* ('existence').

Heidegger comments early on in *Being and Time* that most attempts to analyse existence do so by concentrating on it in an abstract and theoretical way. He attempts to overcome this traditional approach by trying to describe the 'average everydayness' of Dasein. 'Everydayness' is said to incorporate the totality of human existence; that is, our moods, our capacity to be individual and our general involvements with the world.

A major influence on the work of Sartre can be found in Heidegger's suggestion that there is no such thing as 'human essence'. Rather, human beings *are* what they *make of themselves* in everyday life.

This, Heidegger maintains, can be observed in every way of living, for within every way of living, there are three basic elements:

1 the fact that all that exists is 'thrown' into life – where and when is accidental
2 that what we *do*, or indeed *anything* does, defines what we are or what it is
3 the fact that discussions of situations occur

When taken cumulatively, these points suggest that 'we constitute our identity through what we do'. Obviously, such a claim refutes any notion of a meaningful, preordained path for our lives to follow.

Heidegger observed that the normal way to observe an object's existence is to do so only in the context of what it actually does. Consider the following example.

Upon seeing a plane flying overhead for the first time, a child asks his or her parent *What's that?* According to the notion put forward by Heidegger above, the answer given will account for the existence of the plane *not* as an individual, independent existent object, but as an object that serves a purpose within a much wider functionality.

The answer would probably *not* be *That's an aeroplane, which is a heavier-than-air flying machine with wings*. Rather, it might be something like *That's an aeroplane, which takes people to other countries for their holidays*.

When applied to ourselves, this idea leads us to a discussion of another human phenomenon that Sartre would explore; **inauthenticity**. Because of the practices of the community or culture within which we exist, Heidegger suggests that the human inclination is to 'drift along with the crowd'. This, said Heidegger, reduces our ability to grasp and define our own lives, as we are preoccupied with doing what pleases others, or what society expects and demands of us.

However, Heidegger maintained that if we cannot be seen to be existent other than within the communal context, striving to be authentic involves realising a *communal destiny*.

While this conclusion might be very appealing to the religious existentialist (such as Kierkegaard), it does not affirm religion as a method with which to realise any destiny. Heidegger's central assertion remains that the meaning of human life and purpose is to be found 'here and now', during one's life, through experience and action.

Jean-Paul Sartre (1905–1980)

Sartre is the most famous exponent of existentialism. He expressed his ideas not only through philosophy, but also through literature and drama. His influence on twentieth-century thought is profound.

Jean-Paul Sartre

There are three main concerns that Sartre identifies as central to existentialism:

- The first concern is with the *individual* human being, not with general ideas about humanity. It is an individual's uniqueness that makes him important.
- The second is with the *meaning* of human lives, not scientific truths about the world. Sartre is saying that subjective experience is always regarded as more important than objective truth, as Kierkegaard had suggested.
- The third concern is with the *freedom* of individuals. For Sartre, every person has the ability to, and must, choose his or her own attitudes, purpose and lifestyle.

Sartre, like most existentialists, maintained that the only 'authentic' way of life is that which is freely chosen by each individual him- or herself.

You need to know

Sartre used the term **authentic** to describe a way of life that is active and that recognises one's own limitations. It is a way of life that involves *being* an individual, making individual choices and being prepared to stand by the consequences of those choices. The opposite way of life is **inauthentic** – not accepting that we are free to choose who we are and what we do.

Existentialist philosophies have presented themselves in various forms over the years. The most radical division was between religious existentialism (whose exponents include Kierkegaard), and atheistic existentialism (for example, the work of Nietzsche and Marx).

Kierkegaard (like Marx) rejected Hegelian philosophy, but for different reasons. He suggested that the supreme importance lay not with theoretical abstractions, but with the individual and his choices. He maintained that there were three ways of life – the atheistic, the ethical and the religious – between which individuals must choose. He stated categorically that the religious (and in particular, Christian) way was the greatest choice.

Nietzsche was clearly an atheist. As we have seen, he stated the importance of re-evaluating the very foundations and purpose of our lives, as a consequence of 'the death of God'. Therefore any meaning had to be in human terms alone.

These two, along with Heidegger, clearly inspired Sartre enormously. Their ideas can be seen as being reflected in his most famous works. Sartre was also inspired by his own life. His constant focus on the importance of *individual choice* was based on personal experience. After a very lonely and unfulfilling childhood, he was eventually thrown into an environment that confronted him (like all Frenchmen at the time) with pivotal choices every day – the Nazi-occupied France of the early 1940s. The choice at this time was threefold:

- some Frenchmen collaborated with and supported the Nazi occupying force
- some joined and supported the 'French Resistance'
- others simply tried to stay alive by not drawing attention to themselves or to their families

It is clear that under these highly stressful conditions, any choice had to be made with a thorough consideration of the consequences, and absolute acceptance of the responsibility for one's actions. These ideas are prevalent in Sartre's work.

Sartre's Ideas

Sartre claimed that the very idea of God was self-contradictory. He does not spend a great deal of time *proving* this point, as it were, but (like Nietzsche) moves on to consider the consequences of living in a world without God. Sartre does not dismiss 'the God-notion'. He states that God's non-existence is a fact that *must* confront us all in our lives, as the atheist has a profoundly different view of human existence from the theist.

As **Fyodor Dostoyevsky** suggested:

> If God does not exist, then everything is permitted.

Fyodor Dostoyevsky, The Brothers Karamazov, 1879–1880

Sartre contended that the only basis for morality is human freedom. There is no universal justification for the set of values chosen by an individual.

Sartre rejected the very term 'human nature', as it is too general. This is a position that most existentialists would share. We simply 'find' ourselves existing, and must *decide* what to make of ourselves, as Heidegger suggested. However, if we cannot make general statements to which we all can relate, is it the case that there are no true statements about anything? There are some things which we have to do – such as eating, sleeping and relieving ourselves – so Sartre was referring to a lack of true statements about what we *ought* to be. For example, *we ought to tell the truth* is a meaningless statement, as it inherently assumes that always telling the truth will be for the best.

The Conscious Self

Sartre observed that consciousness is always of something other than itself. If I am conscious of your presence in a room, I have recognised you and I am aware that you are in

Something to think about

What do you think Dostoyevsky meant by this remark? What are the implications for the morality of

- a religious believer
- a non-believer

of God not existing?

Something to think about

Based on Sartre's point above, it would appear that any statements that tell us what we *ought* or *ought not* to do are meaningless and untrue. Look again at Sartre's reasoning for this. Then list four or five statements that tell us what we ought or ought not to do. Are there any circumstances in which obeying these commands would be inappropriate?

You need to know

Consciousness is being aware of objects.

the same place as me. Logically, it is necessary to distinguish between human consciousness and whatever the object is. Sartre refers to human consciousness as *le pour-soi* (a being 'for itself') and to non-conscious objects as *en-soi* (a being 'in itself'). The fact that we can distinguish between our own consciousness and the objects of which we are conscious enables us to make judgements about objects, which can be either positive or negative. For example, it is easy for us to make a negative judgement; that is, to say what is not the case (for example, *Laura is not here*). It is in our ability to make these negative judgements that Sartre perceived our freedom. This is because, in consciously understanding *what is not the case*, we are free to imagine what could be the case. He contended that we could never reach a stage or state in which *all possibilities* are fulfilled. Significantly, Sartre thought that we are trying to reach a state in which we become *en-soi* while remaining *pour-soi*. However, he believed that this could never be achieved, as it would constitute a logical absurdity. This is why he described human life as:

> . . . an unhappy consciousness with no possibility of surpassing its unhappy state.
>
> *Jean-Paul Sartre, Being and Nothingness (trans. H. Barnes), Methuen, 1957*

But what does all this freedom mean in everyday life?

Sartre maintained that every aspect of our conscious lives is *chosen* and is *our responsibility*. This includes our emotions; for Sartre, if we are sad, it is because we choose to make ourselves sad. Therefore, I cannot say *I am friendly*, as if this were an objective fact such as *I am male*, because friendliness is a way I choose to be for whatever reason. I am perfectly capable, as a free being, of behaving differently. Therefore, the statement *I am friendly* says nothing about any fact already in existence, but is simply an expression of how I believe others will perceive me.

Therefore, as far as Sartre is concerned, freedom needs to be recognised and accepted. As Kierkegaard did before him, Sartre uses the term **anguish** to describe our consciousness of this freedom. It fills us with anguish precisely because we do not know what we will do! Human beings are unpredictable creatures. For example, consider a performer who *fears* being disliked by his or her public, but *feels anguish* at the thought of being unable to complete the performance because of a nervous disposition!

Something to think about

List any other attributes that we 'choose' according to Sartre's point here.

'Bad Faith'

Sartre believed that the anguish we feel because we are conscious of our freedom can cause us to try to avoid such recognition. Such an attempt, he warned, is illusory. Indeed, he called any attempt to pretend we are *not* free 'bad faith'. He illustrated his point with some examples, two of which are given here:

- A girl is sitting with a man who she knows would like to seduce her. When this man takes her hand, she pretends not to notice. Sartre said that this is because she is trying to avoid having to make a decision as to whether or not she should accept his advances. In doing so, she is pretending that she is not a free and conscious being but, rather, an object.
- The second example concerned a waiter who was obviously over-keen. Sartre claimed that he was trying too hard to be something, which is futile, as no man is essentially anything.

However, if 'bad faith' is the ultimate in self-deception, then sincerity is the ultimate in honesty. But Sartre pointed out that there are inherent problems here also. If you make a statement such as *I am a student*, then you are acting to distinguish between your conscious self (*I*) and the object that you are referring to (*a student*). We can never be what we claim to be!

Sartre's Recommendations

Because Sartre rejected any notion of objective values, he cannot really recommend *any* particular lifestyle to which mankind should aspire. In fact, his only recommendation is that we try our utmost to be authentic, by being fully aware of our choices, and acknowledging that nothing determines them for us. The key implication of this is that *freedom equals responsibility*. The implications of this point are considerable. Our lifestyle, behaviour, character, emotions, attitude to work and relationships are as they are because *we choose* this to be the case.

Sartre illustrated both the importance and the simplicity of freedom in the following example, taken from *Existentialism and Humanism* (1973).

A young Frenchman asked Sartre whether he should help the Resistance effort by going to the aid of the free French forces in England, or stay with his mother in France. Sartre's

Something to think about

Bearing all of these points in mind, is it possible to be an authentic human being? Or, as a race, are we doomed to be a group of people who are always trying to be what we can never be, and claiming to be what we are not?

'No', says Sartre.

Something to think about

Would a religious believer agree with Sartre on this point? If a person did not accept that these things were purely down to personal choice, how might he or she suggest that they were determined?

response was 'You are free, therefore choose.' While this may seem insensitive to the young man's plight, it is illustrative of the belief that there is no prescriptive criteria upon which such a decision could be made.

The conclusion of this is that one simply cannot escape the 'anguish' of freedom. Even choosing to reject one's responsibilities is an exercise in freedom!

Sartre – an Evaluation

There is one central problem inherent within Sartre's philosophy, and it is highlighted by Leslie Stevenson in *Seven Theories of Human Nature* (1974).

If Sartre was suggesting that there is no objective basis for choosing to act and live one's life in a certain way, then it would seem that there is in fact no basis for life! If any 'choice' that one makes is made for no particular reason, other than the fact that we are free to make it, then surely it does not matter what we choose!

As Stevenson contends, it appears that Sartre would describe as 'responsible and authentic' a man who devoted his life to exterminating Jews, if he did so in full knowledge of what he was doing and the implications of it. By the same token, Sartre would dismiss as 'inauthentic' the man who devoted his life to helping the homeless, if he refused to disclose why he was doing so!

Significantly, Sartre did not complete the book he said he would write on an 'ethical code' to correspond with his philosophical position. This was possibly because his position was so egocentric that no ethical code *could* be formed.

Also, towards the end of his life, Sartre became an emphatic advocate of Marxism. Stevenson suggests that this was because the establishment of a Marxist system of government and economy would make it possible for *all* men to exercise their freedom.

Moral Responsibility

So far, we have considered three main philosophical positions, all of which focus on human beings as responsible for their own lives, destiny and sense of purpose. Apart from the more obscure forms of **religious existentialism**, all the schools of thought we have looked at dismiss the notions of God and universal, objective moral laws. This dismissal now requires more detailed investigation. As mentioned at the beginning, most philosophical world-views are either religious or non-religious. Those that are religious frequently exhibit moral codes that are based upon determinist philosophies, whereas those that are non-religious base their concept of morality in the realm of free will, as described by Heidegger, Sartre and others.

Determinist Philosophies as a Basis for Moral Action

These philosophical perspectives, as mentioned above, contend that basically **all** events are in fact **effects**. That is to say, everything that happens does so because it has been specifically caused to happen. If this is true, then we can be sure that the future is as fixed and as certain as the past. For determinists there are no **possible** futures, there is only that which **is to be**. This is because any other outcome would be impossible. William James develops this idea, suggesting that 'any other future complement than the one fixed from eternity is impossible'.

Scientific Determinism

Some believe that rational judgement is also undermined by determinism. This is because most of our beliefs are adopted after (what we consider to be) a process of rational thought. For example, if I spend considerable time working on a geometric puzzle, I would say that my conclusion is the result of a process in which I have made every decision. I would then believe the conclusion to be true. However, if determinism is true, the fact that I have reached this conclusion would, in fact, be causally determined, *not* the result of my thought process. This suggests that it would be possible for an intelligent being accurately to predict the future state of the world.

Scientific determinism is the belief that:

1 every event is caused
2 at any time, only *one* future is possible *because of* the past
3 knowing all the previous conditions and occurrences, and having an awareness of the laws of nature, an agent *could* predict the subsequent history of the universe

This is a view put forward and developed by Pierre Laplace in the eighteenth and nineteenth centuries. Paul d'Holbach (1723–1789) suggested that *everything* was the direct result of the movement of matter – with one thing causing the next.

You need to know

Basically, a **determinist** philosophy suggests that events are predestined. In moral terms, this means that I will be good if 'it's meant to be', or vice versa. In many cases, those that advocate a determinist basis for morality contend that it is God who predestines everything. The 'freewill' approach asserts that *I* and *only I* am responsible for my actions. I do whatever I do, and must be fully accountable for the consequences.

Something to think about

List as many factors as you can think of that influence our behaviour (whether moral or otherwise). Does your list suggest that we are *free* or *determined*?

Something to think about

Have another look at the section on Karl Marx. Before reading on, state whether or not *you* think that Marx was a determinist, and give reasons for your answer.

You need to know

A **libertarian** is the extreme opposite of a determinist. Such a person believes that all people are free to make decisions, and they are therefore *responsible for those decisions*. A further implication is that the past obviously does not determine a unique present, nor does the present lead us to an inevitable future.

This was because he saw reality only in terms of physical matter; he completely rejected the Christian concept of the 'soul', for example. Although many people credit the work of Isaac Newton with instilling the ideas of scientific determinism, more recent commentators suggest that there is much more to scientific determinism than Newtonian physics.

In more recent times, research by certain behaviourists has suggested that freedom *is* in fact an illusion, and that our behaviour is brought about by genetic and environmental factors.

Social/Historical Determinism

J. L. Mackie stated that many of the traditional social/historical theories of determinism (for example, Marxism) are speculative in the extreme. He believed that they do no more than provide **very rough** statistical trends. He claimed that one of the most important arguments against determinism is that we directly experience freedom when we choose. This is because in choosing we are aware of what we could have done otherwise. There are a number of theories that could be considered under this title. As we have already discussed Karl Marx's ideas earlier in this chapter, we will continue to use this example.

From a certain point of view the answer would appear to be that Marx certainly *was* a determinist. Those who advocate this theory focus upon the **inevitable progress of history** through various economic phases, as **guiding human destiny**. In other words, one particular society *caused* the next, and there was nothing anyone could do to change it or prevent it from happening.

However, from another perspective, one must acknowledge that Marx, like many prominent 'Marxists' or communists since, has urged readers and audiences not only to **recognise** that history is moving towards the communist revolution, but also to **act to bring it about**. In other words, some believe that Marx was a **libertarian**, who wanted people to 'seize their own lives' and control their own futures.

Therefore, there exists a conflict of opinion within Marxism today:

1   those expecting 'the Revolution'
2   those trying to bring 'the Revolution' about

Theological Determinism

If the future is determined, does anyone know what it will be like? The school of thought known as 'theological determinism' asserts that as God is an omniscient and transient being, He, and only He, knows what the future holds. However, from the point of view of this chapter, the key question is not who knows what the future entails, but whether or not our lives are determined. According to Ted Honderich in *A Theory of Determinism*, the very idea of determinism questions 'life-hopes, personal feelings, knowledge, moral responsibility, the rightness of actions and the moral standing of persons'.

Some scholars suggest that there is an incompatibility between determinism on the one hand and the concept of moral responsibility on the other. These scholars are referred to as **Incompatibilists** or **Hard Determinists**. The Incompatibilist would assert that if I am to be responsible for my actions, surely I have to be free to choose those actions. If I am to do something because it is pre-ordained for me to do it, is it really my decision? Many would say not. Hard Determinists are not interested in so-called 'human desires' as the motivation for our actions; rather, they look at the causal factors *behind* such desires.

However, there is a group of people who are known as **Compatibilists** or **Soft Determinists**, who dismiss claims that determinism and moral responsibility contradict each other. They suggest that the logical opposite of 'free' is not 'caused', rather it is 'forced'. Therefore, a free act is an act in which the person involved **could have** chosen otherwise, even if it was pre-ordained. As G. E. Moore suggested, we are free in performing actions if we **could have done otherwise** and **would have done otherwise** if we had **chosen to do so**. This applies, according to Moore, even if determinism is true. The Soft Determinist approach allows humans to be more than just physical beings. It suggests that we have an active *metaphysical* side to our existence (possibly 'the soul', possibly what Kant referred to as 'the Noumenal') that can influence our decisions.

A good example of theological determinism can be found in the work of Gottfried Leibniz (1646–1716). He saw God as an infinite and eternal mind that has designed the world as it is. As each thing is caused by something previous to it, a given set of circumstances *would* lead to an inevitable and unique future.

But what about the issue of predictability?

You need to know

Consider the importance of free will as a reason for the existence of evil in the world by looking at the section on 'The Freewill Defence' in Chapter 8.

Leibniz suggests that it will never be possible for humans to predict what will happen, as our minds are imperfect, limited and finite, unlike God's.

What about the issue of evil?

Leibniz suggests that a world in which humans have *apparent* free will must be better than a seemingly perfect world in which there is no evil. He bases this conclusion on the assumption that a perfect God would create a perfect world.

Some Muslim theologians hold a similar idea to Leibniz. In considering **al-Qadr** ('predestination'), they suggest that God **does** predestine our lives, but that there is no contradiction between this and free will, as people have no knowledge of what God has pre-ordained for them. This 'blissful ignorance' means that every choice made by an individual is truly free.

The implication here is that belief in predestination is fully compatible with free will and personal, moral responsibility.

Origination

From a philosophical perspective the logical opposite to determinism is origination. Basically, this is the process of a totally free human choice or action beginning a new chain of cause and effect. It is, to go back to an earlier analogy, the 'flick' that starts the row of dominoes falling. Pivotally, it is a 'flick' that has not been caused, but decided on by a free and conscious human mind. Determinists reject origination, claiming that it is merely a fanciful notion that takes the place of the genuine 'first cause', which is frequently believed to be God.

Something to think about

How might each of the philosophical positions in this chapter (humanism, Marxism and existentialism) affect an individual's moral behaviour?

Essay questions

AS
(a) Describe and explain the Marxist theory of the nature of human purpose and destiny.
(b) Explain and evaluate Marx's view that 'religion is the opium of the people'.

A2
(a) Outline two theories of the nature of human purpose and destiny.
(b) In what ways might the advocates of these theories differ from religious believers, in their outlook on life?

Chapter 12   Miracles

Look it up

The term **miraculous** refers to events that cannot be explained by natural laws alone.

The term **natural law** refers to the concept that certain actions will produce certain consequences, based on the scientific observation of nature. Natural laws rely on past experience to tell us how the natural world operates.

The concept of the miraculous is perhaps the single feature of religion that is most vividly able to capture the imagination of the non-religious. Many people use the word in their everyday vocabulary, often to denote nothing more than a very welcome and somewhat surprising event or series of events. It is not unusual to hear recovery from serious illness being described as 'miraculous', although all that is meant is that it is unexpected, against the odds or simply lucky.

The religious use of the term has tended to denote something more deeply significant than that which is merely surprising. Miracles have been considered so special as to prove that God intervenes within our daily lives. They have been used to establish the existence of God.

This chapter will therefore examine four main areas:

- What is a miracle?
- Can miracles occur?
- Do miracles occur?
- If miracles do occur, what can be deduced from this?

Something to think about

Think of three examples of what you would consider to be miraculous events.

From these examples, what are you taking to be the essential features of a miracle?

What is a Miracle?

The traditional concept of a miracle is generally understood to include two things:

- an interruption to the processes of nature that cannot be explained by natural laws
- an interruption that bears some deeper, usually religious, significance

The first point is made clear by David Hume:

> A miracle may be accurately defined, 'A transgression of a law of nature by a particular volition of the Deity or by the interposition of some invisible agent.'
>
> *David Hume, 'An enquiry concerning human understanding', 1748*

You need to know

To **transgress** means literally to *pass beyond*. A **transgression** usually refers to a *violation* of a law.

Something to think about

Consider what would constitute a 'transgression of a law of nature'.

Is it possible to rule out a natural and as yet undiscovered explanation?

In other words, a miracle is brought about when some 'invisible agent' affects the working of the universe. This definition is, by and large, accepted by philosophers today.

To illustrate the concept of such 'transgressions', Richard Swinburne gives some examples taken from the Bible:

> Levitation; resurrection from the dead in full health of a man whose heart has not been beating for twenty four hours and who was dead also by other currently used criteria; water turning into wine without the assistance of chemical apparatus or catalysts; a man getting better from polio in a minute.

Richard Swinburne (ed.), Miracles, Macmillan, 1989

If we break down Swinburne's examples into their individual stages, we find occurrences that happen frequently within nature. Men can recover from illness, and wine can be produced using water as its main ingredient quite naturally, without any questions being raised. It is not the events themselves in Swinburne's examples which make them remarkable, but the timescale and the order in which they occur. They take place without the generally accepted conditions such that the result can normally be brought about. Although, for example, people have frequently recovered from polio, they have not done so 'in a minute'. When water is normally turned into wine, the process does not happen spontaneously, and nor does it take a mere few seconds. Since these events operate outside the bounds of natural laws, they are considered miraculous.

The transgression of a natural law is not considered sufficient by itself to grant an event the status of a miracle. It is generally considered that miracles need to hold some deeper significance than the transgression itself; that is, miracles are considered to point beyond themselves to some underlying plan or reality. Swinburne expresses the point clearly:

> If a god intervened in the natural order to make a feather land here rather than there for no deep ultimate purpose, or to upset a child's box of toys just for spite, these events would not naturally be described as miracles.

Richard Swinburne (ed.), Miracles, Macmillan, 1989

Something to think about

List all the coincidences you can think of which have led to your eyes being the colour they are.

Why would you not attribute the colour of your eyes to a miracle?

In contrast to Swinburne's examples above, a supernatural healing, believed to be the work of a loving God, could be considered miraculous; for it would have the significance of demonstrating God's nature to the world and demonstrating that He has a plan for everyone.

It is worth referring here to another school of thought upon the nature of miracles. It has been suggested that even those events that do not break any natural law may be considered miraculous, if the sense of divine purpose and significance is strong enough. **R. F. Holland**, an upholder of this position, says that 'A coincidence can be taken religiously as a sign and called a miracle.' If, for example, a religious person prayed for the safety of a friend who was known to be in danger, and if a remarkable and unexpected series of events brought about this person's safety, the one who made the prayer would very likely consider the coincidence miraculous.

Something to think about

Imagine that a young boy strays on to a railway line, into the path of an oncoming express. At the same time, the driver of the train has a heart attack. His hand releases the dead man's handle, and the train comes to a stop less than a metre from the boy.

Would this be considered a miracle or a coincidence?

Is this a miracle or a coincidence?

Can Miracles Occur?

The answer to this question depends upon which definition of miracle we accept. Upon Holland's definition, it is clearly the case that unusual and striking coincidences happen all the time. The difficulty here is that every single event in the world can be attributed to a unique and enormously complex set of coincidences. It is not possible, therefore, to isolate any one of these coincidences and prove that it has been caused by something different from all the others. Holland himself admits that 'it cannot without confusion be taken as a sign of divine interference with the natural order.' David Hume, sceptical at the best of times, flatly denies that such an event could be considered miraculous:

Something to think about

What do you think Hume means by 'the common course of nature'.

> Nothing is esteemed a miracle, if it ever happens in the common course of nature.

> *David Hume, 'An enquiry concerning human understanding', 1748*

What of the more typical understanding of miracle, as an event that interrupts the natural laws of the universe? Here we shall consider three points:

- doubt as to the existence of natural laws
- the argument against miracles from the definition of a natural law
- Hume's critique of miracles

Doubt as to the Existence of Natural Laws

This point is simple, though worth stating. The definition of miracles as breaches of natural laws can only be upheld if we accept that there are natural laws.

Certain **theists** would argue that every single event in the world is totally and directly dependent upon God. As **Brian Davies** explains, for such people 'God is as present in what is not miraculous as he is in the miraculous.' If God is equally present in every action, it would not make sense to speak of His 'intervention'. In reality, however, this is not a serious criticism, since the majority of theists would accept that it is through natural laws that God continues to sustain the world. In other words, God has put into place a set of natural laws which enables the world to govern itself. One reason for His doing so is to give humans a consistent environment, in which we can predict with reasonable accuracy the results of our actions. In this case, it still makes sense to say that in certain exceptional circumstances, God can choose to interrupt the working of His laws.

The Argument against Miracles from the Definition of a Natural Law

It has been argued that our definition of natural laws can preclude the possibility of anything being termed a miracle. **John Hick**, for example, defines natural laws as 'generalisations formulated retrospectively to cover whatever has, in fact, happened'; in which case, bearing in mind that a miracle is a breach in a natural law, he argues, 'We can declare *a priori* that there are no miracles.' Upon this basis, the occurrence of an unusual, previously unwitnessed event should make us widen our understanding of the natural law so as to incorporate the possibility of the new event. There would certainly be no grounds for assuming that this new event breaks the law, for the law itself is only established on the basis of empirical evidence.

Something to think about

When you place a saucepan filled with water on a gas flame, you expect the water to heat up. You know this on the basis of your past experience and the past experience of others. If, one day, you performed the same action and the water turned instead to ice, would you be surprised?

Upon the basis of Hick's argument, you should simply accept that sometimes the gas flame will cause water to freeze. *Why would you not in all probability do this?* Why might it be justifiable to suspect the working of a non-human agent?

Technically speaking, Hick's argument is unassailable. Everyone accepts that natural laws must be widened as and when new discoveries are made. What is now considered impossible may one day be common. It may one day be possible, for example, to communicate with others by thought alone, through the aid of a microchip, implanted in the brain.

Yet this does not mean that certain events might not be found to go completely against our expectations on the basis of all past experience. As a result, we might reasonably look for a cause that is separate from the normal world of our experience. Swinburne, for example, allows that natural laws are not adequately able to cover every single possible happening everywhere. He believes, however, that they are able to give a generally accurate picture of what we should expect to happen in a given situation. He concludes, therefore, that an event such as the Resurrection of Jesus could reasonably be considered miraculous, since it is totally contrary to the normal results of death and since it would not be expected to happen again in similar circumstances. In practice, then, Hick's comment is more of a technical point about the definition of miracles and natural laws. It does not rule out the possibility of events in which a cause outside the world is involved. For this reason, Hick himself admits that there are 'unusual and striking events evoking and mediating a vivid awareness of God'.

Hume's Critique of Miracles

David Hume offers a traditional and comprehensive argument against the occurrence of miracles. Hume's point is not so much that miracles are impossible, but that it would be impossible for us ever to prove that one had happened. He writes:

> A miracle is a violation of the laws of nature; and as a firm and unalterable experience has established these laws, the proof against a miracle, from the very nature of the fact, is as entire as any argument from experience can be possibly imagined. Why is it more than probable that all men must die; that lead cannot, of itself, remain suspended in the air; that fire consumes wood, and is extinguished by water; unless it be, that these events are found agreeable to the laws of nature, and that there is required a violation of these, or in other words, a miracle to prevent them.

> *David Hume, 'An enquiry concerning human understanding', 1748*

Certain miracles, such as the Feeding of the Five Thousand, clearly purported to have many witnesses. For Hume, however, this makes no difference:

> No testimony is sufficient to establish a miracle unless the testimony be of such a kind, that its falsehood would be more miraculous, than the fact, which it endeavours to establish; and even in that case there is a mutual destruction of arguments, and the superior only gives us assurance to that degree of force, which remains, after deducting the inferior.
>
> *David Hume, 'An enquiry concerning human understanding', 1748*

Hume's argument is that laws of nature have been supported innumerably over a period of many hundreds of years. There are literally millions of examples to show that humans, once dead, do not return to life; nor that pieces of metal, when dropped, continue to hang in the air. An apparent miracle, therefore, which contradicts a natural law, would need to outweigh all the evidence that had established the law in the first place. Hume seems to be saying that it would be unreckonably more probable that the miracle be false than that the evidence in favour of the natural law be proved incorrect. It would be more likely, for example, that one was hallucinating than that one was truly witnessing an exception to the law.

This argument clearly requires comment, but Hume does not simply leave matters here. Instead, he goes on to give four further reasons why it is certain that no miracle was ever established.

The **first** is that there has never been

> . . . in all history, any miracle attested by a sufficient number of men, of such unquestioned good-sense, education and learning, as to secure us against all delusion in themselves; of such undoubted integrity, as to place them beyond all suspicion of any design to deceive others; of such credit and reputation in the eyes of mankind, as to have a great deal to lose in case of their being detected in any falsehood; and at the same time, attesting facts performed in such a public manner and in so celebrated a part of the world, as to render the detection unavoidable.
>
> *David Hume, 'An enquiry concerning human understanding', 1748*

Something to think about

If you were to witness *one* exception to the law of gravity, what would you expect to happen next time you dropped something?

Why might an exception to a rule not *necessarily* have to outweigh all those cases that supported a rule?

Something to think about

Does Hume explain precisely what would constitute a reliable witness?

Why might you find it difficult to identify an *actual* group of people whose testimony Hume would, in practice, be willing to accept?

Something to think about

If you *want* to believe that something is true, will you *always* be willing to set aside truth and accept a lie?

Why might your desire for truth outweigh your desire to believe what you want?

Something to think about

Write a list of 'supernatural and miraculous' occurrences that are alleged to have happened, and the nations that have claimed them.

What *types* of nations are on your list?

Do you consider them 'ignorant and barbarous' nations?

Something to think about

If a Christian and a Jew were both, simultaneously, to witness a miracle (as happened in the Bible), what would this say about Hume's argument?

What argument(s) can be used against Hume's fourth criticism?

Hume's **second** reason supports his first, and consists of the claim that those testifying to the miracle will have a natural tendency to suspend their reason and support the claim:

> The passion of surprise and wonder, arising from miracles, being an agreeable emotion, gives a sensible tendency towards the belief of those events, from which it is derived. And this goes so far, that even those who cannot enjoy this pleasure immediately, nor can believe those miraculous events, of which they are informed, yet love to partake of the satisfaction at second-hand, or by rebound, and place a pride and delight in exciting the admiration of others . . . A religionist may be an enthusiast, and imagine he sees what has no reality: he may know his narratives to be false, and yet persevere in it, with the best intentions in the world, for the sake of promoting so holy a cause.

> *David Hume, 'An enquiry concerning human understanding', 1748*

Hume's **third** reason makes the further claim that 'It forms a strong presumption against all supernatural and miraculous relations that they are observed chiefly to abound among ignorant and barbarous nations.'

Hume's **fourth** argument rests upon the premise that the different religions are mutually exclusive. As a result, the miracle accounts arising from each religious tradition, with the intention of supporting it, cancel each other out.

A Critique of Hume's Argument

We have now considered Hume's criticisms in some detail, because they constitute a grave attack made upon the possibility of the occurrence of miracles. There are, however, many flaws to his arguments. For this reason, it can be argued that even the cumulative weight of the criticism does not make it impossible to accept the occurrence of a miracle.

Let us consider first the criticism that a miracle account would need to outweigh all the evidence in favour of a natural law. This is based on the assumption that there must be a mutually exclusive choice between the generally accepted law on the one hand and the miraculous exception on the other. This assumption is hard to justify. The whole point to a miracle is that it is an exception to the rule. As such, its occurrence in no way challenges the force of the general rule, except upon that one occasion. If Hume's argument were to be accepted, we should need to reject a large proportion of the scientific developments in recent centuries. This is because many of these have forced us to accept as possible things that would once have been considered impossible upon the basis of past experience. Brian Davies provides such an example:

> We might say (though rather oddly) that until someone walked on the moon, people were regularly observed not to walk on the moon. And people, in time, have come to do what earlier generations would rightly have taken to be impossible on the basis of their experience.
>
> *Brian Davies, An Introduction to the Philosophy of Religion, 2nd edn, Oxford University Press, 1993*

How strange it would have been if all the people watching the footage of the first men on the Moon had, for the reason that it contradicted previous knowledge, refused to believe what they were seeing. Yet we should need to hold this position if Hume's argument were to hold true.

Richard Swinburne offers an additional argument against Hume's assumption that natural laws, as scientific evidence, will always outweigh the evidence in favour of miracles, based upon mere testimony.

For Swinburne, there are three types of historical evidence that can be used to support miracles rather than the scientific evidence in the form of scientific laws:

- our apparent memories
- the testimony of others
- the physical traces left by the events in question

In anticipation to Hume's counter that scientific laws are somehow more objective, Swinburne emphasises that our knowledge of scientific law is in itself based upon these three types of evidence. If such evidence is not sufficient to establish the occurrence of a miracle, neither is it sufficient to establish the certainty of a natural law.

Regarding the four additional reasons against miracles, a good part of the argument is either unclear or unsubstantiated. Hume stated there had never been a sufficient number of men to provide a valid testimony. He did not, however, explain what a 'sufficient number' would be, nor why he considered previous testimonies insufficient. His claim that miracles 'abound in ignorant and barbarous nations' is hard to accept, since just about every nation has provided such claims. Moreover, the presumption that an eyewitness should require some proof of intelligence before their claim be accepted is objectionable. The fourth objection

Something to think about

What type of evidence gives us our knowledge of natural laws?

How do we know we cannot fly if we jump off a cliff?

How does this compare with the way in which an eyewitness knows that a miracle has happened?

misses the mark in that it assumes that *all* miracle accounts are the mutually exclusive invention of their own religious tradition. Yet although, clearly, the miracles of different traditions cannot support the existence of the whole tradition, there is no reason why the individual miracles themselves may not have occurred objectively, unless they are self-contradictory in themselves.

Hume's arguments against miracles do not therefore mean that miracles *could not* occur. This still leaves two very pertinent questions:

* *Do* miracles in fact occur?
* If they occur, then what exactly do they prove?

Something to think about

What answers would *you* give to the two questions above?

Do Miracles Occur?

Assuming that we have established that it is possible for miracles to occur, there remain four criticisms as to whether or not any miracles have *in fact* occurred:

* some miracle accounts can be explained away as coincidences
* some miracle accounts appear pointless
* other miracle accounts should be rejected upon moral grounds
* yet others are not supported by sufficient evidence

You need to know

Remind yourself of **Holland's** definition of a miracle, at the beginning of the chapter.

Coincidence

The first criticism concerns those events hailed as miraculous upon Holland's definition of the term. Take the following example, given by **Mel Thompson**:

> In July 1995, a Roman Catholic priest suffered a severe stroke and was not expected to live. A fellow priest took the 300 year old mummified hand of an English martyr and placed it on his forehead while he was in hospital. The hand, apparently hacked from his body in 1679 when he was hanged, drawn and quartered, has long been regarded as able to bring about miracles. The priest recovered.
>
> *Mel Thompson, Philosophy of Religion,*
> *Hodder and Stoughton, 1997*

In this example, there is no guarantee that the recovery of the priest is not simply a coincidence – and not even an exceptionally remarkable one at that. Certainly, there is no sense in which what happened here is outside the bounds of nature.

Pointlessness

The second criticism concerns the point that some miracle accounts do not fulfil Swinburne's requirement of attesting to some deeper significance. We can refer to another of Thompson's example by way of illustration:

> In Naples, three times a year, people gather in St Clare's Basilica for a ceremony during which it is hoped that dried blood, believed to be that of St Gennaro who died in 305, will spontaneously liquefy. This 'miracle' is anticipated on a regular basis, and is seen as a good omen.

Mel Thompson, Philosophy of Religion,
Hodder and Stoughton, 1997

Although this phenomenon, were it to occur, would appear to break natural laws, it might not properly be considered truly miraculous for, as Thompson explains, 'There seems no particular reason why this phenomenon should take place, nor why it should be in itself of any religious significance.'

Rejection upon Moral Grounds

The third criticism concerning the actual occurrence of certain miracles is that they may be incompatible with the justice and love of God. Many miracle accounts involve God intervening in the world to bring about some benefit to those who worship Him. If God is all-loving and just, however, surely He would wish to help His followers equally. Why, then, does He choose to intervene by answering the prayers of some, yet not of others? Unless it can be proved that miracles are only effected for the benefit of the righteous, God would seem to be acting irrationally. This proposal is, to say the least, improbable, as it goes against the God of Classical Theism.

Regarding Judaism, for example, can it be that all those who were rescued in the Exodus (people who are portrayed in the Bible as sinful) were morally superior to the 6 million who died in the Holocaust? Yet unless we can confidently say that they were, it seems hard to justify why God should work a miracle on the one occasion and not the other. This argument, incidentally, has particular force when used against those miracles of a relatively trivial nature; involving, for example, minor healings. It does not count against those miracles whose purpose is primarily to demonstrate God's existence, rather than to favour certain followers.

Something to think about

The Jewish tradition argues that in the Exodus account in the Old Testament, God intervened miraculously to save the lives of several thousand Hebrew slaves. In the light of the twentieth-century Holocaust, what moral problems might God's intervention in the past raise for a modern Jew?

Maurice Wiles (1929–) rejects miracles on moral grounds. Wiles proposed that 'God's Action in the World' is a challenge to those who believe that miracles are acts of God that go against the laws of nature. Wiles argues that the world is a single act of God that encompasses the world as a whole. Therefore Wiles concludes that miracles do not occur because God does not intervene in events in the world on an individual basis. If miracles did occur then God would undermine the laws of nature and the accepted order of life, and even if this does happen, why would God choose to perform miracles for some and not others. Wiles asks why 'no miraculous intervention prevented Auschwitz or Hiroshima' and yet there are acclaimed miracles that 'seem trivial in comparison'. Wiles concludes that either God does not intervene in the natural order or He has an arbitrary will that results in His intervention to help the plight of some and ignore the needs of others. If in fact the nature of God is one that may choose to cure an individual of cancer but to ignore the plight of those trapped in the twin towers of New York on 11 September 2001, then Wiles concludes such a God is not worthy of worship.

Insufficient Evidence

The fourth criticism is that many examples of miracles are not supported with enough evidence. If, for example, I were to read an account of a fantastic miracle, witnessed by only one person and related in a tabloid newspaper of dubious reputation, it would surely be justifiable to be highly sceptical about the truth of the claim. This is not to say, of course, that there has never been sufficient evidence, but just that it is conceivable that in some cases there has not in fact been sufficient.

From these objections, we may conclude that *many* of the reports of miracles abounding in today's world may not justifiably be considered miraculous. The objections do not, however, prove that no miracles have happened. It could be argued that miracles such as the Resurrection of Christ, and the delivery of the Qur'an to Muhammad, are exempted from the above criticisms, since they are well supported within their respective faith traditions, and they have the purpose of propounding God's teachings to the world. They may be considered to break natural laws but they do not, in themselves, bestow favours directly upon any individual.

If Miracles do Happen, What can they Prove?

From what we have said so far, no reason has been offered against the possibility of miracles happening. Suppose, then, that a miracle were to occur. What could we deduce from this? Richard Swinburne argues that a miracle would point to the existence of agents other than humans:

> Suppose that E occurs in ways and circumstances otherwise strongly analogous to those in which occur events brought about intentionally by human agents, and that other violations occur in such circumstances. We would then be justified in claiming that E and other such violations are, like effects of human actions, brought about by agents, but agents unlike men in not being material objects. This inference would be justified because, if an analogy between effects is strong enough, we are always justified in postulating slight difference in causes to account for slight difference in effects.

> *Richard Swinburne, The Concept of Miracle, London, Macmillan, 1970*

Something to think about

Imagine that a desert nomad, who had no knowledge of technology, were to be placed in a studio where she heard an opera played through loudspeakers. On the basis of Swinburne's argument, what would she be justified in postulating?

Would she *in fact* be correct in her postulation?

You need to know

Remind yourself of the principle of **Ockham's razor** in Chapter 1 (page 9).

Suppose, for example, that a tumour afflicting a woman were to disappear overnight. Occurrences similar to this occur frequently in the operating theatres of surgeons, and are attributed to human agents. Swinburne's argument suggests that since our case is strongly analogous, we should reasonably postulate an agent similar to humans at work there too. It is justifiable to postulate a non-material cause, however, on account of the 'slight difference' in effects – for example, the fact that no material interference is involved in bringing it about.

Swinburne's argument carries some force; although in some cases a natural, but as yet undiscovered, reason may be the cause of the effect. In some cases at least, therefore, there would be no grounds to suspect the involvement of non-material beings.

Conclusion

Even if we accept Swinburne's conclusions, however, what grounds are there for attributing the miracles to God – and specifically to the omnipotent, all-loving God of Classical Theism? This rather depends upon our prior beliefs. If we already believe in such a God and know Him to act through miracles, it seems reasonable to attribute the miracle to Him. The principle of Ockham's razor could be applied here; where a simple and expected cause is the likely explanation for a certain event, it is not justifiable to invent a more complex one, even if it is a possible alternative.

If, however, there is no prior belief in God, the occurrence of a miracle would not be sufficient to generate belief in such a God; for the miracle could equally well be attributed to an angel or a god who is not omnipotent or omnibenevolent. The miracle could even be attributed to some as yet undiscovered spiritual power deriving from certain human beings. This variety of explanations means that an argument for the existence of God based upon the occurrence of miracles cannot work. Nor can an argument that attempts to prove one religion over another, since there is no proof as to which deity is the originator of the miracle. The occurrence of a miracle can at most strengthen the beliefs of those who already have specific beliefs in and about God.

Essay questions

AS
(a) Explain Hick's argument against the occurrence of miracles.
(b) Assess the view that a belief in miracles is essential for a religious person.

A2
(a) Outline and explain the main features of a religious believer's understanding of miracles.
(b) 'Our knowledge of the miraculous leads to the conclusion that God exists.' Examine and assess this claim.

Chapter 13   Life after Death

Something to think about

What difference is there between 'survival' in the memories of others and the survival of an individual's soul or body after death?

Does the individual's personality survive death in their descendants?

You need to know

One area of debate is whether an individual survives death in the form that they had in life.

This personal identity is referred to as the 'I' of the individual.

Something to think about

Are our body and soul two separate realities, or are we one complex, integrated psycho-physical system?

Is the mind the same thing as the soul?

What is Death?

There is one thing on which all philosophers agree, and that is that our earthly life in our current physical form will end. One definition of death is 'the complete and permanent cessation of all vital functions in a living creature, the end of life'. All philosophers will agree with the first part of this definition, but there is disagreement over exactly what the latter part, 'the end of life', means. Many people accept death as the end of any form of existence. Others would argue that death is not the end of life, and that we continue in some form after death. There are many different ideas of the form that life after death might take. The ideas about our survival after death include:

- the continuation of our genes in our children and their descendants
- that we live on in our lives' 'works'
- that we live on in the memories of others
- the immortality of the soul
- the resurrection of the body
- reincarnation

Body or Soul?

There are two main theories of human nature that have implications for meaningful survival after death:

- **Materialism** is the theory that our minds are inseparable from our bodies
- **Dualism** is the theory that there exist both bodies and minds, distinct from one another, but linked together in some way

Materialism

Those who support Materialism do not accept that there is a separate part to the human body called the 'soul'. An individual is a living, physical body, and nothing more. At death, the body dies and therefore the whole person ceases to exist.

Something to think about

Do you consider yourself to be more than 'a body with a nervous system'?

Is an emotion more than a chemical reaction in your brain?

How do you know this?

Something to think about

Ryle does not accept that it is right to talk of 'mental processes' as a separate function, independent of the body.

Why does he describe this idea of a separate mind as 'the ghost in the machine'?

Materialists believe that an action is the result of a chain of events, and that eventually science will be able to explain everything. Music is nothing but a set of vibrations in the air, a painting is nothing but coloured dots on a canvas, and a person is nothing but a brain attached to a body with a nervous system. What we assume to be emotional responses, such as love or fear, are no more than psycho-chemical reactions in our brain.

Gilbert Ryle

In his work, *The Concept of the Mind* (1949), Ryle argued that the idea of the soul – which he described as 'the ghost in the machine' – was a 'category mistake'. He argued that it was a mistake in the use of language. It resulted in people speaking of the mind and the body as different phenomena, as if the soul was something identifiably extra within a person. He used the example of a foreigner watching a cricket game and asking 'But where's the team spirit?' The foreigner expected 'the team spirit' to be something identifiably extra to the players, umpires, scorers and equipment. Ryle argued that any talk of a soul was talk about the way in which a person acted and integrated with others and the world. It was not something separate and distinct. To describe someone as clever, irritable or happy did not require the existence of a separate, invisible thing called a mind or soul. Such terms simply refer to the way in which someone behaves:

> When two terms belong to the same category, it is proper to construct conjunctive propositions embodying them. Thus a purchaser may say that he bought a left-hand glove and a right-hand glove, but not that he had bought a left-hand glove, a right-hand glove and a pair of gloves ... Now the dogma of the ghost in the Machine does just this. It maintains that there exist both bodies and minds; that there occur physical processes and mental processes; that there are mechanical causes of corporeal movements. I shall argue that these and other analogous conjunctions are absurd; but, it must be noticed, the argument will not show that either of the illegitimately conjoined propositions is absurd in itself. I am not for example, denying that there occur mental processes. Doing long division is a mental process and so is making a joke. But I am saying that the phrase 'there occur mental processes' does not mean the same sort of thing as 'there occur physical processes' and therefore, that it makes no sense to conjoin or disjoin the two.

Gilbert Ryle, The Concept of Mind, 1949

There are two forms of Materialism; the hard and soft versions.

Hard Materialism

'Hard' materialists do not accept that an individual's characteristics are anything more than physical ones. Any idea of consciousness is nothing more than brain activity. The mind cannot be separated from the body. When the body dies, then so does the brain.

Soft Materialism

'Soft' materialists do not accept that all characteristics are physical ones. Consciousness is more than just a brain process. The mind and body are related and do not act independently of each other, but the body often displays inner emotions. A physical symptom may be caused by something that is troubling the mind. There is nothing that we can do independent of our bodies and, therefore, our personal identity must involve our bodies, since without our bodies we cannot be fully identified. As with hard Materialism, the belief is that when the physical body dies, then so does the mind.

Materialists consider that there is no scientific evidence for the existence of a soul, and that as such an area is inaccessible to scientific activity then it would never be possible to prove whether or not a soul exists. Materialists do not accept that it is possible to locate the soul in any part of the body. The body is matter alone, so there cannot be a soul.

The materialist argument for not accepting survival after death may be summarised as follows:

- life depends on a functioning brain, nervous system and physical body
- death involves the destruction of the brain, the nervous system and the physical body
- therefore a person's life ends at death, as without a physical form life cannot be supported

Richard Dawkins rejects any concept of an immortal soul. Dawkins believes that the human animal is nothing more than the sum total of his or her individual DNA. For Dawkins, life on earth came to be not as a miraculous creation but as a natural consequence of the process of evolution. In his book *The Selfish Gene*, Dawkins argued that in nature, the battle for survival is not between each species of plant and

Something to think about

How do you think the **logical positivists** would view the idea of a soul? Remind yourself of their philosophy by re-reading Chapter 2 (page 10).

You need to know

Look back at Chapter 6, pages 79–80, and remind yourself of Darwin's theory of evolution.

animal, but between the genes that encode the very nature and operation of each entity. Dawkins has developed a website, 'The Evolution of Life', which 'creates' electronic life-forms and demonstrates how they evolve generation by generation, at the same time showing how their 'fitness' to survive and multiply responds to changes in their computer-generated universe.

Although Dawkins rejects the existence of an immortal soul in favour of a random evolutionary process, he still believes in human dignity and purpose through the marvellous way in which an individual's genetic code is passed on to future generations. For Dawkins, the mere fact that humans have evolved to a stage where they are trying to discover the meaning of life is far more marvellous than any creation myth. Dawkins does not think that humans should worry about the meaning of it all and their place in a hostile universe, as they *are* the universe.

Dawkins argues that human thinking has gone awry because people have tried to find meanings to life, including following a religious doctrine that teaches the rewards of paradise. If people rejected notions of an after-life and a God and learnt to reason as scientists, then they would become better humans. This is because science can answer questions about the origin of life and provide evidence to support the answer, but religion can only depend on faith.

Something to think about

How is Dawkins's theory about the evolution of species different from the evolutionary theory of Darwin and how is it similar?

You need to know

The **resurrection of the body** is the belief that after death it is not just an individual's soul that survives but the body as well. The individual is raised from the dead in a bodily form.

Re-creation Theory

Not all materialists accept that death is the end: instead, some believe that there is life after death. As the physical body cannot be separated from the 'soul' (mind), there is only one way this could happen and that is if the whole body continues after death. This survival would have to involve the resurrection of the body.

A dead body is known to decay in the grave, or to become ashes after cremation. This raises the question of how a resurrection of the body could take place. This presents those materialists who accept life after death with a problem. If, for a materialist, survival must include both body and soul, then life after death would have to be in a form similar to life in this world. It would have to be possible to recognise the resurrected person as the same individual that he or she was before death. Any other form would mean that the personal identity (the 'I') of the individual had not survived death.

Something to think about

What problems are raised by acceptance of the resurrection of the body after death?

Something to think about

Would a replica body still be 'I'?

Is a replica body identical to the person who has died, or is it a clone of 'me' and, therefore, not really me?

Something to think about

Read **St Paul's** teaching on resurrection in Thessalonians 4.

What are your views of Hick's and St Paul's teaching about the resurrection of the body?

John Hick

Hick argued that, given certain circumstances, it would be possible that the dead could exist after death as themselves, if an *exact replica* of them were to appear. This replica could be identified as being the same person who had died, and therefore, according to Hick, would be the same person. God is all-powerful and therefore it is no problem for God to create a replica body of the dead person. This replica will be complete with all the individual's memories and characteristics. Hick considered that although death destroys us, God would re-create us

> ... as a resurrection replica in a different world altogether, a resurrection world inhabited only by resurrected persons. This world occupies its own space distinct from that with which we are now familiar. That is to say, an object in the resurrection world is not situated at any distance or in any direction from the objects in our present world, although each object in either world is spatially related to every other object in the same world.

John Hick, Philosophy of Religion, Prentice-Hall, 1990

Hick considered that he was demonstrating that the resurrection of the body is logically possible, and so it is only a small step to say that a person can therefore experience bodily resurrection in a place where resurrected bodies dwell.

Hick's view is compatible with a Christian understanding of the resurrection of the body. St Paul wrote:

> Someone will ask, 'How can the dead be raised to life? What kind of body will they have?' You fool! When you sow a seed in the ground it does not sprout to life unless it dies. And what you sow is a bare seed, perhaps a grain of wheat or some other grain, not the full-bodied plant that will later grow up. God provides that seed with the body he wishes; he gives each seed its own proper body. And the flesh of living beings is not all the same kind of flesh, animals another, birds, another, and fish another. And there are heavenly bodies and earthly bodies; the beauty that belongs to heavenly bodies is different from the beauty that belongs to earthly bodies. The sun has its own beauty, the moon another beauty; and even among stars there are different kinds of beauty. This is how it will be when the dead are raised to life. When the body is buried, it is mortal; when raised, it will be immortal. When buried, it is ugly and weak; when raised, it will be beautiful and strong.

When buried it is a physical body; when raised it will be a spiritual body. There is, of course, a physical body, so there has to be a spiritual body.

I Corinthians 15: 35–44, Good News Bible, Lion Publishing, 1976

St Paul taught that after death the body will be raised, but it will be transformed and will become a spiritual body, as unlike its earthly form as the seed is from the plant into which it grows. This is one way to explain how an individual keeps the personal identity that he or she had in life but is able to achieve eternal life in a bodily form.

Re-creation and the Problem of Personal Identity

Even if others can recognise me in my 'new' body, and I have the same memories as before I died, many philosophers do not accept that a replica body is still the same 'I' that died. It is a question of which of the following statements is accepted as correct:

First I existed in this world, then I died, and then I existed again in the next world

First I existed in this world, then I died, and then God created someone else who is exactly similar to me

Hick tried to solve the problem with a series of thought experiments, to prove that the 'I' that existed in this world is the same 'I' as resurrected in the next. He imagined a man called John Smith, who lived in the United States. One day, his friends watched as Smith suddenly vanished without trace. At the same moment as he disappeared, a replica Smith appeared in India. According to Hick, this Smith

> . . . is exactly similar in both physical and mental characteristics to the person who disappeared in America. There is continuity of memory, complete similarity of bodily features including fingerprints, emotions and mental dispositions. Further, the 'John Smith' replica thinks of himself as being the John Smith who disappeared in the United States. After all possible tests have been made, and have proved positive, the factors leading his friends to accept 'John Smith' as John Smith would surely prevail and would cause them to overlook even his mysterious transference from one continent to another, rather than treat 'John Smith' with all of John Smith's memories and other characteristics, as someone other than John Smith.

John H. Hick, Philosophy of Religion, Prentice-Hall, 1990

Something to think about

Before you read the next section, do you agree with Hick that the John Smith who materialised in India is the same John Smith who disappeared in the United States?

Hick continued by supposing that John Smith died. God re-created John Smith in the next world and this re-created 'John Smith' was the same person.

Something to think about

For a materialist to accept life after death, then there has to be the resurrection of the body, as there is no personal identity without it. The body and mind are inseparable.

Is it also necessary for a believer to accept the resurrection of the body if there is to be reward or punishment, in Heaven or Hell, in the afterlife?

Something to think about

What do you think that the Spanish artist Angeles Santos was trying to say about the afterlife in his painting 'Un Mundo' ('A World')?

'Un Mundo', painted in 1929 by Angeles Santos

Dualism

A dualist approach to mind and body argues that it is the mind that determines our personality, and that the body is an outer shell for the real self. The body is contingent and therefore is destined for decay, but the mind, associated with the higher realities, such as truth, goodness and justice, is immortal. If a man's life is spent in contemplation of these higher realities, then his soul can enter eternity after the death of the physical body. This belief that the soul continues after death is known as the **immortality of the soul**.

You need to know

Substance is something that is able to exist independently of something else. A substance is able to exist on its own.

You need to know

Remind yourself of the philosophies of **Plato** and **Aristotle** by reading Chapter 1 (pages 2–3).

Plato

Writing in *The Republic*, Plato stated that the soul belonged to a level of reality that was higher than that of the body. He thought that the soul is a substance and is immortal. This view was derived from his theory of ideas, which he called **forms**. For everything in existence, Plato accepted that there was the perfect idea (form). For example, for every man there is an ideal man; for every dog, there is an ideal dog; and so on. Every individual thing participates in these universal ideas. The idea is prior to the individual instance of it, and is thus more real. Ideas are not physical things, so they must belong to a **spiritual realm** of reality, which is more real than the material realm. The soul is that which can grasp the realm of ideas. It is not matter, which is gross and unthinking. The physical world is the world in which the body exists and through which we receive sense-impressions. The soul is immaterial and is capable of knowing eternal truths beyond the world. The soul wants to travel into the realm of heavenly ideas and to understand them; the body wants to be involved in worldly matters to do with the senses. The soul is trying to steer the mind to this realm. Knowledge is the recollection of the acquaintance that we had with the forms before our immortal souls became imprisoned in our bodies. The aim of the soul is to break free of the chains of matter and flee to the realm of ideas, where it will be able to spend eternity in contemplation of the true, the beautiful and the good. The thinking being can survive without the physical body. The body would not survive death but the soul, the real essence of the person would continue – and for Plato this is our personal identity, which forms the 'I'.

Plato's Allegory of the Cave

Plato used an allegory of an underground cave with an entrance open to the light to explain his distinction between body and soul. He compared humans to prisoners chained from birth in this cave. They are chained in such a way that they can see only what is in front of them, and are prevented by the chains from turning their heads. Above and behind them there is a fire blazing at a distance, and between the fire and the prisoners there is a raised way and a low wall that makes the shadows cast on the wall appear on a stage. The prisoners are not aware that these are only shadows of the real world and think that they are seeing reality. A released prisoner goes out of the cave and at first the light will blind him to the fact that what he saw in the cave was an illusion and what he is now seeing is reality. As the prisoner goes upwards he becomes accustomed to the light, and the closer he gets to it, the clearer his vision becomes until eventually he will understand his proper place in the universe and the truth about himself.

When the released prisoner remembers the cave and his fellow-prisoners who still only see shadows, he will pity them. When the prisoner is returned to his cave and once more sees only shadows, he will have recollections of the reality behind the shadows. Those who have never seen the truth reject his explanation that these are only shadows of reality.

Plato explained that the cave is the world of sight, the light of the fire is the sun, and the journey upwards out of the cave is the ascent of the soul into the intellectual world. Plato argued that the idea of good appears last of all, and is seen only with an effort; and

> . . . when seen, is also inferred to be the universal author of all things beautiful and right, parent of light and of the lord of light in this visible world, and the immediate source of reason and truth in the intellectual; and that this is the power upon which he who would act rationally, either in public or private life, must have his eye fixed.

The Republic

Something to think about

How might a believer use Plato's Allegory of the Cave to support a belief in the existence of God?

Plato argued that before we were born we had knowledge of the Forms but we 'forgot', and thus lost, this knowledge. However, it is possible to grasp the Forms again by asking the right questions, in other words through logic. For Plato, this was also an argument for the immortality of the soul and the distinction of the soul from the body.

Plato is teaching that humans need to become enlightened to free them from ignorance and darkness, but teachers cannot force this knowledge on people. The power and capacity of learning exists in the soul already. Just as the eye was unable to turn from darkness to light without the whole body, so too knowledge can be gained only by a person willingly seeking it. Eventually the search will lead to understanding of the Form of the Good and people will turn from physical pleasures such as eating and drinking and concentrate instead on spiritual matters.

Something to think about

In what ways are the dualisms of Plato and Aristotle similar, and in what ways are their philosophies different?

Something to think about

If it is only an individual's thoughts that survive, does this mean that personal identity has ceased to exist? Am 'I' no longer in existence?

Aristotle

Aristotle considered the 'soul' to be the part of the body that gives it life. It is what turns the physical form into a living organism of its particular type. For example, a dog has a doggy soul, and a human has a human soul. There is no problem for Aristotle about how the soul and body work together. Soul and body are inseparable. The soul develops the person's skills, character or temper, but it cannot survive death. Body and soul are a unity and when the body dies, the soul ceases to exist. *This would appear to be materialistic*, but Aristotle believed that the body and the soul were different. Human beings have a soul or self that is capable of an intellectual life. Only humans can reflect on feelings and sensations, and grasp 'universals' (goodness, as opposed to an individual good thing). In this way we come to understand eternal truths.

For the ancient Greeks, the **psyche**, our sensations and emotion, were on the 'body' side of the mind/body dualism. If a person was hungry, then the body would feel pangs of hunger; but the mind would dwell on the universal concept of hunger rather than the individual pangs of hunger. For the Greeks, mental activity (the **nous**, which is the thinking mind) was distinguished from the body and its sensations. Many Greeks thought that it was this aspect of the soul that survived death.

You need to know

Remind yourself of the philosophy of **St Thomas Aquinas** by reading Chapter 1 (pages 3–4).

St Thomas Aquinas

Aquinas agreed with Aristotle that it was the soul that animated the body and gave it life. He called the soul the **anima**, that which 'animates' the body:

> Now that the soul is what makes our body live; so the soul is the primary source of all these activities that differentiate levels of life: growth, sensation, movement, understanding mind or soul, it is the form of our body.

St Thomas Aquinas, Summa Theologica

Something to think about

Why was it important to Aquinas, as a Christian, that each soul should have an individual identity?

According to Aquinas, the soul operates independently of the body. Aquinas believed that only things that are divisible into parts decay. The soul is not divisible, and therefore, on the basis of Aquinas' argument, it is able to survive death. However, through the link with a particular human body, each soul becomes individual. So, even when a body dies, the soul that departs retains the individual identity of the body to which it was attached.

You need to know

Remind yourself of **Descartes'** philosophy of the reality of existence in Chapter 1 (pages 4–5).

Cartesian is the term used to refer to the influence of ideas and concepts developed by René Descartes.

Something to think about

List examples of ways in which the mind can affect the body and ways in which the body can affect the mind.

Cartesian Dualism

René Descartes included in the 'mind' all the feelings and sensations that he could describe, but which he could not locate physically. He accepted that everything that is non-physical becomes part of the mind. He concluded 'I think therefore I am', and therefore that the mind is distinct from the body, although the two interact. The mental reality is not empirical and therefore not in the world of space. The mind is not located in the body, and is not the same as the brain. Descartes' dualism of mind and body rested on certain ideas, which included the following:

- The mind is a 'non-corporeal' substance, which is distinct from material or bodily substance. The mind and body are different things.
- Every substance has a property or a special character. So, for instance, the property of the mind-substance is consciousness and the property of bodily or material-substance is length, breadth or depth. The mind is a substance 'whose whole essence is to think' and so takes up no space. The body is material, whose essence is to take up space.
- In contrast to the mind, the body is that which is extended. It has a material form, which can be described in forms of extensional features such as its size, shape, position or movement.

For Descartes, 'ideas' were in the mind, not out there in the world waiting to be grasped. Cartesian dualism may be summarised as follows:

- The mind is the place in which all feelings, sensations and thoughts are known only to the person experiencing them.
- The body performs all physical activities. These are observable to all.
- The mind and body interact with each other, as the mind can cause events to occur in the body and the body can cause events to occur in the mind.
- The mind and body are separate.

Descartes concluded that as our identity comes from our ability to think and reason, then it was conceivable that we could survive without our bodies and remain the same person. He did not accept that we need our bodies to live an intellectually aware and active life. Therefore, Descartes

Something to think about

I am dying of a heart condition. I am informed that the technique exists to transplant my brain into the body of someone who has died of a brain tumour. I agree and my brain is transplanted into this new body. The body works perfectly and all my memories are intact, but I look totally different. My friends and family no longer recognise me, while the friends and family of the person into whose body my brain has been transplanted greet me in the street. Who am I? Am I the person who died of the brain tumour or the person whose brain was transplanted? Could I be a new identity altogether?

Something to think about

Are you a soul that is temporarily lodged in a physical body?

believed that the mind could survive the death of the body. For him, the mind is 'I', which thinks and makes us who we are. We can drastically change our bodies and our physical appearance without changing our personalities, and even if a person were to undergo a radical physical transformation, we would still be able to recognise that person by reference to his or her character and memories.

Descartes considered that when an individual dies, that person's soul is able to continue with God after death, as the same individual that existed in a physical form on Earth:

> Our soul is of a nature entirely independent of the body, and consequently . . . it is not bound to die with it. And since we cannot see any other causes which destroy the soul, we are naturally led to conclude that it is immortal.

> *René Descartes, Discourse on the Method, 1637*

Is Dualism Correct?

Many philosophers are concerned that the separation of body and mind (soul) raises questions for discussion. These challenges to Dualism include the following questions:

- *Is our identity only the result of memories and actions in the mind?* If we get a new body, then does this have no influence on how we behave or how others react to us? **Bernard Williams** rejected this conclusion. Williams argued that memories are not a good guide to identity. Memories and personality can be fabricated and personal identity cannot be proved through mental activity alone. He believed that identity comes from physical characteristics as well. Personal identity depends on the way in which we recognise each other, and without our bodies we cannot be fully identified.
- *What about the causal effects between mind and body?* We know that there are things that we do to the body that affect the mind. For example, the use of alcohol or drugs changes personality.
- *Modern science has shown links between the mind and the brain, so how can the mind survive on its own?* Surgeons can split the brain and create 'two minds'. The mind appears to be causally dependent upon the 'brain'.
- *If minds are non-physical objects, how can the mind cause anything to happen in the physical world?* For example, I think of running for the bus; but if my mind is not linked to my body, then why does the physical act of running for the bus take place?

Reincarnation

If the survival of personal identity after death were to depend on the resurrection of the body, then reincarnation would have to be rejected as a means by which an individual survives death. Reincarnation involves an individual's soul inhabiting a new body, which may be totally different from that of the previous life. In each reincarnation the 'soul' lives a different life in a different body.

If the survival of personal identity after death were to depend on memories, then reincarnation would have to be rejected as, in the majority of cases, the memories of previous lives are either non-existent or are deeply buried in the subconscious.

Buddhists deny that there are souls. Buddhists accept that there is an interconnection between each life lived by a person. Each life is interconnected with each previous life through the law of **karma**. The 'I' is not the person who is living his or her current life, but the union of all lives lived. There are causal connections between different lives, and it is through these connections that each life is part of the same person. The Buddhist monk Nagasena explained this form of connection using the analogy of a chariot:

'Explain to me what a chariot is. Is the pole the chariot?'

'No, reverend Sir!'

'Is then the axle the chariot?'

'No, reverend Sir!'

'Is it then the wheels, or the framework, or the flagstaff, or the yoke, or the reins, or the goad-stick?'

'No, reverend Sir!'

'Then is it the combination of pole, axle, wheels, framework, flagstaff, yoke, reins and goad which is the "chariot"? '

'No, reverend Sir!'

'Then is this "chariot" outside the combination of pole, axle, wheels, framework, flagstaff, yoke, reins and goad?'

'No, reverend Sir!'

'Then ask as I may, I can discover no chariot at all. Just a mere sound is this "chariot". But what is the real chariot?'

'Where all constituent parts are present, the word "a chariot" is applied. So likewise where the skandhas are, the term "a being" commonly is used.'

E. Conze, Buddhist Scriptures, Penguin, 1983

Evidence for Life after Death

There are several ways in which evidence for life after death is believed to have been found:

- 'near-death' experiences (NDE)
- regression to past lives under hypnosis
- 'sightings' of dead people
- spiritualism

'Near-death' experiences

Advances in modern technology have resulted in more people who have been declared clinically 'dead' subsequently being resuscitated. **Dr Raymond Moody** realised that the descriptions by these people of what happened to them while they were 'dead' were so similar that it must be more than coincidence. His research into the phenomenon of 'near-death' experiences demonstrated that there were common features to the experiences, which included the following:

- at the moment of death, the person has a feeling of being outside the body and of floating above it
- the 'dead' person is able to observe what is happening and the setting in which events are taking place
- there is heightened awareness and an absence of physical pain
- movement is unrestricted, and the person is able to pass through walls
- there is a sense of indescribable bliss, ecstasy and peace
- there is rapid movement down a tunnel, with a bright light at the end
- dead relatives and friends are waiting at the end of the tunnel
- at the end of the tunnel is a beautiful place, where the person feels in the presence of a divine being
- in the presence of this divine being, individuals are shown a panoramic view of their lives, consisting of everything that they have done, and this is displayed all at once
- individuals are made aware of the effects of their actions, and of how these actions affected others
- they see themselves as they really are, and are able to judge themselves objectively
- they realise that the most important thing is to show love to others
- finally, they are told that it is not their time to 'die' and they are returned to their physical bodies

Something to think about

Remind yourself of the features of a **religious experience** in Chapter 3, and consider why many would claim that a 'near-death' experience is a religious experience.

Something to think about

The main challenge to 'near-death' experiences is precisely that they are near death. Those who reject the experience as evidence of life after death argue that the individual did not die and that the experience had other causes, such as oxygen starvation. What other reasons might those who reject the experience give to account for what happened to the 'dead' person?

Regression to Past Lives under Hypnosis

If people have had earlier lives, then there is a belief that memories of these past lives ought to reside in the subconscious. For example:

Something to think about

Do you think that the experience of *déjà vu* is a memory from a past life or an electrical discharge in the brain?

- There are people, especially children, who claim to have memories of former lives. Descriptions of past lives are given, which can be partly confirmed by historical records.
- Others appear to have regressed to earlier lives under hypnosis. Some of these memories have been investigated, and found to be accurate accounts of people and places from the past.

Not all investigators accept these 'memories' as evidence of reincarnation, and other reasons are put forward to explain why an individual possesses such knowledge. The question arises as to whether memories of a former life can be classed as 'proof' of earlier lives:

- the individual might be recalling information gained in childhood, and attributing it to a past life
- there could be a cultural gene that passes down information about the lives of our ancestors
- some memories may result from psychological problems, and be manifested as memories of earlier lives when in fact they are suppressed events from this life

'Sightings' of Dead People

Dr Deepak Chopra pointed out that bodies are comprised of energy. They may appear to be solid, but the truth is that they are in reality just an impulse of energy. When an individual dies, the energy field may retain his or her image, and may be perceived as a ghost. He considered the 'ghost' to be an individual's consciousness, manifesting itself through the remaining energy.

Others argue that ghosts are apparently manifestations of dead people. It is doubted that they are hallucinations, because they are often seen by more than one person. There have been sightings at the same place, by different people, at different times. However, if a ghost is not a sighting of a dead person, then other explanations for the phenomenon include the following:

- hoaxes or elaborate tricks could make people think that they have seen a ghost

Pevensey Castle, reputedly one of the five most 'haunted' places in Britain

- the 'stone tape' theory suggests that just as magnetic tape is able to record events and play them back so, in certain conditions, stones will record dramatic events and 'play them back' when the same conditions are present
- ghosts could be the result of mistaken identity, or the power of suggestion could lead to the mistaken belief that a ghost has been sighted

Spiritualism

Communication between the spirit world and the living is regarded by many as evidence of life after death. Many mediums have passed on messages from departed spirits that contain accurate information, which was previously unknown to the medium. These messages give comfort to the bereaved, as they suggest that their loved one is still 'alive' in another dimension, and that at some future date they will be able to join them.

Investigations of some mediums have proved that they are frauds. Others appear to be genuine, and to be able to demonstrate that something extraordinary is happening when they pass on messages. This could be communication from departed spirits or it could be some form of telepathic access to the minds of those who are still living. There is evidence to support both points of view.

You need to know

Spiritualism is the belief that it is possible to communicate with departed spirits. The communication between those who have 'passed over' and those in this world takes place through a medium. A medium is an individual who is believed to have the ability to receive messages from those in the spirit world and pass them on to the living.

Something to think about

If spiritualism were proved to be true, in what form would individuals survive their death?

Cryogenics is the branch of physics dealing with the production and effects of very low temperatures.

Something to think about

What answers might be given to the questions raised by cryogenics?

Cryogenics

One possible application of cryogenics is the freezing of terminally ill patients who are near death, so that their bodies do not decay. The aim is that the frozen body will be revived from this state of 'suspended animation' when medical science is able to provide a cure.

In addition to a number of challenging scientific dilemmas, this idea raises other issues related to life after death:

- If a person is revived at some future date, should he or she have been considered dead in the interim period?
- If the person is considered to have been revived 'from the dead', then is this life after death?
- The physical body might be revived, but will the soul return to the body?

Essay questions

AS
(a) Outline the main features of a 'near-death experience'.
(b) Examine and assess the claim that near-death experiences are subjective experiences and therefore are not evidence for life after death.

A2
(a) Describe and explain the main evidence given by a believer to prove that there is life after death.
(b) Explain and assess the claim that a belief in life after death is no more than wishful thinking.

Chapter 14   The Synoptic Paper

At the end of the A2 course all students have to take the Synoptic Assessment. The assessment is a compulsory examination worth 20 per cent of the total mark. Students do not have to learn new material for the Synoptic Paper. The questions on the paper are asking students to bring together the areas of religion studied at AS and A2 and answer questions in greater depth than on the earlier papers. Students should not prepare for the Synoptic Paper by studying model answers but by preparing the chosen topics in depth to be able to answer the specific question set on the examination paper.

If students are to do well on the Religious Studies Synoptic Paper then they need to show that they:

- have knowledge and understanding of the subject content in the areas studied during the course
- have knowledge and understanding of the connections between elements of areas studied during the course
- are able to draw together the knowledge, understanding and skills learned in the different areas studied during the AS and A2 Religious Studies courses
- are able to relate the areas studied to specified aspects of human experience
- know which areas of study from the Religious Studies examination specification they have followed are to be studied for the Synoptic Paper. These areas will be explicitly mentioned in the Religious Studies GCE specification
- are able to support arguments with appropriate examples and illustrations from the areas studied at AS and A2.
- are able to make comparisons and contrasts between the areas studied at AS and A2
- are able to make a critical assessment of mainstream opinions on the area studied
- are able critically to evaluate different points of view and reach an appropriate conclusion

Students who have followed the Philosophy of Religion specification will have studied another area as well. Both of these areas are brought together on the Synoptic Paper. When students go into the examination room, it is important that they are certain of the areas studied during the course in order that they choose the right question for them from those on the paper. Even if students think that they can answer a question on the paper from an area they have not studied, it is unlikely that they will have sufficient depth of information to answer it to a good standard if it has not been researched with the synoptic paper in mind.

It may be helpful to go through the specifications studied during the GCE course and make a list of the areas to study in depth that are relevant to the topic(s) to be studied for the Synoptic Paper.

An Example of a Study Plan for the Synoptic Paper

The following example of a study plan is based on the requirements for the AQA Synoptic topic 'Life, Death and Beyond'. The student preparing this plan has studied:

AS Units – an introduction to Religion and Human Experience; an introduction to Religion and Science; an introduction to Religion and Ethics

A2 Units – studies in Religion and Ethics; studies in the Philosophy of Religion

Topic	Illustrative Material
Religious perspectives on the nature of human life	Different understanding of the nature of human life as expressed within one religion or religious textual tradition
	Ethical implications for this religious tradition of medical issues related to life after death, such as abortion, euthanasia, use of embryo and foetus in research
	Challenges to the sanctity of life from medical ethics and the response of the religion studied to the challenges
Concepts of spiritual life	Mysticism as evidence of life after death
	Concept of soul and the nature of personal identity as evidence of survival after death
	Challenge of a Materialist's view of human nature

Topic	Illustrative Material
The relative importance of the present life and life after death	Immortality as an aspect of Kant's theory of ethics
	The implications of religious views on the consequences of the way life is lived now for life after death, e.g. heaven or hell
	Consequences of actions in Utilitarianism for life after death
	Determinism; religious perspectives
	Death as an integral part of creation
	Miracles as evidence of God's involvement in human affairs
	Challenge of existentialism to beliefs in an afterlife
	Problems of evil and implications for the afterlife
The symbolism of life and death	Sources of authority that have informed the believer about life and death e.g. the Bible
	Variety of beliefs about life after death based on general understanding of the interpretation of teaching within the religious tradition chosen, including symbolism related to the afterlife
Eschatological and apocalyptic teaching	Main features of a religious tradition's belief in an afterlife, and beliefs about judgement, Heaven and Hell
	Importance of eschatological/ apocalyptic teaching for the faith chosen
Beliefs about death and beyond	Variety of beliefs about life after death
	Validity and verification of near-death experiences
	Is a near-death experience a natural experience (result of oxygen starvation of the brain or endorphins) given a religious interpretation?
	Is it reasonable for other people to accept these experiences as evidence of life after death?

Does Religious Language have Meaning or Purpose?

Religious Language has a Purpose

Religious language is non-cognitive

R. B. Braithwaite said that it does not convey facts, but is a means of expressing emotion and morality.

Religious language consists of **analogies** that allow people to talk about God and faith:

- **St Thomas Aquinas** – analogies of proportion and analogies of attribution
- **Ian Ramsey** – models/qualifiers

Religious language is **symbolic**:

- **Paul Tillich** – symbols point us to 'being itself'
- **J. R. Randall** – religious language is not factual but takes us beyond to the ultimate reality

Religious language is a language game

Ludwig Wittgenstein stated that each human activity has its own language = 'the game'. If you are not in the 'game', you will not understand the language and the result is that it will appear meaningless to you. Therefore if you are not a believer any talk about God and faith will be meaningless and appear to have no purpose.

Meaningfulness of Religious Language

Verification Principle

A statement is only meaningful (logical) if we know how it can be proved true or false; either because it is an analytic statement or through empirical methods.

Logical positivists (Vienna Circle) considered religious language meaningless because it could not be tested empirically, and was not analytic.

A. J. Ayer developed the strong and weak versions of the argument.

Falsification Principle

A statement is only meaningful if we accept that evidence may count against it. Religious language is considered meaningless because believers will not allow anything to count against their beliefs.

Antony Flew argued that religious language dies the 'death of a thousand qualifications' because believers do not allow anything to count against their beliefs, and keep qualifying beliefs when anything appears to count against them. Flew used **John Wisdom's** Parable of the Gardener to demonstrate how believers and unbelievers express different reactions to the same 'facts'.

Criticism of verification and falsification

John Hick criticised the principle on the grounds of eschatological verification.

R. M. Hare's 'bliks'.

Basil Mitchell – a believer is expected to have faith, even when the evidence appears to go against the beliefs.

Richard Swinburne – things have meaning even if we know we can never prove them true or false (toys in the toy cupboard).

Philosophy of Religion for A Level
This page may be photocopied
© Nelson Thornes Ltd, 2002

What is a Religious Experience?

A **religious experience** is a spontaneous or induced, mental event over which the recipient has relatively little control. It is often accompanied with the gaining of certain knowledge. The experience is always unique.

Prayer

Prayer refers to a method of communication between man and God.

F. W. H. Myers regarded prayer as part of one's psychological well-being. However, he contends that we do not know how prayer operates.

St Teresa of Avila categorised prayer:

1 The prayer of quiet

2 The prayer of union

3 Ecstasy (including spiritual marriage)

Mystical experience

Mystical experience involves:

- gaining knowledge of an 'ultimate reality'
- being free of the limitations of space and time
- experiencing a sense of unity with the Divine
- experiencing a sense of bliss

William James characterised mystical experiences as follows:

1 **Ineffability** – the fact that the experience cannot be described in human terms

2 **Noetic quality** – the fact that certain knowledge is gained through revelation, not sensory perception

3 **Transiency** – the fact that the experience is out of proportion, in terms of time and space

4 **Passivity** – the fact that the experience is out of the control of the individual

Conversion

Conversion (in religious terms) is a process that leads to the adoption of a religious attitude or way of life.

Psychologically, this process occurs when religion becomes the central focus of a person's mind, often to the exclusion of other things.

Types of conversion:

1 Volitional

2 Self-surrender

Examples of conversion:

1 Intellectual conversion

2 Moral conversion

3 Social conversion

Conversions are often seen as 'miracles' by those who experience them, because of the often profound and, in some cases, permanent effects.

Anselm

Proslogion 2: 'God is that than which nothing greater can be conceived.' Even the unbeliever must have a definition of God in order to dismiss it as a concept.

If this definition is accepted, God must exist in reality, as that which exists in reality will always be greater than that which exists purely *in intellectu*.

Proslogion 3: It is possible to conceive of a being, the existence of which is **necessary**.

God must be such a being if He is 'that than which nothing greater can be conceived'. This is because a being that possesses necessary existence will always be greater than a contingent being.

Ontology: the Study of Being

An *a priori* argument.

Malcolm

If God is 'that than which nothing greater can be conceived', He cannot be **brought** into existence; nor can He simply **happen to come** into existence (as this would require the input of a greater being and would render God limited and finite).

Therefore, God's existence is either **necessary** (if He **does** exist), or impossible (if He **does not**).

Unless God's **necessary** existence presents us with a logical contradiction, we must accept it.

'Reductio ad absurdum'

These are all examples of '*reductio ad absurdum*' arguments; they begin with a proposition, and attempt to prove (through logical reasoning) that it would be 'absurd' to reject the proposition.

Descartes

'God is a supremely perfect being.'

'Existence' is a perfection.

To think of God without existence, therefore, is like thinking of a triangle without its three sides.

It is therefore **illogical** to consider the concept of God without the concept of existence.

Plantinga

'Possible worlds.'

There is a possible world in which there is a being with 'Maximal Greatness'.

A being only has 'Maximal Greatness' if it exists in every world.

Therefore, such a being exists in **our** world.

This, however, does not mean God.

A problem exists: even if the being exists in every world, there could exist, in each separate world, an individual being that is greater.

Therefore, Plantinga suggests 'Maximal Excellence'.

If one applies this **and** 'Maximal Greatness' to the being, one can conclude that there **is** a God **whose existence follows from His essence**.

Gaunilo

'The Most Perfect Island.' (See notes.)

While Anselm never compares two things of a like kind, Gaunilo is occupied with comparisons of similarities (i.e. islands).

This criticism of Anselm does not work, as it assumes that it is coherent to conceive of an island than which none more perfect can be conceived; it is **not** coherent.

As Plantinga suggests, islands have no **intrinsic maximum**; that is, they can always be bettered.

Kant

Kant has two basic objections; first, that there is no contradiction in dismissing both a subject **and** its associated predicate (i.e. God **and** existence). This successfully challenges Descartes.

Kant also maintains that 'existence is not a predicate'. If it were, it would be something that a thing either had or lacked (such as blue eyes). This creates a paradox, however, in saying that something **does not** exist: How could such a thing lack (or indeed possess) anything?

Philosophy of Religion for A Level
This page may be photocopied
© Nelson Thornes Ltd, 2002

How Successful is this Argument?

Frege

' "Existence" is a second-order predicate.'

Frege distinguishes between first- and second-order predicates. He suggests that first-order predicates tell one something **about** the subject, whereas second-order predicates tell one about concepts.

It would seem that Anselm is regarding existence as a **first-order** predicate, which it cannot be, as it tells one nothing **about** the subject.

A critique of Malcolm

Malcolm argues that stating that God possesses **necessary** existence means that one can conclude logically and acceptably that God must exist. Brian Davies challenges this: he believes that Malcolm has failed to recognise that the word 'is' can be used in different ways.

On the one hand, it can be used to **describe** something ('the horse is brown'), and on the other it can be used to explain that there actually is something ('there is such a thing as a dragon'). While the first use is clearly descriptive, Davies argues that the second use tells one nothing, and yet leaves the listener having to **suppose** the existence of the subject. However, this is unacceptable, as one could literally define **anything** into existence!

A critique of Plantinga

Some would dismiss Plantinga by attacking the whole concept of 'possible worlds'.

However, criticism can also focus upon his assumption that claiming there is a being with 'maximal excellence' in every world means that such a being must exist in our world. This is not the case. All that follows is that 'maximal excellence' is possible, and therefore God is possible, **not actual**.

Does the Cosmological Argument Prove the Existence of God?

The **cosmological argument** proves the existence of God from the idea that there is a **first cause** of the universe.

The Big Bang

This scientific theory has proved how the universe began. It can be used to either support or reject the cosmological argument.

Proponents of the argument

Aquinas seeks to prove the argument through:

- motion (change)
- cause
- contingency

The *kalam* **version** seeks to prove the argument through the following:

- the universe is not an actual infinity and had a first cause
- this first cause of the universe must already have existed
- this first cause caused the universe to exist

Leibniz believed that there had to be a sufficient reason for the universe to exist and that the reason is God.

Opponents of the argument

Kant would not accept that there is any evidence to support God as a first cause of the universe. We do not have sufficient knowledge to support such an idea.

Hume argued that Aquinas contradicted himself by saying that things cannot move themselves or be uncaused, and then arguing that God is both, unmoved and uncaused.

There may be a first cause of the universe but it does not have to be the God of Classical Theism.

A critique of the kalam argument

Recent scientific discoveries have demonstrated that things do come into existence without a direct cause.

Why does the universe have to be caused?

Why cannot it always have been there?

Does the Design Argument Prove the Existence of God?

The **design (teleological) argument** proves the existence of God from the idea that:

- there is design, order and purpose in the universe
- there must have been a designer
- this designer is God

St Thomas Aquinas

Aquinas sought to prove the argument through the way in which things in the world appear to be directed towards a specific purpose. The purpose is evidence of design. The designer is God.

William Paley

Paley used evidence from nature to prove the argument. He argued that the way in which things fit together for a specific purpose cannot have happened by chance. For example, a bird's wings for flight or the eye for sight are evidence of design. The designer is God.

The Anthropic Principle

The **Anthropic Principle** considered that there is evidence that there is design in the universe and world for the specific purpose of the development of intelligent life. Natural selection could be part of this design. The designer is God.

(**F. R. Tennant** and **Richard Swinburne** support the principle.)

The Aesthetic Principle

The **Aesthetic Principle** argued that humans are able to appreciate beauty. This is not a requirement for survival and so cannot be the result of natural selection. It must have been the product of design.

(**F. R. Tennant** developed this argument.)

Criticism of the argument

David Hume was a major critic of the argument. He argued that:

- There may be design, but this does not prove it is God. The universe could be the work of many designers, or of an apprentice designer.
- We do not know enough about the world to conclude that it is the work of one designer. Human experience would demonstrate that complicated projects are the result of many designers – not just one.
- The flaws in the design of the world, such as death and disease, would suggest that the design was not a good one. This counts against the benevolent God of Classical Theism.

The Epicurean Hypothesis argued that, given sufficient time, the random particles that make up the universe would come together to give the appearance of design. Random chance caused the universe and world to exist in its present form – not design.

Charles Darwin's *The Origin of Species by Means of Natural Selection* (1859) demonstrated why there appeared to be design in the world. Life has developed as the result of evolution. The survival of the fittest and natural selection have given the appearance of design.

Does the Moral Argument Prove the Existence of God?

The **moral argument** is based on the view that God is required to explain the existence of morality in the world.

It rests upon the assumption that morality cannot be explained otherwise.

It proceeds in two main ways:

1

Morality comes straight from God

Newman took this line of argument, seeing the conscience as God's voice within us.

Owen similarly argued that objective laws presuppose God as the law-giver.

2

Rational consideration of the objective nature of morality suggests that God exists

Trethowan linked morality to the concept of value. Moral obligation towards others suggests that others have value. God is required as the source of this value.

Kant emphasised the objective nature of moral obligation. He said that this only makes sense if there is a source to this objective duty, who is able to meet its demands. This source is God.

Criticisms of the moral argument

1 Morality could simply be produced by the brain. It could be a mechanism developed through life in society, in close conflict with others.

2 There may be no such thing as an objective moral law:

   Fletcher argued that morality required greater flexibility.

   Jung argued that nothing could be known about what was objectively true.

3 An objective law could be explained without reference to God.

   It could be a natural law in the same way as physical natural laws.

4 The moral argument can at most only prove the existence of a law-giver.

   It cannot prove the existence of the omnipotent and omnibenevolent God of Classical Theism.

Why do Evil and Suffering Exist?

Moral evil is caused by human beings, whereas **natural** evil exists independently of human actions.

Both types of evil result in the **suffering** of innocent people.

The problem of evil

For religious people, the existence of suffering and evil poses a challenge to belief in the God of Classical Theism. This challenge makes God's existence either **improbable** or **impossible:**

- It makes it **improbable** since an all-knowing and all-powerful God would be able to prevent suffering and evil. An all-loving God would want to prevent suffering and evil. That He does not calls into question His omnipotence, omnibenevolence or existence. **David Hume** took this viewpoint.

- It makes it **impossible** for those whose definition of God includes the concept of **infinite goodness,** where God's goodness is understood to equal our definition of the term. Upholders of this point of view argue that the existence of *any* evil removes the infinity of God's goodness. **Aquinas** considered this point of view.

A **theodicy** is an attempt to **justify God in the face of evil**.

Augustine's theodicy

- God is omnipotent and omnibenevolent
- God created a perfect world
- Angels and humans brought **moral** evil into the world through abuse of free will
- **Natural evil** results from the breakdown of the natural order following moral evil
- Evil is an **absence of good,** not a substance, so God cannot have created it
- Everyone was present in Adam, so everyone deserves to suffer as a punishment
- God's mercy means that some will be saved and go to Heaven

Criticisms

- Evil cannot create itself out of perfection (so, **Schleiermacher**)
- It is **not** fair for us to suffer, since we were **not** all in Adam – likewise, science tells us that humans were **never** created in perfection
- The existence of Hell suggests evil was part of God's plan – He is unfair to send some to Heaven

Why do Evil and Suffering Exist?

Irenaeus' theodicy

- God is omnipotent and omnibenevolent
- He did **not** make a perfect world, because true goodness has to be developed rather than ready made
- True goodness requires free will, which justifies the potential for evil
- Actual evil (moral *and* natural) is justified by its power to enable us to develop – the world was made as a place of 'soul-making' (**Hick**), not as a paradise
- Everyone will be rewarded in Heaven

Criticisms

- The idea that everyone will go to Heaven is unfair and removes the point of obeying God
- The theodicy does not explain why suffering should be so **excessive** – nor does it explain **pointless** evil, which benefits no one
- **D. Z. Phillips** argues that an **omnibenevolent** God would not make people suffer for any purpose

Philosophy of Religion for A Level
This page may be photocopied
© Nelson Thornes Ltd, 2002

The freewill defence

- This develops Irenaeus' argument as to the value of free will
- The **main debate** centres on **whether God could have created free beings which would always choose to obey Him**
- If God could have done this (as **Mackie** held), the freewill defence **fails**
- **If the freewill defence fails, so do the theodicies of Augustine and Irenaeus**

Process theodicy

Process theodicy was developed by **David Griffin:**

- God is loving but **not omnipotent**
- God's role in creation was limited to setting off the evolution process
- God cannot prevent moral or natural evil, since the world and its creatures are beyond His control
- God suffers along with His creation

Criticisms

- It is not a **theodicy**, since it offers no defence of the God of Classical Theism
- God was not justified in His decision to start evolution when he could not control the process – it is unfair that some prosper while others suffer
- It is unjustifiable to simply 'come up' with a new definition of God to try to explain evil and suffering

Monism

- God is omnipotent and omnibenevolent
- The world is a single entity – when considered in this way, it is good
- Evil does not exist in itself, but results from 'human erring belief'
- Evil is therefore an illusion

Criticisms

- Evil **does** exist
- Even if evil is an illusion, it still exists to those who believe that it does
- This theodicy is dangerous, because it removes the significance of evil

What Views do Psychologists Hold about Religion?

Psychologists have argued that religion has a psychological cause that has nothing to do with the objective existence of God.

Freud's explanation for religion

Religion is an **illusion**, created by the mind as a mental defence against, first and foremost:

- **inner psychological conflict** (in this sense, religion is a neurotic illness)

It also offers protection against:

- the tensions and demands of life in society
- the dangers and loneliness of the natural world

Religion as a response to inner psychological conflict:

- the developing child undergoes the **Oedipus complex**
- this results in powerfully **ambivalent** feelings towards the father
- these feelings are **repressed** into the **unconscious** as a defence mechanism
- repression is not completely effective
- the repressed emotions reappear in **dreams** and **neurotic symptoms**
- **religion is the chief neurotic symptom**

Religion as a neurotic symptom:

- religion shares with other neurotic symptoms an emphasis on **compulsive attention to detail**
- powerful feelings of guilt are produced when the demands of religion are not met
- the figure of **God** is the equivalent to the **father figure**
- God is regarded with the same **ambivalence** as the father figure
- belief in God is the **last stage** in a series of developments, including **animism** and **polytheism**

Criticisms

1. The theory of the primal horde, which helped to explain the development from the Oedipus complex to religion, has been discredited
2. The Oedipus complex theory has been discredited
3. Freud's claims depend upon the subjective interpretation of a very narrow selection of evidence
4. Freud's argument for the termination of religion ignored religion's positive aspects

Religion eases **the tensions and demands of life in society** by giving a reason for suffering and offering God as the explanation for society's laws.

Religion eases the fear of **the danger and loneliness of the natural world** by offering protection and comfort against the forces of nature.

Freud concluded that religion should be overthrown, since it has resulted in conflicts of its own making and has impeded human progress. It should be replaced with science.

What Views do Psychologists Hold about Religion?

Jung's explanation for religion

- Religion stems from the **archetypes**
- These are situated in the collective unconscious mind
- An archetype is part of the structure of the mind, which innately generates certain kinds of images
- **God-images** are generated by the **God-archetype**

Jung's judgement as to the worth of religion:

- religion is a positive entity
- religion helps the individual maintain mental health through the process of **individuation**
- individuation is governed by the **self-archetype**
- individuation is the innate drive which integrates and harmonises all the elements of the psyche – it results in a mentally balanced individual, who can relate better to others

How individuation is a religious process:

- any process which is **archetypal** can be termed **religious,** since Jung's definition of a religious experience is one that **alters consciousness** and derives from **outside the conscious mind** – an archetypal experience fits this definition
- the images produced by the self-archetype which effect the process of individuation are the **images of God** and other religious images – therefore, Jung can affirm that religion is central to the individuation process

Criticisms

1 Jung's methodology is flawed. He creates necessary truths out of personal, unquantifiable opinion. This means that his conclusions rest on unsound premises. His argument that we cannot know anything of God's objective existence is based on the assumption that this must be the case. The empirical evidence is not tested.

2 Jung's theory of the archetypes has been attacked, suggesting another cause for religion.

3 Jung's individuation theory assumes that religion is only useful as a symbol for psychic wholeness. He fails to explain a major dimension of religion, which is the importance of the specific God-images in their own right.

Scientific Changes in the World-view

Plato (c. 429–347 BC)

- The universe is a vast finite space
- The spherical Earth is at the centre
- The motion of heavenly bodies is circular, uniform and constantly regular

Aristotle (384–322 BC)

- An infinite geocentric universe
- The eternal Earth is at the centre of a series of eight revolving concentric spheres
- On each sphere are the Sun, the Moon, the stars and the five known planets
- The spheres are crystalline, invisible and move around the Earth in perfect circles
- The region above the Moon is perfect, infinite and made of the unchanging substance called quintessence – all movement in this region is circular
- The region below the Moon is imperfect, finite and corruptible – everything is made out of the four elements (fire, water, earth and air)
- As the natural state of things on Earth is to be at rest, any movement is unnatural and in straight lines
- Everything is moved by the Prime Mover

Ptolemy (c. CE 100–170)

- A geocentric universe
- The planets move in epicycles attached to a larger sphere

St Thomas Aquinas (CE 1224–1274)

- A geocentric universe
- God is the Prime Mover and cause of everything
- The Earth is not eternal, but was created by God
- The Earth is flat and motionless
- The Earth is corrupted by sin, and constantly changing
- Above the Moon is the perfect realm of God, in which the heavenly bodies move in perfect circles

Nicolaus Copernicus (CE 1473–1543)

- A heliocentric universe
- The Earth goes around the Sun, along with the other planets
- Only the Moon revolves around the Earth
- Heavenly bodies travel in perfect circles

Scientific Changes in the World-view

Johannes Kepler (CE 1571–1630)

- A heliocentric universe
- The planets move in elliptical orbits around the Sun
- The physical universe follows a mathematical design
- God has imposed order on the universe

Isaac Newton (CE 1642–1727)

- There are universal laws throughout the universe
- These universal laws of motion and gravity explain the movement of the planets

Pierre Laplace (CE 1749–1827)

- The gravitational pull on the planets by the Sun is self-correcting, so that they do not collide
- Everything in the universe is determined, so the hand of God is not needed to keep the heavenly bodies in place
- Science will explain everything one day, so there is no need of God

Tycho Brahe (CE 1546–1601)

- A geocentric universe
- The Earth is at the centre, with the Sun and Moon orbiting it
- The other planets orbit the Sun
- Comets move in straight lines, so movement above the Moon is not always circular
- Comets appear to move through the crystalline spheres
- Stars come into existence, so the region above the Moon is not unchanging

Galileo Galilei (CE 1564–1642)

- A heliocentric universe, observed through a telescope
- The Moon has craters and mountains, so it is not perfect
- Jupiter has moons and Venus has phases, so the region above the Moon is not unchanging
- The movement of the planets is natural and not the work of a prime mover
- Galileo distinguished between celestial and terrestrial laws

---

Religion and Science Separate

- 'God of the Gaps' – God is used to explain what science cannot
- Deism – a clockwork universe which God set going and left

Scientific Changes in the World-view

Charles Darwin (CE 1809–1882)

• Life on Earth has evolved through the survival of the fittest and natural selection

↓

Pierre Teilhard de Chardin (CE 1881–1955)

• Evolution is part of God's plan
• Evolution will lead towards the Omega Point
• Everything will be integrated with Christ

↓

Albert Einstein (CE 1879–1955)

• The speed of light is constant
• Time slows down the closer one gets to the speed of light
• Matter is not solid and releases energy
• Time, space, energy and mass are related to one another

↓

Steady-State theory (mid-twentieth century)

• The universe has no beginning or end
• The universe is a process of continuous creation

Quantum theory (late twentieth century)

• Matter is not solid
• The smallest components of matter do not obey fixed laws
• It is not possible to predict their behaviour with certainty

Big Bang theory (late twentieth century)

• The universe originated with a 'big bang'
• Time began when the Big Bang occurred

Science is left with the question of what caused the Big Bang and why it happened.

Was it a spontaneous event or the work of God?

How do We Account for Our Existence?

The theistic approach

God/gods give us the **gift** of life. Life is sacred; it has sanctity. As such, the **meaning** of life is to fulfil God's requirements and ensure our eternal future (be this reincarnation or 'after-life').

The 'evolutionary' view

We are the consequence of chemical/biological events which were/are inevitable, and which are not controlled by anyone/anything but themselves. This view is supported by Richard Dawkins.

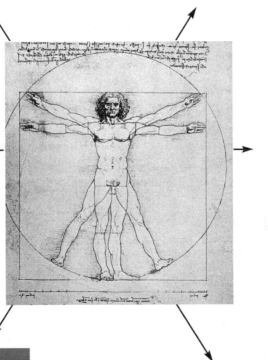

The humanist approach

We justify our own existence through our words, actions, ambitions, emotions and experiences.
We help ourselves and we help others. This gives us meaning and purpose.

The determinist view

Our existence is entirely preordained. Our thoughts, actions and motivation are 'in the hands of fate' (God or otherwise). Therefore, we are unable to justify our own lives as individuals.

The altruistic approach

Our lives can be justified through our help towards other people, seeking only to further **their** lives, and with scant regard for our own.

The hedonist/egoistic view

The sole meaning of our existence is to generate as much **personal pleasure** as is possible (in whatever form this may take).

Religion and Human Nature

Humanism

A world-view that recognises and celebrates the fact that all human beings have their own unique capabilities, and therefore have no need for 'God' to find purpose to life.

- - - - - - - - - - -

Religious humanism

Religion is purely functional: it provides a basis for morality and serves mankind. No doctrine is ever allowed to subvert the 'higher purpose' – i.e. real human needs.

- - - - - - - - - - -

Secular humanism

A philosophy of defiance. Human beings are what they strive to make of themselves. There are no 'absolute truths' (religious or otherwise) – we must simply evaluate each situation on its merits and use our considerable talents to deal with it.

Marxism

Man's consciousness is determined by his **social** and **economic** being.

- - - - - - - - - - -

Feuerbach

Religion is an 'expression of alienation'; the only way for man to free himself from this is through the realisation of **human** destiny.

- - - - - - - - - - -

Marx

Man cannot find his purpose in religion; this is 'the opium of the people' – a fantasy which dulls the mind to the harsh economic truths around us. Man is a productive being who fulfils all his needs through work. The establishment of a communist society will give **all** men the opportunity to fulfil their needs.

Existentialism

Kierkegaard

A response to the Hegelian notion of an objective 'absolute spirit' that leads us all to a shared destiny.

Kierkegaard states that Hegel looks at humankind too generally: he does not focus on the most important element, which is **the individual**. It is only through **subjective choice** that we find our destiny (and, therefore, purpose). Kierkegaard maintains that the most beneficial choice is a 'leap of faith' to Christianity.

- - - - - - - - - - -

Nietzsche

'God is dead', so we must account for our existence and purpose in some other way, or risk facing the consequences of 'nihilism'.

There is no 'absolute truth' regarding being; rather, life can be viewed as a succession of power struggles and relationships ('will to power'). Morality and purpose can only be built on **strength**.

- - - - - - - - - - -

Heidegger

Human beings **are** what they **make of themselves** in everyday life.

We grasp our own destiny and purpose through the way we live our lives, and must be careful not to 'drift along with the crowd'.

- - - - - - - - - - -

Jean-Paul Sartre

We are free beings: therefore we must choose what to do, which determines what we are.

- The very idea of God is self-contradictory
- There are no universal laws or absolute truths to keep us in check
- This means that there is no ultimate meaning inherent in human life
- The only foundation for our behaviour and our morals is human freedom
- We are free to choose everything about ourselves – attitudes, emotions, actions and character
- Any attempt to escape the responsibility that comes with this freedom is 'bad faith'
- We must strive to avoid 'bad faith' by trying to be 'authentic' in everything that we do; this involves accepting our freedom and the responsibility that it entails
- This will enable us to ascertain our true purpose

Philosophy of Religion for A Level
This page may be photocopied
© Nelson Thornes Ltd, 2002

What are Miracles?

Miracles are considered to be *either*:

- events which contain striking coincidences (**Holland**) or
- events in which a natural law is broken (**Hume**)

Whichever view is taken, it is also understood that they must have some **deeper significance** (**Swinburne**).

Arguments against the existence of miracles as coincidence

It could never be proved that such an event involved miraculous intervention. It could always have been a simple coincidence.

Arguments against the existence of miracles as violations of natural law

1 **Certain theists** argue that **everything** depends on God, whether violation or not.

- **Most,** however, argue that God governs the world through regular laws

- - - - - - - - - - - - - - - - - - - -

2 **Hick** argued that any apparent violation of a natural law could be explained through an exception to that law.

- **Swinburne,** however shows that events can be unexpected enough to be considered violations of what we should normally expect to happen

- - - - - - - - - - - - - - - - - - - -

3 **Hume** argues:

- It is **always more likely** that the testimony of a miracle is incorrect
- Such testimony is generally unreliable
- Natural laws have been observed to function an uncountable number of times
- Evidence for a miracle would have to outweigh all the evidence for the natural law
- Miracle accounts from different religions cancel each other out

Criticisms

- Swinburne argues that natural laws are based on the same kind of testimony as miracles
- Since miracles are **exceptions** they do not have to outweigh the natural law
- Miracle accounts from different religions may cancel out the religions, but not always the miracles

---

What can miracles prove, if they occur?

- They could be attributed to psychic or other natural powers about which, as yet, we know little
- They could be attributed to a non-material, personal being or beings (**Swinburne**)
- This may or may not be the **God of Classical Theism**

Is there Life after Death?

Do we have souls?

Are our minds inseparable from our bodies?

▼

Materialism

Do we exist as the two separate distinct parts of a physical body and a soul?

▼

Dualism

How can we survive death?

- **Materialists** who accept life after death would argue that survival after death would have to include **the resurrection of the body**. As our physical bodies decay, then after death we will have to receive a replica body (**John Hick**). But is a replica body really 'I'?

- **Dualists** accept the **immortality of the soul**. The body decays but the soul continues after death (**René Descartes**).

Do we have more than one life?

Reincarnation accepts the **transmigration of souls**. At death, the soul leaves the body that it currently inhabits and eventually starts another life in another physical body.

Each life is influenced by the **karma** from the previous lives. The aim is to achieve perfection, so that the need to be reborn ends and a state of bliss is achieved. Personal identity is lost as the soul becomes one with the Ultimate Reality.

Is there evidence to support life after death?

- **'Near-death' experiences** – is the person really 'dead' and visiting the afterlife, or are NDEs hallucinations resulting from oxygen starvation or illness?

- **Regression to past lives** – is the person remembering past lives or remembering experiences and knowledge gained earlier in this life?

- **'Sightings of dead people'** – are these sightings of the spirits of the dead, hallucinations or a 'tape' of past events?

- **Spiritualism** – are mediums contacting the dead, or are they thought-readers of the living?

Is it life after death?

- When people remember the things that we have done, or us, is this life after death?

- If we have descendants, do we live on in their genetic make-up?

- If we are kept in a cryogenic state at the point of death, with a view to revival at some future date, have we died?

Index

Page numbers in italics indicate illustrations.